THE HERITAGE OF

SPANISH

C·O·O·K·I·N·G

THE HERITAGE OF
SPANISH
C·O·O·K·I·N·G

TEXT
ALICIA RIOS

RECIPES
LOURDES MARCH

Random House New York

Copyright © 1992 Weldon Russell Pty Ltd.

Published in Australia by Weldon Russell Pty Ltd, a member of the Weldon International Group of Companies, Sydney, and in Great Britain by Ebury Press, an imprint of Random House UK Ltd, London.

Publisher: Elaine Russell
Managing editor: Dawn Titmus
Senior editor: Ariana Klepac
Editorial assistant: Margaret Whiskin
Translator: Annie Bennett
Copy-editors: Mary Flower, Jill Wayment, Roderic Campbell
Picture researcher: Teresa Avellanosa
Design concept: Susan Kinealy
Designer: Catherine Martin
Food photographer: Alejandro Pradera
Caption writer: Roderic Campbell
Indexer: Garry Cousins
Production: Jane Hazell

Library of Congress Cataloging-in-Publication Data

Rios, Alicia.
    The heritage of Spanish cooking / Alicia Rios and Lourdes March.
    256 p. 33.5 x 24.5 cm.
    Includes index.
    ISBN 0-679-41628-5
    1. Cookery, Spanish.   I. March, Lourdes. II. Title.
TX723.5.S7R53   1992
647.9546—dc20   92-53633

Produced by Weldon Russell Pty Ltd, 107 Union Street, North Sydney, New South Wales 2060, Australia

Typeset by Post Typesetters, Brisbane, Australia
Printed by Tien Wah Press, Singapore

A KEVIN WELDON PRODUCTION

Manufactured in Singapore
24689753   23456789   98765432
First American Edition

Front cover: *Still-life with watermelons and oranges*, Luis Meléndez (1716–80); PRADO MUSEUM, MADRID

Back cover: *The Seville Fair* (detail), Manuel Rodríguez Guzmán (1818–67); PALACIO DE RIOFRIO, SEGOVIA

Endpapers: *Stripping the maize* (detail), Benlliure y Gil (1855–1937); SPANISH MUSEUM OF CONTEMPORARY ART, MADRID

Opposite title page: *The era*, Francisco de Goya (1746–1828); PRADO MUSEUM, MADRID

Title page: *Still-life*, Pablo Picasso (1881–1973); PICASSO MUSEUM, BARCELONA

Opposite contents: *Afternoon tea at the edge of the Manzanares* (detail), Francisco de Goya (1746–1828); PRADO MUSEUM, MADRID

Microcosm, Manuel Lopez Villaseñor (born 1924); PRIVATE COLLECTION

CONTENTS

Still-life, Luis Meléndez (1716–80); PRADO MUSEUM, MADRID Traditionally, the northwest region of Spain supplied the most succulent oysters — like those the French writer

Alexandre Dumas found so pleasing.

INTRODUCTION

The Iberian peninsula has been the melting-pot for a great diversity of cultures, each of which had some role in influencing the ultimate formation of the cultural mosaic that is Spain. However, the degree of influence differed in each case, for geographical and historical reasons. For instance, Roman cultural influences, which were in any case weakened because of Spain's distance from Rome, became even further modified as a result of the Germanic invasions. Again, in the Middle Ages, while the rest of Europe was undergoing a slow process of evolutionary change, the Arab invasion of Spain brought with it yet more new influences to be absorbed. Finally, with the European colonization of America, it was Spain that became the gateway for all that was brought back from the New World to Europe.

Geography has also been an important factor in the development of Spain's culinary diversity. Spain's climate and topography is extremely varied: it ranges from some of the highest mountains in Europe to tropical islands. This has given rise to a great variety of culinary produce and customs. The continental climate is suitable for cereal crops and sheep-rearing, while fruit and vegetables are grown in warmer, irrigated areas. The extensive Spanish coastlines produce a great wealth of fish.

The earliest known settlers in this land of plenty were the Iberians in the south, and the Celts in the north. In the center these groups mixed, forming the "Celtiberians." Contact, based on trade, existed between the Iberian peninsula and the eastern Mediterranean as long ago as the fourth or fifth millenium BC. This eventually led to the establishment of Phoenician settlements on the Iberian peninsula around 1000 BC. Extensive trading contacts continued and new settlements were established on the Atlantic and Mediterranean coasts, not only by the Phoenicians but (from about the eighth century BC) by Greeks, too.

Carthage (situated near present-day Tunis, in North Africa), itself originally a Phoenician settlement, established an empire stretching from Egypt to the western Mediterranean and including much of the Iberian peninsula by the third century BC. The Romans captured the area roughly corresponding to what is now Andalusia from Carthage at the beginning of the second century BC but did not effectively control the peninsula (which the Romans called Hispania) until about 130 BC. Roman control lasted from then, for almost 500 years. It was ended by the invasions of Germanic

Book of Hours (unknown painter, fifteenth century); NATIONAL LIBRARY, MADRID
A book of Hours set out the prayers for each day of the year and was richly illustrated with scenes appropriate to the day and season. Being commissioned by a nobleman, it depicted in intimate detail daily life on his estates — his household, his tenants and their cultivation practices and the produce of his lands.

Santa Cristina de Linya, Jaime Ferrer I (fourteenth-fifteenth century);
SOLSONA MUSEUM, LERIDA
The *retablo* (a wooden altar-piece) is a common decorative feature of Spanish churches. Ferrer's choice of Manises pottery — with its characteristic, stylized floral design — for the table-setting reflects its widespread fame at this time. Manises, near Valencia, was then one of the great centers of Mudejar (Arab-influenced) pottery-making. The use of Gothic letters in the design, such as the "Ave Maria" on the plate, dates from the first half of the fifteenth century.

tribes, such as the Vandals and Visigoths, at the beginning of the fifth century AD.

This period ended with yet another invasion in AD 711, when Roderic, the last Visigothic king in Spain, was defeated by the Moslem invaders from North Africa. The Moslems quickly gained control of the greater part of Spain, leaving only a few, small Christian states in the north. By the early eleventh century the Christian advance southward had begun, their success aided by Moslem disunity. By 1248 only Granada remained under Moslem control, and it finally fell in 1492.

ORIGINS OF SPANISH FOOD

The Romans, when they came, were interested in exploiting the commercial potential of their Hispanic colonies. Being good agriculturalists, and fond of food, they were already experienced in the cultivation and use of many different kinds of foods found throughout their vast empire. Consequently, they soon realized that Hispania was ideal for the cultivation and supply of certain basic foodstuffs, including wheat, olive oil, wine and salted fish.

Cereals became an integral feature of the Mediterranean diet, and the practice of bread-baking, established under the Romans, gradually developed over the centuries. In Spain a great many recipes use bread, either as a base or as an additional ingredient. This is an example of low-cost cooking which, nevertheless, shows great creativity. Small chunks of bread in soup came to be a fundamental source of carbohydrates in the diet; garlic soup is a good example of this ingenious custom. Bread is also used in other dishes as a thickener: fried ingredients are pounded in a mortar then added to thick *gazpachos.*

Thanks to the Romans, the primitive oleaster (native wild olive tree) was turned into the Mediterranean olive tree and cultivated on a large scale. Hispania became the most important supplier of olive oil in the empire and oil became a basic element of Spanish cuisine. It provides flavor, smoothness and unity for uncooked ingredients, richness for cooked dishes, thickness for stews and protection for roasts. It is the primary medium for frying foods, producing excellent results with wonderful textures. Different kinds of oil should be used for each of these techniques: the quality of its flavor and aroma makes extra-virgin oil ideal for salads; for stews and other cooked dishes. However, where some of these qualities are destroyed by heat, a refined olive oil is usually sufficient, depending on the strength of flavor desired. Spanish cooks are well aware of these different requirements when buying olive oil, which is labeled according to the degree of acidity.

The Straits of Gibraltar provide a privileged natural trap for catching fish of the tuna family in large numbers. Long before the Roman techniques had developed for catching and salting this fish, an activity known as the *almadraba* provided one of the main exports in Roman times and even today vestiges of the pre-Roman art of salting fish are still to be found in Spanish markets.

Roman cooking methods — roasting, broiling (grilling) and baking — also had an impact on Spanish cuisine.

One result of the Germanic invasions was that Spanish cuisine had more exposure to medieval cuisines elsewhere in Europe and took on a more international flavor. When the Roman empire broke up, Spain had to learn to value food sources that, although less commercially viable than before, were no less indigenous. Thus, under the Visigoths, livestock farming developed and a taste was acquired for certain foods the new invaders brought from their homelands.

The Visigoths must have been very pleasantly surprised to discover the delights of the Iberian pig. It is less domesticated and leaner than the rosy pink breeds of their northern countries, but it has a wonderful flavor, which is the result of feeding solely on acorns. The Iberian pig has since become established as one of the prime elements of Spanish stock raising. We are also indebted to the Visigoths for bringing vegetables such as spinach, radishes and certain legumes to the Spanish fields which provided an ideal place for their cultivation.

THE MEDIEVAL ERA

With the absence of any single unifying power, in medieval times the regions of Spain gradually began to develop their distinct character. This encouraged the production of local cheeses. The interesting variety and quality of Spanish cheeses has gone unnoticed in the past owing to insufficient standardization and quality control. But only recently large-scale production has started of a wide range of cheeses, following the results of historical research carried out to establish their appropriate guarantees of origin.

Of all the characteristics of Spanish cuisine, perhaps the most original features were introduced by the Arabs. The Arab conquest — because it was so complete — created a unique opportunity for Moslem culture to fully penetrate the predominantly European character of Spain of that time. In addition, the continuing Arab presence on the peninsula — which was to last for over 700 years — meant that the influences they brought had sufficient time to become fully absorbed and integrated with the pre-existing Spanish characteristics. The Arabs found in Spain their promised paradise. With their understanding of the importance of water for food production, and assisted

St John the Baptist and St Catherine (detail from a *retablo*), the Master of Sigüenza (fifteenth century); PRADO MUSEUM, MADRID
St John the Baptist and St Catherine are shown dining in Heaven. To the medieval mind, the closest earthly parallel to such a meal would have been a royal banquet. The activity surrounding this banquet reminds us that music, too, played its part as an accompaniment to food.

by the favorable climate, the Arabs took great areas of the harsh Spanish soil and transformed them into oases.

The Arab presence in Spain led to the introduction of all the agricultural produce of the Middle East suitable for growing in this climate: citrus fruit, rice, eggplants (aubergines), sugar cane, herbs and spices. The use of saffron, cinnamon, cumin, caraway, cilantro (coriander) and mint is a distinctly Arab touch, and has since become an essential feature of the most traditional dishes of Spanish cuisine. However, many of these influences have remained largely unacknowledged: partly because such herbs and spices became so established in Spanish cooking as to seem only Spanish, and partly because of the general hostility towards Arabs and Arab culture which occurred in the years following their expulsion from Spain. Visitors cannot therefore expect to find obviously Arab dishes on menus in Spain.

Perhaps the most characteristic feature of the Arab influence on Spanish cooking is the combination on one plate of various finely chopped and intricately prepared ingredients, together with menus where this diversity is also reflected in the different dishes served at a meal. Highly seasoned and spiced meat and fish are used to make little rissoles or fillings. Hotpots are mixtures of vegetables and meats cooked in or with the broth (stock). The Arabs were instrumental in the development of the importance of poultry, rice and fried foods.

This period also saw the appearance of the first culinary documents. Some of

Rebecca and Eliezer, Bartolomé Murillo (1617–82); PRADO MUSEUM, MADRID
Rebecca offered Abraham's servant a drink of water. She thus fulfilled the law of hospitality toward a stranger — as much a Spanish theme as it was biblical. And the graceful bearing and elegance of these women suggests Seville, whose people were Murillo's favorite subjects.

them contain interesting references to the gastronomy and cuisine of this long period of interaction between the Arabs and the Spaniards, such as in the treatise by Ibn Razin al Tuyibi al Andalusi, written between 1243 and 1328. This, in turn, stimulated the production of medieval culinary literature, which was in general heavily influenced by the powerful Arab culture.

MODERN SPAIN

The events of 1492 made it a key year for Spanish history: the reunification of Spain, achieved by the conquest of Granada, the last Arab kingdom; and the European "discovery" of America. All this occurred during the reign of the Catholic monarchs, Fernando and Isabel. And, to it, we can add another event — the start of the definitive national cuisine. The final factor that determined the appearance of this cuisine was the importation of new foods from the New World. Following the European discovery of America, various foods were brought first to Spain and later spread to the rest of the world. It was not that Spain was seeking new foods at the time. In fact, one of the reasons behind these early voyages of discovery was to go to the places of origin of already familiar foods which were difficult to obtain. Spices had been in great demand in Europe ever since they were brought back from the Middle East by returning Crusaders. Although it was known that spices came from the East, much of the motivation behind Columbus's voyage was a belief that new routes could be opened up to the sources of supply by traveling west. The prospect of access to the lucrative spice trade led navigators across the Atlantic, and their discovery of America was an unexpected result of this search for new trade routes.

At the beginning, these New World foods were regarded as fanciful eccentricities, sometimes even dangerous. The aggressive red of the solanaceous plants, such as tomatoes and bell peppers (capsicums); the baffling bitterness of the black cocoa bean, or the monstrous ear of corn; the subterranean potatoes, which were to become an essential resource for a Europe full of hungry people — were all threatening in their unfamiliarity.

Because it was certain individual foods that were being imported, rather than a complete cuisine, this led to ad hoc combinations of new and old ingredients. This, in turn, stimulated the creative processes in Spanish and other European cuisines. Tomatoes were added to the pale Arab *gazpachos*, providing vitamins, sweetness and color. Bell peppers were an ideal receptacle for stuffing, as this was the first-known vegetable that did not need to be hollowed out beforehand.

The explorers who had gone in search of the traditional spices of the Indies came across two novelties: the sweet vanilla of the Caribbean and the piquant paprika plant. This plant produced a milder, sweeter pepper when acclimatized to Spanish soil and weather conditions. The powder from the dried peppers was used to produce *pimentón* or paprika, a purely Hispanic creation. Paprika made from mild peppers is widely used in countless dishes which have shaped the character of Spanish cuisine. The practice of using paprika in the curing of pork-meat products led to the creation of the now famous *chorizo* sausage.

Some of the most notable creations made with these new ingredients include the mixture of bell peppers, tomatoes and other vegetables known as *pisto* (vegetable stew), the golden potato omelet and a wide range of other potato-based dishes.

Tilework from the Municipal Market in Manises, Valencia (nineteenth century). All local markets would have been noisy, busy places, bustling with shoppers and echoing with the cries of sellers. The overturned basket gives a hint of the hurly-burly. What differentiated one from another, of course, was the aroma of regional specialties. *Botifarra* is a Catalan sausage. The white variety being made from ground pork and spices and the dark red or black variety made from blood.

on the direction of Spanish cuisine, which gradually adopted a more international character. Cookbooks, too, tended to reflect this new culinary direction.

Nevertheless, traditional Spanish, and especially regional, cooking did not disappear. It was strongly maintained, chiefly in the domestic setting of people's homes. By the end of the nineteenth century traditional Spanish cooking was becoming increasingly valued and had begun to appear on restaurant menus. Cookbooks once again reflected this change in taste, and began to show more appreciation and knowledge of Spanish culinary tradition. Even at this time, however, French cuisine remained influential as can be seen from the popularity of a book by Angel Muro, *El Practicón*, which was published in Madrid in 1894.

The water-carrier of Seville, Diego de Velázquez (1599–1660);
WELLINGTON COLLECTION, LONDON
Water-carriers remained necessary in Spanish towns for centuries after Velázquez painted this one. By the 1830s little about them had changed, to judge from the English traveler and Hispanophile George Borrow's description of them in their "dress of coarse duffel and leathern skull-caps, seated in hundreds by the fountain sides, upon empty water casks, or staggering with them filled to the topmost stories of lofty houses."

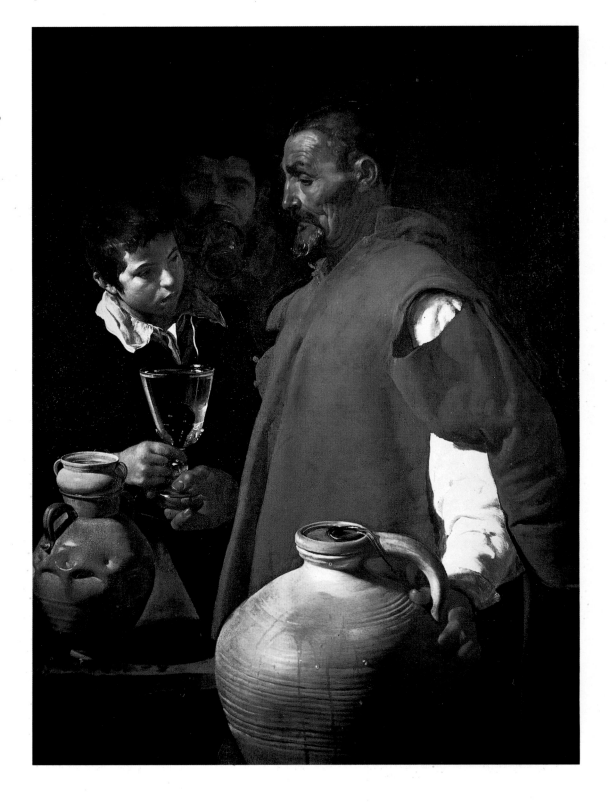

EATING HABITS

There are three principal mealtimes in Spain: first thing in the morning, at midday and at the end of the day. The most unvarying of these is the midday meal, which is the most important and substantial, as it is in the majority of Mediterranean countries. This is also normally the most formal meal, as it usually means the presence of the whole family and takes place at a set time. What people have for breakfast depends both on the type of work they do and the climate in the part of the country where they live. Traditionally, the warmer the weather, the lighter the breakfast. Manual laborers used to eat breakfast later, eventually leading to the establishment of another meal, called the *almuerzo*, between breakfast and the midday meal. Paradoxically, a parallel can be drawn between this meal of the agricultural worker and the *aperitivo* (appetizer) of the upper classes. While the purpose of the *almuerzo* was to maintain strength, the *aperitivo* was meant to stimulate the appetite for the large midday meal.

However, in addition to the three main meals, the *almuerzo* and *aperitivo*, in the late afternoon, there is the *merienda*. If any excuse were needed to account for this bonus, then we need only mention that dinner, which is as large a meal as lunch, is eaten so late in Spain that nothing comes between it and bedtime. Nevertheless, these customs are changing in line with the demands of modern lifestyles and similar working schedules to those in other countries. When Spanish people are on holiday, however, they soon revert to their old customs, and the same goes for eating out, when the classic forms take precedence. Dinner at home is probably the only meal

The market of El Borne, Barcelona, viewed from the church of Santa María del Mar (unknown painter, late eighteenth century);
City History Museum, Barcelona
By the late eighteenth century Barcelona had become a great, prosperous city through trade and industry. Its port had only recently been granted royal licence to trade directly with the Americas, and the fruits of this trade soon found their way into the city markets, like El Borne.

Still-life with bread, Manuel Prego (twentieth century); PONTEVEDRA MUSEUM Sardines, some onion and a hunk of fresh, crusty bread — the basis for a typically simple, inexpensive but tasty meal.

which is most becoming simplified and lighter these days.

The number of courses and the type of food for a typical meal in Spain is determined by social factors. Until the civil war (1936–39), an extensive menu was synonymous with high social standing. For lunch the upper classes had three courses, together with garnishes and side-dishes, and followed by dessert. The first course was usually an egg dish or some sort of not-too-complicated exotic recipe; the second and third were preferably fish and meat, but could be two kinds of meat.

This typical menu is taken from *El Practicón*, by Angel Muro: *First Course:* Scrambled Eggs with Tomato, *Second Course:* Galician-style Clams, *Third Course:* Stewed Rabbit with Fresh Fava (Broad) Beans, *Dessert:* Rice Pudding.

The civil war taught Spanish people how to eat frugally. The poor state of the national economy meant that meals became restricted to just one course. From then on, Spaniards took more interest in nutrition and became less troubled at being served smaller amounts of food in general and of animal proteins in particular.

Present-day meals never go beyond the basic idea of two courses. Following age-old beliefs, one is carbohydrate-based and one is mainly protein. This basic structure is then extended with appetizers, salads, garnishes and desserts, according to circumstances. A typical modern meal might be along the following lines: *First Course:* Vegetable Medley, *Second Course:* Lamb Chops with Sautéed Potatoes and Lettuce and Tomato Salad, *Dessert:* Santiago Almond Cake or Fresh Fruit.

Regarding drinks, wine — preferably red — would normally be served with both these meals, and espresso coffee would be drunk after the dessert. On special occasions, meals are rounded off with liqueurs and whatever cakes or sweets are typical of the occasion.

Spanish cuisine, therefore, embraces many different kinds of influences, and takes advantage of high-quality, staple foods of great nutritional value grown throughout the country. In addition, Spain has developed its own individual style of cooking, based on foods fried in olive oil, as well as different kinds of stews and hotpots.

For all these reasons, most Spanish people feel very passionately about their cuisine. When they are away from home, Spanish people go to great lengths to seek it out — for some expatriates it is the only element of Spanish culture that cannot be replaced.

Still-life, Ginés Parra (twentieth century); PRIVATE COLLECTION

A café at the beginning of the century, José Jiménez Aranda (1837–1903); PRIVATE COLLECTION   Cafés served alcohol as well as coffee, and sometimes both together —

as in the *carajillo*, a *cafe solo* laced with the sharp Spanish brandy. But, as elsewhere in Europe, cafés were also important meeting-places for the exchange of ideas.

APPETIZERS, TAPAS AND SALADS

Appetizers (*aperitivos*) are, like salads, complements to main meals. *Tapas*, on the other hand, constitute small meals in their own right, usually eaten at midday in the course of a *tapeo*. One of the pleasures of living in Spain is to go on a *tapeo*: to move leisurely from bar to bar in order to sample the delights of the *tapas* on offer. And, naturally, it is customary to accompany each plate of *tapas* with a judicious glass of whatever one prefers to drink. Neither *tapas* nor *aperitivos* are regarded as mere adjuncts to drink. An *aperitivo* is some light food, like olives for example, taken for the purpose of stimulating one's appetite for the main meal. A *tapa* is like an elegant, miniature, self-sufficient dish to be consumed, as the fancy takes one, either complemented with a drink or not.

APERITIVOS

Including an *aperitivo* as part of a meal is a useful way of bridging the sometimes unbearable wait while the main dishes are being prepared. In the past, during long formal meals, plates of ham, *salchichón* (sausages), olives and other light foods were left on the tables. This was in case the diners felt like something to nibble between courses of the menu. This precursor to our appetizers greatly surprised travelers, as is revealed by the comments of writers such as the Frenchman Bartolomé Joly in his *Journey Around Spain* of 1603–04, and A. Jouvin in his voluminous book *The Traveler of Europe* in 1672.

TAPAS

It is thought that the word *tapa* comes from the habit of using scraps of food to cover the jugs of wine in inns and taverns (*tapa* means lid). Having drunk the contents of the receptacle, the customers often ended up eating the "lid" too. Today, however, there is a great variety of *tapas*, some very simple, others bordering on *haute cuisine*. *Tapas* are the delight of teetotallers, whose abstinence is more than compensated for by these tasty dishes.

The *tapeo* consequently has become a hedonistic, characteristically Spanish custom, closely linked to the morning wine crawls that are a typical feature of Sundays

The merienda (design for tapestry), Francisco Bayeu (1734–95); PRADO MUSEUM, MADRID
Bayeu was painter to the court of Charles III. Goya became his apprentice, later marrying his sister. Picnics were very fashionable at court, and not necessarily lavish, either. Simple but satisfying, *chorizo*, bread and wine make an excellent afternoon snack (or *merienda*).

The café, Antonio Esquivel (1806–57);
FINE ARTS MUSEUM, BILBAO
Some famous cafés were adopted by a
particular clientele and used by it
like a club. The atmosphere that dos
Passos, the American writer, found in a
Madrid artistic café in 1916 was little
different from similar earlier cafés. "At
three or so, one sat drinking coffee or
anis in the Gato Negro, where the
waiters have the air of cabinet ministers
and listen to every word of the rather
languid discussions on art and letters
that while away the afternoon hours."

and festive days. The present-day custom has its origins in the days when women
would hurry back home after the religious service to prepare the festive lunch, and
the men, having to pass the time until the meal was ready, collected at the local
bars. They did not restrict themselves to just one establishment, in their desire to
sample the different dishes available.

Each regional cuisine has contributed its specialties over the years, enriching
Spain's repertoire of *tapas*. The north specializes in seafood, the Levante region in
vegetables and the south in fried fish. The central region brings together all these
contributions, adding its own local stamp, which is what most qualifies a regional
dish as a *tapa*. Central Spain also features sausages and other meat dishes among
its range of *tapas*.

Tapas can be categorized into three main types, according to how easy they
are to eat: *cosas de picar, pinchos* and *cazuelas*.

Cosas de picar (meaning "things to nibble") basically refers to finger food —
in other words, anything that can be easily picked up with the finger and thumb
alone, without the need for any other implement. A paper napkin may sometimes
be needed afterwards, however, with certain fried dishes.

Of all the different kinds of finger food, the supreme example must be, for its
sheer Spanishness, the olive. There is such astonishing variety in a simple olive —
in the colors it can have, from distinct shades of green to deepest black; in its size,
from tiny to huge. And there are so many ways to treat olives. Each region has its
own way of dressing olives, featuring the most characteristic spices. Pitted olives can
be stuffed with almost anything from red bell peppers (capsicums) to anchovies and
almonds.

As soon as an implement is required to manipulate the food, such as a toothpick, we enter the world of the *pinchos*. *Banderillas* are pickles on a stick, thus named because the red bell pepper makes them look like the *banderillas* (decorated darts) used in a bullfight. Toothpicks may also be necessary to get at a crumbly piece of potato omelet or a piping-hot chunk of *morcilla* blood sausage.

Cazuelas ("little dishes"), together with forks, are required when the food comes in a sauce — for example, *albóndigas* (meatballs) or shrimp (prawns) fried in garlic. These *tapas* are samples of the specialties of particular places, and are served with bread, which can be used to mop up the sauce.

SALADS

A salad is a dish that is both accessible and cheap and Spain, being a Mediterranean country, is not short of suitable ingredients for making salads. All salads use fresh garden produce and are served cold, although some ingredients may have been cooked beforehand. Salads were originally a cheap form of eating for the lower classes, and were regarded as a sorry alternative to meat.

It was the Romans who introduced the taste for salad but the singular Spanish habit of starting meals with a salad goes back to the Arabs. The fertile *huertas* (vegetable gardens) produced an enormous variety of suitable ingredients. These were dressed with olive oil, the juices of citric fruit and countless aromatic herbs to produce different kinds of salad, such as *tabbulah*, which was prepared with cereals, vegetables and aromatic herbs.

The Spanish habit of serving salads first seemed well established by the seventeenth century and drew comment from French travelers in Spain at the time, who were unused to such practices. Bartolomé Joly noted, in *Journey Around Spain* (1603–04), "First comes the fruit, which they eat, unlike us, first of all, salads, oranges both whole and in sugared slices..." Marie Catherine Jumel de Barneville, countess of Aulnoy, described in a letter written in 1679 how, after having been received by the Queen Mother, Mariana of Austria, she attended luncheon, and observed, "They served dishes in front of the Queen; the first were iced melons, salads and milk, of which she ate a lot before eating the meat..." Salads were also served for *meriendas* (afternoon tea) at home and in the country.

Despite the abundance of suitable ingredients, the Spaniards have traditionally not made good salads. Juan de la Mata, in his *Arte Repostería* (1747), was one of the few culinary writers to illustrate the Spanish way of preparing salads of all kinds. However, other countries less generously endowed with the sort of produce suitable for salads have created surprising combinations, which are gradually being incorporated into Spanish cuisine. There are, nevertheless, some delicious salad recipes to be found around Spain that are relatively unknown only because salads generally do not travel well. Some magnificent local salads feature baked vegetables, cooked legumes (pulses), salted fish and aromatic herb dressings. Away from their places of origin, all seem as interesting and different as, for example, a Swiss salad might, showing that salad is a regional specialty. The most widely known version of salad is made simply with lettuce and tomato, and dressed with oil, salt and vinegar; when onion, olives, canned asparagus tips, canned tuna and hardcooked (hardboiled) egg are added, it is called *mixta*.

Camacho's wedding (detail), José Moreno Carbonero (1860–1942);
ROYAL ACADEMY OF SAN FERNANDO, MADRID
The food for this wedding, in Cervantes' *Don Quixote* (1605–15), was so bounteous that Sancho Panza was given "three hens and a couple of geese" just as an appetizer. Preparation of another snack involved "two cauldrons of oil, larger than dyers' vats" for frying puddings, which were then taken out and "plunged into another cauldron of warmed honey."

Breakfast at the Alhambra, Mariano Fortuny (1838–74); PRIVATE COLLECTION, BARCELONA
The Alhambra, the fortress-palace of the Moorish rulers of Granada, is a place of great beauty and resplendent gardens and courtyards. As a setting for the morning coffee and *churros*, there are few locations more enchanting or magical.

OCTOPUS WITH PAPRIKA AND OLIVE OIL

Pulpo a feira   Serves 4–6

In Galicia octopus is a delicacy with an extraordinary flavor and, not surprisingly, it is enormously popular. Only an experienced cook can tell just when it is ready — neither tough nor overcooked. This dish is typically eaten on local holidays and market days and is also traditional during Lent. Like the Galician people, it has spread throughout Spain and is eaten in Galician bars and restaurants as a *tapa*.

1 fresh octopus, about 2 lb (1 kg)
kosher (coarse) salt
⅓ cup (3 fl oz/90 ml) olive oil
1 teaspoon sweet paprika
1 teaspoon spicy paprika

Pound the body and tentacles of the octopus with a pestle, taking care not to damage the suckers.

Heat some unsalted water in a large pan. When it comes to a boil, turn the bag of the octopus head inside out, then, holding on to the sides with the tentacles facing downward, dip it slowly in and out of the water 3 times. Drop it into the water and boil for 30–45 minutes, according to thickness. Prick to check if it is soft, then remove the pan from the heat and set aside for about 15 minutes.

When you are ready to serve, take the octopus out of the pan, snip into fairly small strips or chunks and arrange on a plate. Season with salt, then drizzle with the oil and sprinkle with the 2 kinds of paprika. Serve hot or warm.

CLAMS IN WHITE WINE SAUCE

Almejas a la marinera　　　　　Serves 4

In Spain clams, cockles and other mollusks are used to create limitless dishes according to both local tradition and individual inspiration. The definition of *a la marinera* varies along the Spanish coastline. In some places it denotes highly seasoned clams cooked with onion and tomato, while on other parts of the coast, bell peppers (capsicums), carrots and even rice or breadcrumbs are added, with local wines served as a condiment. High-quality clams are very expensive and are now regarded as a luxury *tapa*.

2 lb (1 kg) small clams
salt
⅓ cup (3 fl oz/90 ml) olive oil

2 cloves garlic, finely chopped
2 teaspoons breadcrumbs
⅓ cup (3 fl oz/90 ml) water
⅓ cup (3 fl oz/90 ml) dry white wine
2 teaspoons chopped parsley

Soak the clams in salted water to release any sand, shaking them around occasionally.

Heat the oil in a heatproof casserole and brown the garlic. Add the clams and sauté on low heat until they open. Mix the breadcrumbs with the water and add to the casserole along with the white wine.

Cook on low heat for 10 minutes, gently moving the casserole back and forth to thicken the sauce.

Sprinkle with the parsley and serve very hot.

Octopus with paprika and olive oil (left); clams in white wine sauce (right)

GREEN BELL PEPPERS, TOMATOES AND TUNA WITH PINE NUTS

Pimiento, tomate y atún con piñones   Serves 4

This summer dish can now be made all year round, although it comes into its own when tomatoes are in season and are tasty and red. It belongs to the *pisto* family because it is fried, but is still very nutritious. It should be served with large chunks of bread and plenty of local red wine. It also makes an excellent pie filling. Although the original recipe calls for tuna in brine, tuna in oil can be used instead.

¾ cup (6½ fl oz/200 ml) olive oil
½ cup (2 oz/60 g) pine nuts
1 lb (500 g) green bell peppers (capsicums),
    finely chopped

4 lb (2 kg) ripe tomatoes, peeled and chopped
salt
2 teaspoons sugar
6½ oz (200 g) tuna in brine, flaked

Heat the oil in a skillet (frying pan), then remove from the heat and add the pine nuts. Toss quickly over low heat, taking care not to let them burn. Remove from the pan and set aside.

Fry the bell peppers in the same oil. When they start to brown, add the tomatoes and cook until the mixture is reduced and the oil starts to come to the surface. Add a little salt and the sugar. Add the pine nuts and tuna, mix well and cook for another 5 minutes.

Serve hot or cold. The flavor improves if the dish is left for a day before eating.

Green bell peppers, tomatoes and tuna with pine nuts

Potato omelet

POTATO OMELET

Tortilla de patatas   Serves 4

In Spain the humble potato omelet, the *tortilla*, is revered like a priceless work of art. Round, yellow and resplendent, it is worshiped like a sun god. It is perhaps the most versatile and widely accepted dish in Spanish cuisine. It can be eaten hot or cold, while sitting down at a table or standing at the counter of a bar, in a sandwich on the train or as part of a picnic in the country.

The popular writer of fables from the Canary Islands Tomás de Iriarte observed in the mid-eighteenth century:

. . . then someone invented *la tortilla*
and now everyone cries *¡Qué maravilla!*

1½ lb (750 g) potatoes
1⅓ cups (11 fl oz/345 ml) olive oil
salt
6 eggs

Peel and rinse the potatoes, then slice finely and pat dry with a cloth.

Heat the oil in a deep skillet (frying pan) and add the potatoes. Deep-fry on medium heat, with a lid on, for 20–30 minutes, stirring occasionally. The pieces should be soft but not brown. When the potatoes are cooked, remove from the pan and drain in a colander. Add a little salt.

Beat the eggs lightly, just enough to mix the whites and the yolks. Add salt if necessary. Mix in the potatoes, stirring with a fork.

Heat a little of the oil again — just enough to cover the base of the skillet — and add the egg mixture, shaking the pan to avoid sticking. Cook for 2 minutes, or until just set.

Cover the pan with a wide plate or lid, then, holding it firmly with the flat of your hand, turn the pan upside-down. Slide the omelet from the plate or lid back into the pan and cook the other side for 1–2 minutes. It should be quite runny inside. Transfer to a large plate and serve.

Kitchen scene (nineteenth-century mosaic);
CERAMICS MUSEUM, BARCELONA
The amount of garlic hanging up suggests that *all-i-oli* was made regularly here. A kitchen so well supplied probably belonged in a great house, and it looks like the sort of kitchen where nothing is wasted — not even escaping eels.

SPICY POTATO CHUNKS

Patatas bravas   Serves 4

Patatas bravas are a great favorite in *tapas* bars where these crunchy bright red triangles never fail to delight. Alternating tasty mouthfuls of spicy potato with sips of beer or wine is a sensuous experience indeed. Maybe we subconsciously remember how the erotic prowess of the indigenous inhabitants of the West Indies was attributed to their eating a lot of potatoes!

*2 lb (1 kg) potatoes, cut into even-size large
    chunks*
olive oil for deep-frying
*2 tablespoons (1 oz/30 g) all-purpose plain
    flour*
½ teaspoon paprika
1 cup (8 fl oz/250 ml) beef broth (stock)

*2 tablespoons (1 fl oz/30 ml) white wine
    vinegar*
1 small piece chili pepper
salt
2 or 3 tablespoons tomato sauce (purée)

Fry the potato chunks in plenty of oil on low heat for 20–30 minutes. Just before the end of cooking time, turn up the heat to brown the pieces. Transfer to a casserole.

Prepare the spicy sauce by heating 1 tablespoon of the oil in a pan. Add the flour and paprika, then gradually add the broth, stirring constantly. Add the vinegar and chili pepper, then cook for 8 minutes, stirring constantly.

Check the seasoning. Remove from the heat, add the tomato sauce and mix well.

Serve the potatoes lightly coated with the hot sauce.

GARLIC MUSHROOMS

Champiñones al ajillo   Serves 4–6

Al ajillo means frying some kind of vegetable, fish or meat in very hot oil flavored with garlic and perhaps chili peppers. Favorite *al ajillo* foods include shrimp (prawns), chicken and rabbit. The secret of preparing mushrooms in this way is to continue frying until the juice evaporates, producing a concentrated flavor and a golden color. Nowadays the mushrooms are usually broken with the fingers to preserve the texture and stop them from turning black. Previously they were cut into thin slices and lemon juice was sprinkled on and rubbed in by hand to keep the mushrooms white.

⅓ cup (3 fl oz/90 ml) olive oil
*4 cloves garlic (3 sliced lengthwise and 1
    finely chopped)*
1 small piece chili pepper
*2 lb (1 kg) button mushrooms
    (champignons), wiped clean, sliced and
    sprinkled with the juice of ½ lemon*
salt
freshly ground pepper
2 teaspoons chopped parsley

Heat the oil in a heatproof casserole and fry the sliced garlic and chili pepper. When they start to brown, add the mushrooms, season with salt and pepper and cook over high heat for 10–15 minutes, stirring occasionally.

Before removing from the heat, add the chopped garlic and parsley. Serve immediately in individual earthenware dishes.

Spicy potato chunks (left); garlic mushrooms (right)

Shrimp in batter (left); salt cod soldiers (right)

SHRIMP IN BATTER

Gambas en gabardina   Serves 4

Gambas en gabardina means "shrimp (prawns) in rain-coats." This somewhat unorthodox name has a technical explanation. Only substances containing starch fry well; fish are starch-free, and are therefore usually coated beforehand with flour or breadcrumbs. In this recipe the batter is a protective covering, preventing the oil from soaking through to the inside while also keeping the shrimp moist.

8 oz (250 g) small shrimp (prawns) in their shells
¾ cup (3 oz/90 g) all-purpose (plain) flour
1 pinch salt

1 pinch saffron
⅓ cup (3 fl oz/90 ml) beer, approximately
olive oil for deep-frying

Remove the heads, legs and two-thirds of the shells of the shrimps, leaving the tail joints on.

Mix the flour, salt and saffron, gradually adding the beer to form a thick batter.

Dry the shrimp thoroughly on paper towels. Holding them by the tail, dip each one in the batter.

Fry in batches in plenty of very hot oil until golden. Remove with a slotted spoon or fish slice. Drain in a colander, then transfer to paper towels. Serve immediately.

36

SALT COD SOLDIERS

Soldaditos de Pavía   Serves 4

This *tapa* consists of a piece of salt cod fried in an egg batter. Sometimes this *tapa* is then wrapped in a strip of baked red bell pepper (capsicum). This decoration is reminiscent of the uniform of the Hussars, founded by General Pavia in the last third of the nineteenth century, who wore a red band across a blue background, hence the name.

1 lb (500 g) fleshy dried salt cod
olive oil for marinade and deep-frying
juice of 1 lemon
1 teaspoon sweet paprika
ground white pepper
⅙ oz (5 g) fresh yeast
warm water
¾ cup (3 oz/90 g) all-purpose (plain) flour
1 pinch saffron, chopped
salt

Cut the cod into thin strips, 2½ in (6 cm) long and ¾ in (2 cm) wide. Soak for 12 hours, changing the water twice. Drain and dry the strips, then cut in half lengthwise.

Make a marinade using ⅓ cup (3 fl oz/90 ml) of the oil, the lemon juice, paprika and a little ground white pepper. Add the cod strips and marinate for at least 1 hour.

Meanwhile, prepare a batter by dissolving the yeast in a little warm water, then adding the flour, chopped saffron and a little salt. Gradually add more warm water to form a smooth, custardlike consistency.

Set aside in a warm place to develop (about 15 minutes).

Dip the cod strips into the batter, coating them evenly, then fry in hot oil until crispy and golden.

Andalusian pilgrimage, B. de Martin (mid-nineteenth century); FINE ARTS MUSEUM, GRANADA

Still life, Penagos (1889–1954); MAPFRE VIDA CULTURAL FOUNDATION

ANDALUSIAN SALAD

Ensalada andaluza   Serves 4

In ancient times Mediterranean cultures grew lettuce (documented from AD 500), curly endive, carrots, asparagus, parsley, leeks and garlic and made use of countless wild aromatic herbs to prepare stimulating salads. These were dressed with olive oil, vinegar made from grapes, figs or peaches and salt. In the caliphate of Al-Andalus, the recipes were enriched with green onions (spring onions) and orange and lemon juice. In *Arte de Reposteria* (1747), Juan de la Mata lists a mindboggling array of ingredients used in salads in the eighteenth century.

> Any kind of green Salad, such as Celery, Cardoons, Italian Salad, others called Repelada, Lettuce, Escarole, bitter and sweet Chicory, and other appropriate Herbs for this purpose, should be cleaned thoroughly and served according to individual taste. Some people mix the leaves with Tunny fish, Anchovies, Bottargas, as the eggs of the Tunny fish are called, all cut into pieces: take note, the eggs have to be hard, and the Tunny fish must be boiled and well desalted. Some like to dress their salads with a couple of cloves of crushed Garlic mixed with a little Vinegar, Oil, Pepper and Salt. Instead of Garlic, a lot of people add Cumin or Oregano, which is a truly tasty addition to any kind of Salad. Others make Salad with Tunny, Anchovies or Bottargas, dressed with Onion, Parsley, Salt, Pepper, Oil and Vinegar.
>
> Juan de la Mata, *Arte de Reposteria*, 1747

1 curly endive, finely shredded
3⅓ cups (1 lb/500 g) olives, pitted
1 small onion, peeled and chopped
1 clove garlic, finely chopped
1 tomato, chopped
1 teaspoon fresh tarragon, finely chopped
salt
1 egg, hardcooked (hardboiled)
3 tablespoons (1½ fl oz/45 ml) olive oil
2 tablespoons (1 fl oz/30 ml) white wine vinegar
3½ oz (100 g) tuna in oil, flaked

Put the curly endive, olives, onion, garlic, tomato and tarragon in a salad bowl. Add a little salt.

Crush the yolk of the egg in a mortar, then slowly trickle in the oil and vinegar, stirring with the pestle. Pour over the salad.

Chop the eggwhite and sprinkle over the top along with the flaked tuna. Add a little salt. Serve.

Andalusian salad (left); diced vegetable salad (right)

DICED VEGETABLE SALAD

Pipirrana   Serves 4

Pipirrana is one of the most popular accompaniments to summer meals and is one of a variety of salads comprising finely chopped ingredients, which are mixed thoroughly and then tossed with the dressing. It should be left to marinate for a while for the flavors to blend properly and is very refreshing on hot days.

2 green bell peppers (capsicums)
4 large tomatoes (13 oz/410 g approximately)

2 onions (6½ oz/200 g approximately), peeled
2 Kirby cucumbers or 1 small cucumber, peeled
2 eggs, hardcooked (hardboiled) (optional)
1 small can tuna (optional)
¼ cup (2 fl oz/60 ml) olive oil
2 tablespoons (1 fl oz/30 ml) white wine vinegar
salt

Dice all the ingredients finely into ½ in (1 cm) cubes and dress with the olive oil, vinegar and salt. Mix thoroughly.

Chill for at least 1 hour before serving.

The feast of San Isidro, Francisco de Goya (1746–1828); PRADO MUSEUM, MADRID

BAKED TOMATOES

Tomates al horno   Serves 4

This simple oven-baked dish can either form part of a selection of appetizers or be served as a first course with slices of cured ham and bread with olive oil, and it is delicious either hot or at room temperature. The tomatoes should be ripe and freshly picked to provide as much rich Mediterranean flavor as possible.

4 medium-size, not overripe tomatoes
  (1 lb/500 g)
salt
2 cloves garlic, peeled
1 tablespoon finely chopped parsley
3 tablespoons (1½ fl oz/45 ml) water
2 tablespoons (1 fl oz/30 ml) olive oil
freshly ground pepper
1 tablespoon dry breadcrumbs

Preheat the oven to 400°F (200°C/Gas 6).

Wash the tomatoes, slice in half, then place cut-side up in an ovenproof baking dish and sprinkle with salt.

Crush the garlic with the parsley and a little salt in a mortar. Add the water.

Spoon this mixture onto the tomatoes, drizzle on a little oil, then sprinkle with a pinch of pepper, a little salt and the breadcrumbs.

Bake for approximately 30 minutes. Serve.

TOASTED VEGETABLE PLATTER

Escalivada   Serves 4

In Catalan *escalivar* means "to toast over flames." *Escalivada* is, therefore, a salad of toasted vegetables. It is a rustic summer dish, usually made in the countryside over a campfire. Eggplants (aubergines) and bell peppers (capsicums) are the most usual ingredients, as they can withstand the direct heat, cook easily and do not contain a lot of water. Nevertheless, onion and tomato can be added. The secret is the smoked flavor produced by the embers, which produces much tastier results than when vegetables are toasted in an oven. Nowadays it is even found as an appetizer on restaurant menus. It should be liberally sprinkled with top-quality olive oil.

4 large eggplants (aubergines)
8 fleshy red bell peppers (capsicums)
⅓ cup (3 fl oz/90 ml) olive oil
salt
2 cloves garlic, peeled and finely chopped
  (optional)

Bake or charcoal-grill the eggplants and bell peppers. Set aside for 10–15 minutes in a covered dish (this makes them easier to peel).

Peel the bell peppers and remove the seeds.

Peel the eggplants and trim off the stalks.

Cut the bell peppers and eggplants into strips, then arrange on a serving dish and dress with oil and salt.

Chopped garlic can be sprinkled on top if desired. Serve.

Baked tomatoes (left); toasted vegetable platter (right)

Salt cod layered salad

SALT COD LAYERED SALAD

Poti-poti   Serves 6

Poti-poti means "disarray" or "jumble." This recipe is a variation on the Catalan salads featuring slivers of dried raw cod (*bacalao*), and the *bacalao* has to be soaked for an hour or two before eating. Sometimes it is served with local sausages or with slices of bread with oil, ham and tomato, perhaps sprigs of raw cauliflower, or other fresh seasonal vegetables, making a complete meal.

3 lb (1.5 kg) potatoes
*8 oz (250 g) dried salt cod, flaked and soaked
    for 24 hours in 2–3 changes of water*

*4 large tomatoes (about 13 oz/410 g), cut into
    segments*
*1 onion (about 3½ oz/100 g), peeled and cut
    into thin segments*
2 red bell peppers (capsicums), finely chopped
8 oz (250 g) small green olives
2¼ cups (10 fl oz/310 ml) olive oil
salt

Wash the potatoes and boil, unpeeled, in salted water for 30–45 minutes. Allow to cool a little, then peel and cut into ¼ in (0.5 cm) strips.

Put the potatoes in a deep serving dish, cover with a layer of cod, then add the tomatoes and onion, followed by the bell peppers and olives.

Dress with olive oil and salt. Serve cold.

WHITE BEAN SALAD

Judias blancas en ensalada   Serves 4

This salad, an example of the much-vaunted "Mediterranean diet," is simple, austere and honest — rather like the people of Aragón who created it a very long time ago — and is a good example of how ingredients can be combined to form nutritional and tasty dishes. It was probably eaten during times of abstinence as it contains only vegetables. It has an outdoor, country feel and is a good choice for a picnic with olives, cheese, cold cuts and a ripe tomato salad.

*13 oz (410 g) dried white beans, soaked
    overnight*
1 onion (5 oz/155 g), peeled and chopped

4 cloves garlic, peeled
1 bay leaf
salt
¼ cup (2 fl oz/60 ml) olive oil
*2 tablespoons (1 fl oz/30 ml) white wine
    vinegar*

Put the beans in a pan with water to cover. Bring to a boil, then drain and heat again with cold water.

Add the onion, garlic and bay leaf, and simmer gently until the beans are tender (1½–2 hours). Add salt toward the end of the cooking time. Drain and dress with the oil and vinegar. Serve at room temperature.

White bean salad

Cristiano, Anselmo Guinea (1854–1906); DIPUTACION DE VIZCAYA A well-made *potaje*, using fresh vegetables from the garden, was a satisfying repast to offer guests —

especially when, like this one, steaming with tantalizing aromas and accompanied by thick hunks of freshly baked bread.

GAZPACHOS, SOUPS AND HOTPOTS

There has been a growing tendency in recent years to interpret *gazpacho* as having only a limited meaning. Nowadays the term is mainly used to refer to a cold vegetable soup, along with such well-known variations as borscht (made from beets/beetroot), vichyssoise (from leeks) and, the most international and commonplace, cold tomato soup. Historically, however, what the term implied was much more complex.

The name was originally used to refer to a rustic yet creative combination of ingredients in a mortar, improvised according to whatever was available, but always based on the constant components of bread, water, oil, salt, vinegar and garlic. This resulted in many different kinds of *gazpacho*, many of which might have been cold but not all necessarily were.

Bread is used to provide thickness and heartiness. There are some very early *gazpachos* where the bread is left in small pieces and not blended in with the other ingredients. If the bread is pounded in the mortar, it blends with the water and oil.

Gazpachos can therefore range in consistency from very liquid to almost solid, which might surprise those who think *gazpachos* should only be thin. Vinegar plays a crucial role in the creation of those thin, refreshing *gazpachos* that are associated with warm weather. The presence of vinegar provides a link to Roman culture, as it was the Romans who popularized throughout their empire the use of vinegar as an all-purpose refreshment. As the recipes in this chapter show, the basic distinction between one *gazpacho* and another lies in the different consistency each one has and in the strangest additions, which may include raisins, hardcooked (hardboiled) egg or little pieces of fish or ham.

Olive oil is the first ingredient added to the mortar by a humble Spanish *gazpacho* alchemist, and then salt. In addition to all its other virtues, salt acts as a catalyst, breaking down the vegetable fiber and extracting the juices. Garlic, the final basic ingredient, is the seasoning most widely used in the Mediterranean area.

Refreshing summer *gazpachos* are the best-known and most highly esteemed variety, especially by visitors. Consequently, *gazpacho andaluz* is now an essential first course on hot summer nights. The cold *gazpachos* have gradually come to include

Man and child, unknown Andalusian painter (late nineteenth century); FINE ARTS MUSEUM, VALENCIA

The old fruit-seller, Diego de Velázquez (1599–1660); NATIONAL MUSEUM, OSLO
Perhaps the old woman is being given a bowl of soup while waiting to sell her fruit. Velázquez had a gift for portraying ordinary people as real, not sentimentalized. The muted use of color — predominantly ochers and browns — and the simplicity of this composition, focusing on her care-worn face, are characteristics of this painter's style.

those vegetables that can be eaten raw and therefore provide most freshness and vitamins.

Even though nowadays *gazpacho andaluz* is the most common variety — as well as the most liquid and refreshing — it should still be remembered that, in classic Spanish cooking, the term *gazpacho* originally applied to the concept of a cuisine created by combining ingredients in a mortar. In *Don Quixote*, Sancho Panza refers to this when he complains, "I would rather get sick of eating *gazpachos* than be at the mercy of an impertinent doctor trying to starve me to death."

SOUPS

The inhabitants of Spain used to be — and still are — very fond of soup. It featured prominently in Spanish literature and in customs such as *sopa boba conventual* which was provided by religious communities to feed the poor of their parishes. As well, there were the "soup students," a group of scholars who complained that soup was their staple food throughout the university term. They even featured a wooden soup spoon in the coat of arms of their student capes, which are still used today by the groups of minstrels known as *tunos*. Spanish picaresque literature made much of the risks involved in eating soup, when other foods were unavailable.

In recent years, however, the quality of soup has suffered as a direct result of the production of food on a commercial scale. The success of any soup depends on there being a certain trust in the ingredients that have gone into it — a trust that is difficult to sustain when the soup is made in a factory. It also needs to be treated carefully, given that it is usually too hot to be eaten quickly and is very easy to spill.

Yet, whether simple or elaborate, soup is intimately associated with Spanish home life. And it has always been considered to be the food that is easiest to digest, hence the *puchero para dolientes* and *puchero de enfermo* (both meaning "invalid soup") and *puchero reconfortante* (comforting soup) of classic Spanish culinary literature.

In the past, three basic categories of soup used to be made in Spain: those containing meat, those suitable for fast days (which mainly meant that vegetables were included) and healthy soups. Nowadays soups tend to be classified either by the nature of their ingredients — whether vegetables, fish or meat is used. for instance; or else by how they are prepared — whether liquid or solid ingredients or an extract is used.

Ingredients vary from region to region according to what each region produces. The austere fields of the north of Spain, being limited in what they cultivate, provide the basic materials for vegetable soups such as the one based on leek and potato. But in the south there is a wider range of vegetables which are gently fried with seasonings before the water is added.

Menudillo soups are broths containing pieces of ham, chicken livers, chicken breast and hardcooked egg. The most Spanish of soups, however, is the *olla*, where solid foods are cooked in a broth and can be eaten separately.

Seafood is sometimes used in its own right, as is the case with shellfish soups, while *marinera*-style soups rely more on the flavor of the seafood, which is used to make the basic broth (stock).

Cooking blood-sausage (eighteenth-century tilework);
GIMENO WORKS, MANISES, VALENCIA
This type of sausage (*morcilla*), similar to a blood-pudding, was a common ingredient for *cocidos*.

Dinner on the boat, V. Alvarez Salas (1871–1919); MUSEUM OF GIJON, ASTURIAS

HOTPOTS

Potajes (hotpots) represent a very ancient form of cooking — although more sophisticated than roasting. It is a way of cooking whose only requirements are a fireproof pole to hold a pot over the fire so that the pot can be removed before its contents start to burn, and water to cook the ingredients in.

The pot used for this cooking method was the *olla*, a type of stewing pot with handles that is narrower at the top than at the bottom. And its beginnings can be traced back to the ancient cooking culture that used bell-shaped utensils, which originated in the Iberian peninsula, later spreading throughout Europe and the rest of the Mediterranean. The campanulate pot, so called from its characteristic shape with the opening reminiscent of a bell, was the great contribution made by prehistoric Spanish ceramics to the culture of the Bronze Age.

Hotpots provide a convenient and nutritious meal. The only work involved is a great deal of stirring — all the different ingredients are combined with all sorts of seasonings in water to soften them and make them digestible.

Different kinds of *potaje* have gradually become established in Spanish cuisine — distinguished by whether they contain meat or ingredients more suitable for times of fast — but all contain some kind of legume (pulse), and one or more vegetables. The hotpots for fasting days usually also include dried salt cod. In the days before refrigeration, salt cod could be transported throughout the country with no danger of its deteriorating in the heat, and the protein it provided was very welcome on fasting days.

Merienda *(afternoon snack) in the* countryside, Lucas Villamil (1824–70);
SAN TELMO MUSEUM, SAN SEBASTIAN

The addition of sausages meant that certain *potajes* underwent a change of identity and adopted new names. Thus, for example, there is *fabada asturiana* made from dried white beans, blood sausage and smoked beef, while the blanket term *lentejas* usually refers to lentils cooked with *chorizo* sausage and bacon fat.

Chickpeas play an especially important role in hotpots. The best example of their use nowadays is in the *cocido*, a derivative of the medieval *olla*. By the middle ages the word *olla* had come to refer as well to the food cooked in that type of pot. This food was sometimes called *poderosa* (powerful), when its ingredients were considered to be a reflection of the financial standing of the person making it, and on other occasions was labeled *podrida* (rotten), if it had been overcooked. The Jewish *adafina* is a hotpot which also falls within this category. It is put on the stove on Friday night to cook slowly, so that it is ready for eating the next day, as if it were some kind of manna from heaven, made without any human intervention. *Cocido* no longer includes the hardcooked eggs of *adafina*, although sausages have become an established element.

Cocido is any very complete hotpot, including not only chickpeas and sausages, but also beef and poultry, potatoes and other vegetables. For a very long time now it has been the basic meal of the Spanish people. Perhaps the most well-known version is *cocido madrileño* ("*cocido* from Madrid"). There is a song which used to be very popular, called *Cocidito Madrileño*, which compared this dish with the most prestigious foods, and *cocido* came out on top! The Hotel Ritz in Madrid, one of the most expensive in the world, features *cocido* on its menu one day a week, although it is really the typical meal of manual laborers and, according to the song, was cooked in garrets.

Still-life for October, Diego de Velázquez (1599–1660);
CAJA DE AHORROS COLLECTION, ZARAGOZA
Pomegranates, the centerpiece of this autumnal display, are unusual as a fruit in that the center consists only of small seeds, each one coated with a juicy pulp. It is this highly sharp, pulpy coating which is eaten by being sucked from around the seeds. The pulp produces a rich, dark red juice for flavoring sweets and for making *granadina*, a syrupy extract used as a drink-base. Pomegranates are supposed to have been introduced into Spain by the Moors — according to one tradition, by Abd-al-Rahman, first of the Ummayad emirs of Cordoba, who imported them from Baghdad in the eighth century.

Chilled almond and garlic soup with grapes

CHILLED ALMOND AND GARLIC SOUP WITH GRAPES

Ajo blanco con uvas   Serves 4

Almond-flavored *ajo blanco* comes from Málaga, and is usually served with fresh muscat grapes (peeled and seeded), small pieces of fish or sometimes apples or melon. A marble or metal mortar and a wooden pestle are used to obtain the almond milk, and the almond and olive oils emulsify perfectly with the garlic, salt and bread. A truly authentic *ajo blanco* is diluted with water fresh from a well or a pitcher standing in the shade. It is considered a crime to add ice cubes.

1½ cups (8 oz/250 g) almonds
5 oz (155 g) bread, with crusts removed
2 cloves garlic, peeled
salt

⅔ cup (5 fl oz/155 ml) olive oil
1 tablespoon sherry vinegar
4 cups (1 qt/1 l) very cold water
1 lb (500 g) muscat grapes, peeled and seeded

Blanch the almonds for 2 minutes in boiling water to loosen the skin. Drain and rub the loose skins off with a tea towel.

Soak the bread in a small amount of water.

Crush the almonds, bread, garlic and salt in a large mortar or bowl. Mix thoroughly with the pestle, gradually drizzling in the oil to form a spongy paste. Mix in the vinegar, then add the cold water.

Transfer to the refrigerator.

Just before serving, check whether the soup needs more salt or vinegar, then add the grapes and serve well chilled.

52

CADIZ FISH SOUP

Sopa de pescado gaditana   Serves 4

This delicious and highly distinctive fish soup is prepared in the fishermen's taverns of Cádiz. The basic ingredients are white fish and vegetables, flavored and colored with golden-fried onion. A magic touch is provided by wine and orange juice, traditionally squeezed from the wonderful bitter fruit from the trees decorating the town of Cádiz. The soup is affectionately known as "dog gravy" — maybe because originally it was made with extremely flavorsome fish bones and heads.

1¼ lb (600 g) white fish (with head), sliced
2 leeks, cleaned and sliced lengthwise
2 carrots, scrubbed and sliced horizontally
3 cups (24 fl oz/750 ml) water
¼ cup (2 fl oz/60 ml) dry white wine
salt
¼ cup (2 fl oz/60 ml) olive oil
1 onion (6½ oz/200 g), finely sliced
juice of 1 orange
French bread (allow 4–6 thin slices per person)

Put the fish head, leeks, carrots, water, wine and salt in a pan and cook for 30 minutes to make a broth. Strain and reserve about 2 cups (16 fl oz/500 ml) of the liquid. Keep hot.

Salt the fish on both sides and set aside.

Heat the oil in a heatproof casserole and fry the onion on a low heat. When it starts to brown, add half the hot broth and cook for about 15 minutes, or until the onion is very soft. Add the rest of the broth and the slices of fish, then cook over low heat for 10 minutes.

Add the orange juice and serve with the slices of bread.

Cádiz fish soup

ANDALUSIAN GAZPACHO

Gazpacho andaluz   Serves 4–6

T he wife of Emperor Napoleon III, Eugenia de Montijo of Granada, was responsible for Andalusian gazpacho becoming popular in France. Today tourism has led to this soup being made throughout the world.

Gazpacho is delicious, natural, nutritious, thirst-quenching and always available. The formula may be simple, but it actually takes practice to make it well. Kitchens in southern Spain always have a supply on hand, ready to pour into glasses as a refreshing summer drink or serve in a dish garnished with a variety of finely chopped ingredients. Gazpacho is delicious at any time and is an ideal offering for making visitors feel at home. The gazpachos of olden times, such as the soup mentioned by Juan de la Mata in *Arte de Repostería* (1747), contained none of the ingredients from the New World as these foods had not yet become an integral part of Spanish cooking.

The most common Gazpacho is known as the Capon de Galera, which is made as follows: take the crusts of a one-pound loaf of bread, without the crumbs, toast them and soak in water: afterwards put them in their Sauce, composed of Anchovy bones, and a couple of cloves of Garlic, well ground, with Vinegar, Sugar, Salt and Oil, all thoroughly mixed, letting the bread soften in the garlic. Then put it all on the plate, adding all or some of the ingredients and vegetables of the Royal Salad.

Juan de la Mata, *Arte de Repostería*, 1747

3½ oz (100 g) stale bread, with crusts removed

2 lb (1 kg) very ripe tomatoes, peeled

1 green bell pepper (capsicum) (3½ oz/ 100 g), finely chopped

2 cloves garlic, peeled

¼ cup (2 fl oz/60 ml) white wine vinegar

⅔ cup (5 fl oz/155 ml) olive oil

2 teaspoons salt

Garnish

1 small onion (4 oz/125 g), finely chopped

1 firm, ripe tomato (3½ oz/100 g), peeled and finely chopped

1 green bell pepper (capsicum) 2 oz (60 g), finely chopped

2 oz (60 g) cucumber, peeled and finely chopped

1 egg, hardcooked (hardboiled) and finely chopped

3½ oz (100 g) stale bread, diced

Soak the bread for the soup in about ⅔ cup (5 fl oz/155 ml) of water. Squeeze out the excess liquid.

If working by hand, crush the bread and all the other ingredients in a large mortar, then drizzle in the oil slowly, mixing to a smooth consistency. If using a food processor put all the ingredients in the bowl and blend to a fine purée. You may need to do this in 2 or more batches. Check the seasoning.

Pour into a bowl, cover and chill for at least 1 hour.

Put the garnish ingredients in individual bowls and serve with the gazpacho.

Cold water can be added to thin the soup just before serving if desired.

CHILLED RICH TOMATO SOUP

Porra antequerana   Serves 4

P orra is a thick gazpacho, a smooth yet stiff mixture, the result of constant pounding in the mortar to bind all the ingredients with the olive oil without the mixture separating. Originally a simple country recipe, *porra* is a good example of how the artful people of Málaga have contrived to find ways to alleviate the discomforts of their long, hot summers.

8 oz (250 g) dense-textured bread

4–5 cloves garlic, peeled and chopped

salt

1 lb (500 g) ripe tomatoes, peeled and chopped

1 cup (8 fl oz/250 ml) extra virgin olive oil

3 tablespoons (1½ fl oz/45 ml) white wine vinegar or lemon juice

3 eggs, hardcooked (hardboiled) and chopped

3½ oz (100 g) cured ham, diced, or 1 small can tuna in brine

Soak the bread in 2 cups (16 fl oz/500 ml) water for a few minutes until soggy. Remove the crusts and squeeze out as much excess liquid as possible.

If working by hand, crush the garlic with a little salt in the mortar, then add the tomatoes, followed by the bread. Blend with the pestle, trickling in the oil and then the vinegar to form a smooth paste — do this carefully to prevent the mixture from separating. Season.

If using a food processor, purée the garlic, tomatoes, bread and salt, then add the oil gradually, followed by the vinegar. Season at the end. Place in the refrigerator.

Garnish with the hardcooked eggs, and ham or tuna, and serve well chilled.

Andalusian gazpacho (back); chilled rich tomato soup (front)

Garlic soup (top); Madrid chicken giblet soup (bottom)

GARLIC SOUP

Sopa de ajo   Serves 4

This is a humble but exquisite soup, made with dense-textured bread and garlic fried in oil, then flavored with paprika. There are more luxurious or well-to-do versions where *chorizo* sausage, triangles of cured ham and even poached eggs are added. Although originally a peasant soup, it is everyday fare in the cities, especially in Castile. In Catalonia thyme is added to the cooking water. The soup is said to have special purifying virtues and is highly regarded as a pick-me-up — ideal for the morning after the excesses of the night before.

4 cups (1 qt/1 l) water
¼ cup (2 fl oz/60 ml) olive oil
4 cloves garlic, peeled
10 oz (315 g) dense-textured French bread, thinly sliced
1 teaspoon paprika
salt
4 eggs (optional)

Put the water on to boil.

Heat the oil and fry the garlic in a skillet (frying pan) or heatproof casserole. Add the slices of bread and brown. Stir in the paprika, then pour in the boiling water. Add the salt and cook for 15 minutes. Serve.

If desired, break an egg for each person into the soup in the final few minutes of the cooking time. Wait until the white sets before serving.

MADRID CHICKEN GIBLET SOUP

Sopa de menudillos a la madrileña   Serves 4

The broth (stock) left over from *cocido* (see page 60) is traditionally used up the next day to make chicken giblet soup, which may include livers, spleen and often ham and finely chopped hardcooked (hardboiled) egg. This soup is a good example of the resourceful *petit bourgeois* cuisine of the cities, designed to make a dish go as far as possible. It is, however, an elegant, comforting soup which is suitable for serving to guests.

⅓ cup (3 fl oz/90 ml) olive oil
1 small onion (4 oz/125 g), finely chopped
1 clove garlic, finely chopped
5 oz (155 g) chicken giblets, finely chopped
8 oz (250 g) tomatoes, peeled and finely chopped
1 tablespoon finely chopped parsley
salt
6½ oz (200 g) French bread, thinly sliced and toasted in the oven
4 cups (1 qt/1 l) cocido broth (stock) (use other chicken broth if unavailable, but flavor will not be as good) (see page 60)

Preheat the oven to 350°F (180°C/Gas 4).

Heat the oil in an ovenproof casserole and fry the onion and garlic. When they start to brown, add the giblets and sauté for a few minutes. Add the tomatoes, parsley and a little salt, then cook for a further 15 minutes.

Add the toast slices and the broth, then transfer to the oven for 15 minutes. Serve immediately.

Shepherds, tilework (eighteenth century);

Leek and salt cod soup

LEEK AND SALT COD SOUP

Porrusalda   Serves 4

Basque–French cuisine is famed for being refined and skillful. It is, however, also hearty and has a very distinctive character. Simple and homely, it requires passionate dedication. Basque–French fish dishes have an international reputation, particularly the cod preparations featured in all recipe books. This simple cod soup is a traditional dish from the mountain *caseríos* (hamlets). While especially appreciated during meatless days, it is also a welcome dish at other times.

10 oz (315 g) dried salt cod, soaked for 12 hours
⅓ cup (3 fl oz/90 ml) olive oil

4 cloves garlic, peeled
4 medium leeks, chopped
2 lb (1 kg) potatoes, cut into chunks
salt

Drain the cod, remove the skin and bones, then break the flesh into small pieces.

Heat the oil in a heatproof casserole and fry the garlic, then add the leeks, followed by the potatoes.

Cover with water, bring to a boil and add the cod. Turn down the heat, cover, and cook slowly over low heat for 45 minutes.

Check the seasoning. Serve.

THICK TOMATO SALMOREJO

Salmorejo   Serves 4

The word *salmorejo* derives from the Latin *salmuria* or *salmuera*, meaning a highly saline aqueous medium. Nowadays, however, *salmorejos* — gazpachos without water — are quite different. Garlic, bread, salt and oil are laboriously pounded in a mortar to produce a thick cream, then vinegar and water are added. The more modern version also includes tomatoes. The recipe came originally from Córdoba, but it is now found throughout Andalusia, with each village adding its favorite extras: ham and egg, almonds, ground cumin, mint, and even partridge and rabbit in some mountain villages.

2 cloves garlic, peeled

1 egg yolk

4 large, ripe tomatoes (1½ lb/750 g), peeled and chopped

1 thick slice (1 oz/30 g) French bread

⅓ cup (3 fl oz/90 ml) olive oil

salt

2 tablespoons (1 fl oz/30 ml) white wine vinegar

1 small onion and 1 green bell pepper (capsicum), finely chopped
or
2 oz (60 g) ham and 1 hardcooked (hardboiled) egg, finely chopped

Blend the garlic, egg yolk, tomatoes and bread in a large mortar. Add the oil carefully to obtain a thick mixture. Season at the end with salt and vinegar.

Serve garnished with either onion and green bell pepper or ham and hardcooked egg.

MONKFISH SOUP WITH MAYONNAISE

Gazpachuelo   Serves 4

The humble *gazpachuelo* from Málaga started out as nothing more than egg yolks beaten with olive oil, pieces of boiled eggwhite, a few drops of vinegar and lemon or bitter orange juice, and diluted with fish or shellfish broth (stock). It is an example of the seasonal versatility of gazpachos, as this version is eaten hot and is more of a winter dish. A richer version is made with a fish base, combined with mayonnaise, thin slices of fish and finely chopped ham, with a glass of wine poured in just before serving.

6½ oz (200 g) small clams

salt

13 oz (410 g) monkfish, in chunks

1 onion, chopped

2 bay leaves

Fishing scene, Joaquín Sorolla (1863–1923); PRIVATE COLLECTION

Thick tomato salmorejo (front left, and back); monkfish soup with mayonnaise (front right)

2 tablespoons (1 fl oz/30 ml) dry white wine
1 lb (500 g) potatoes, cut into ¼ in (0.5 cm) slices
⅓ cup (3 fl oz/90 ml) thick mayonnaise
French bread (allow 4–6 thin slices per person)

Wash the clams and soak in salted cold water to release the sand.

Put the monkfish in a large heatproof casserole with cold water to cover. Add the onion, bay leaves and white wine. Bring to a boil, cook for 1 minute; remove from the heat and set aside.

Put the clams in a heatproof casserole, add water to barely cover and cook over low heat. When the shells open, remove from the heat and discard the shells. Strain and reserve the cooking water.

Strain the broth from the monkfish into a heatproof casserole and set aside. Remove the skin and bones from the fish, then flake the flesh and cover with a little of the strained clam broth. Cover and set aside.

Boil the potatoes in the fish broth for 30 minutes. Strain and reserve the broth.

Put the mayonnaise in a tureen and gradually add the broth from the potatoes and the clam broth, stirring with a wooden spoon.

Add the fish, clams and potatoes and check the seasoning.

Toast the slices of bread and serve with the soup.

59

Madrid meat and chickpea cocido

MADRID MEAT AND CHICKPEA COCIDO

Cocido madrileño   Serves 6

The *cocido madrileño* is a very traditional local specialty. The range of ingredients varies according to individual means. From its working-class origins, *cocido* has risen to the lofty heights of the aristocracy. Versatile and ad hoc, its many varieties reflect the climate and culture in which it has developed. It is related to the Jewish *adafina*, Moroccan hotpots, North African couscous, the *pucheros* and *ollas* of Latin America and European *pot-au-feu*. It turns into two courses when served: the soup, and the chickpeas served with vegetables and the meats.

1 lb (500 g) beef shank (shin)

½ chicken, boned (approximately 13 oz/410 g)

3½ oz (100 g) pork fat

3½ oz (100 g) cured ham

1 lb (500 g) chickpeas, soaked overnight

1 salted pig's foot (trotter), soaked overnight

½ small onion (4 oz/125 g), stuck with a clove

salt

8 oz (250 g) green beans, trimmed

8 oz (250 g) green cabbage, chopped

6½ oz (200 g) golden thistles, cleaned and chopped or large white ribs of Swiss chard (silverbeet)

9½ oz (300 g) Swiss chard (silverbeet), washed

6½ oz (200 g) chorizo (paprika-flavored cured pork sausage)

6 small potatoes (1¼ lb/600 g), peeled

few strands saffron

2 morcilla blood sausages (black pudding) (6½ oz/200 g)

2½ oz (75 g) vermicelli

¼ cup (2 fl oz/60 ml) olive oil

1 clove garlic, peeled

tomato sauce as accompaniment (optional)

Put 13½ cups (3 qt/3 l) cold water in a wide-based pot. Start heating, adding the beef shank, chicken, pork fat and ham. There should be enough water to cover all these ingredients. Skim off any foam. When it comes to a boil, add the chickpeas and the pig's foot and bring back to a boil, then add the onion and salt, turn down the heat and simmer gently for about 3 hours.

Cook the beans, cabbage, thistles and Swiss chard with the *chorizo* in a separate pot for 30 minutes. Add the potatoes and saffron and cook for a further 20 minutes. Boil the blood sausages in a separate pan, taking care to keep them whole.

Strain off the broth from the 2 pots, then mix together. Check the seasoning and add the vermicelli.

Drain the green vegetables and sauté in the oil in a skillet (frying pan) with the garlic clove. Transfer to a serving dish. Slice the *chorizo* and blood sausages and arrange alongside the vegetables. Add the potatoes, leaving them whole.

Drain the chickpeas thoroughly and transfer to a large serving dish. Cut the beef into small chunks and arrange on top of the chickpeas. Chop up the ham, pork fat, chicken, and pig's foot and arrange around the edge of the dish.

The 2 dishes should be served at the same time, accompanied, if desired, by tomato sauce served in a sauce boat.

CHICKPEA AND SPINACH HOTPOT

Potaje de garbanzos y espinacas Serves 4

T he origin of the *potaje* goes all the way back to the invention of pottery and cooking in a moist medium. The Roman cook Celio Apicio, probably of Andalusian origin, recorded some recipes which could be precursors to modern *potajes*. From the fourth century onward *potajes* were a traditional meal during Lent, usually mixing some kind of pulse with vegetables and sometimes other ingredients too. Salt cod used to be included but was given up as a symbol of penitence. A variety of *potajes* is described by Ruperto de Nola in *Libro de Guisados* (1520), Diego Granado in *Libro del Arte de Cocina* (1599), Francisco Martínez Montiño in *Arte de Cocina, Pastelería, Vizcochería y Conservería* (1611) and Juan de Altamiras in *Nuevo Arte de Cocina* (1745). The exquisite chickpea hotpot is still very popular in Madrid.

> If you have some broth [stock] from chard [silverbeet], or spinach [English spinach], use it to soak the Chickpeas, or if not with the broth from Codfish; when they have been soaked, washed and scalded, cook them in a little new oil. When they are cooked, put some fried onion to them, with all the spices, crushed with a few cloves of garlic. Season with salt, and if you want to thicken them, put a sixth part of rice: if it be a festive table, put to it an almond sauce, and eggs; for the poor people, it is enough to pound a ladle of chickpeas with egg yolks, and the whites you can use for eggs in omelet; with one egg, and two whites, you can make an honest omelet, because you can happen upon some peculiar people, who will call you to account over one egg, and I speak from experience. If you can, combine the Chickpeas with the hard heads of the Codfish, cooking them with the Chickpeas, and a few heads [bulbs] of garlic, which produces a good flavor; but this depends on the heads: make use of them only if they are good, because otherwise your guests will sometimes let you know, and I hope you will learn from experience, and not be caught out. If guests arrive unexpectedly, pound some herbs to make the contents of the bowl go further, and no one will be any the wiser.
>
> Juan de Altamiras, *Nuevo Arte de Cocina*, 1745

1 lb (500 g) chickpeas, soaked overnight

2 lb (1 kg) fresh spinach (English spinach), washed and chopped

1 lb (500 g) potatoes, peeled and cut into chunks

salt

2 eggs, hardcooked (hardboiled)

¾ cup (6 fl oz/185 ml) olive oil

1 thick slice French bread (1 oz/30 g)

2 cloves garlic, peeled

Chickpea and spinach hotpot

1 onion (3½ oz/100 g), finely chopped

1 teaspoon paprika

Heat plenty of water in a large pot. When it comes to a boil, add the chickpeas; cover and simmer over low heat.

Add the spinach, potatoes and a little salt and cook slowly for a further 30 minutes.

Chop up the whites of the hardcooked eggs. Reserve the yolks.

Heat the oil in a skillet (frying pan). Fry the slice of bread, then remove from the pan and set aside. Fry the garlic in the same oil, remove and set aside. Slowly sauté the onion until it starts to brown. Add the paprika, stir, then quickly pour this mixture over the chickpeas. Crush the fried garlic and bread with the egg yolks in a mortar, then add to the chickpeas along with the chopped eggwhite.

Check the seasoning. Cook gently for another 15 minutes. Taste to check that the chickpeas are cooked, then serve.

The Madrid Fair, Manuel de la Cruz (1750–92); MUNICIPAL MUSEUM, MADRID
The Madrid Fair is a grand farewell to summer and everyone is out enjoying the street-life before the chill winter winds strike.

MAJORCAN DRY VEGETABLE SOUP

Sopas mallorquinas de verduras   Serves 4

This dish, made with vegetables and dense-textured bread, takes on all the flavor of the excellent local olive oil. It is still made according to the original recipe.

⅔ cup (5 fl oz/155 ml) olive oil

3 cloves garlic, finely chopped

3 green onions (spring onions), chopped

2 leeks (white part only), finely chopped

2 tomatoes (6½ oz/200 g), peeled and finely chopped

½ teaspoon paprika

4 large cabbage leaves, washed and shredded

3½ oz (100 g) green beans, chopped

2½ oz (75 g) shelled peas

3½ oz (100 g) spinach (English spinach), shredded
salt

3½ oz (100 g) coarse-textured, unsalted whole-wheat (wholemeal) bread, thinly sliced

Heat ⅓ cup (3 fl oz/90 ml) of the oil in a heatproof casserole. Gently fry the garlic, green onions and leeks. Do not allow them to brown. Add the tomatoes, followed by the paprika. Stir with a wooden spoon. Add the cabbage and continue cooking, stirring frequently. Add a small amount of water. Add the green beans and peas and cook for 15 minutes. Add the spinach, another ladle of water and some salt, then cover and cook for a further 10 minutes. Drain well and reserve the cooking water.

Lay half the bread in a heatproof casserole and sprinkle with a little oil. Cover with a layer of vegetables, then another layer of bread drizzled with oil. Put the rest of the vegetables on top and moisten with a little of the cooking liquid. Drain off any excess as the dish should be dry. Sprinkle on some more oil and place, uncovered, in a warm oven for a few minutes to dry out before serving.

Majorcan dry vegetable soup

TOLOSA RED BEAN SOUP

Alubias rojas a la tolosana   Serves 4

Beans occupy a privileged position in Spanish cuisine and feature in many dishes. In Segovia beans are the main ingredient of a dish called *con todo* ("with everything") — a reflection of their popularity. There are many varieties, shapes and colors of beans and each region has its favorites. The Basques prefer red (kidney) beans and like to stew them with the best ingredients from their larders and the gardens surrounding the rustic hamlets set on green hills.

1 lb (500 g) red (kidney) beans, soaked overnight
1½ onions (1 finely chopped)
½ cup (4 fl oz/125 ml) olive oil
3½ oz (100 g) pork fat
8 oz (250 g) pork spareribs
salt
½ green cabbage, shredded
2 blood sausages (black puddings) (3½ oz/ 100 g each)
2 cloves garlic, peeled and crushed

Put the beans in a large pot and cover with cold water. Add the half onion, 2 tablespoons (1 fl oz/30 ml) of the oil and the pork fat. Cook on low heat. Add more cold water as the beans cook and the broth reduces. When the beans are half cooked (after about 1¼ hours), add the spareribs and check the seasoning. Cook for another hour or so, or until the beans are soft and a thick broth has formed.

Heat ¼ cup (2 fl oz/60 ml) of the oil in a skillet (frying pan) and fry the remaining chopped onion until it starts to brown. Add the beans and cook slowly.

Boil the cabbage in a separate heatproof casserole or pot. When it is half cooked (about

Tolosa red bean soup (left); Canary Island hotpot (center); Alto Aragon lentil hotpot (right)

15 minutes), add the blood sausages and check the seasoning. Cook for another 15 minutes, then drain and transfer to a serving dish.

Heat the remaining oil in a skillet. Fry the garlic and add to the cabbage.

Serve the bean soup piping hot, accompanied by the cabbage and sausage.

CANARY ISLAND HOTPOT

Puchero canario   Serves 4

The people of the Canary Islands are proud of the traditions of their ancient cuisine which had a substantial influence on the culinary habits of Latin America, especially Cuba and Argentina. The pine nuts and currants in this everyday dish reflect its connection with the classic flavors of Iberian cooking. The Canarian stamp *par excellence*, however, is provided by the tomatoes, considered to be not only the most beautiful in the world but also the tastiest.

12 oz (375 g) chickpeas, soaked overnight
16 almonds
2 tablespoons pine nuts
⅓ cup (3 fl oz/90 ml) olive oil
1 onion (5 oz/155 g), finely chopped
8 oz (250 g) tomatoes, finely chopped
2 tablespoons currants
salt

Cover the chickpeas with water and cook on low heat.

Meanwhile, crush the almonds and pine nuts in a mortar.

Heat the oil in a skillet (frying pan) and sauté the onion over low heat. When it starts to brown, add the mixture from the mortar, fry for 1 minute, then add the tomatoes and currants. Continue cooking on low heat for 15 minutes.

Add this mixture to the chickpeas, season with a little salt, then cook very slowly for about 1 hour, or until the chickpeas are tender. Serve.

ALTO ARAGON LENTIL HOTPOT

Lentejas al estilo del Alto Aragón   Serves 4

Life in Alto Aragón, in the Pyrenean valleys, may be somewhat austere, but this does not stop the inhabitants from expressing their fondness for good traditional cooking in the

Jaime I the Conqueror, tilework in Plaza de España, Seville (1920)

form of hearty dishes such as lentils with leeks and ham. The famous Aragonese cold-cured sausages are the secret of this magnificent, warming winter soup.

2 cups (12 oz/375 g) brown lentils
1 ham bone
⅓ cup (3 fl oz/90 ml) olive oil
2 leeks, chopped
1 onion (5 oz/155 g), chopped
1 tomato (4 oz/125 g), peeled and chopped
1 blood sausage (black pudding) (about 3½ oz/ 100 g), chopped
5 oz (155 g) button mushrooms (champignons), chopped and sprinkled with the juice of ½ lemon
salt
a few drops dry anisette liqueur
⅓ cup (3 fl oz/90 ml) muscatel wine

Boil the lentils with the ham bone.

Heat the oil in a skillet (frying pan), then add the leeks and onion. When the mixture starts to brown, add the tomato and cook over medium heat for 10 minutes, then add the blood sausage and mushrooms and cook for a further 10 minutes.

When the lentils are almost ready (after approximately 40 minutes), add the vegetable and sausage mixture and a little salt, then cook for 40 minutes.

Taste to check whether the lentils are done. Before removing from the heat, sprinkle on a few drops of anisette and add the muscatel. Serve immediately.

Merienda *(afternoon snack) at the Venta de Cerero* (tapestry), Ramón Bayeu (1746–93); BOURBON PALACE, EL ESCORIAL, MADRID A *venta* was a basic type of roadside inn, at

which often the only food provided would be for the animals. Travelers were commonly expected to provide their own food.

EGG DISHES, BREAD AND SAVORY PIES

The common factor that links the three food groups included in this chapter is that in each case no wastage is involved — every last morsel is eaten up. The shell is the only part of an egg which is discarded. Tiny pieces of leftover bread are popped into our mouths rather than thrown away. And *empanadas* are savory fillings with edible containers.

EGGS

The fact that we have overcome any possible squeamishness about eating the embryo of a bird is of great advantage to us nutritionally. Perhaps it was the extraordinary aesthetic qualities of eggs when they are being cooked that encouraged us to do this. Nuñez Alonso, a present-day Spanish writer thought that we owed the discovery of the fried egg to its beauty — shining, bright yellow enamel framed in white porcelain — and even went so far as to imagine the beauty of a vault decorated with fried eggs.

The egg plays an important role in the kitchen. It is very versatile, adopting different forms depending on how it is used. It can be used on its own or gradually added to other foods, achieving its greatest splendor in cake-making.

Throughout the history of cooking, the egg has taken on various associations: as a saving grace for abstainers at the most difficult times of their fasting; as a cure or source of strength for invalids and convalescents; and, strangely, as a symbol of the Resurrection, which is the origin of *monas de Pascua*, buns encrusted with eggs. These buns are baked at the beginning of spring to coincide with Easter celebrations and so this symbol represents both nature's return to life and the resurrection of Christ. In baroque painting, therefore, the appearance of eggs consciously placed in the foreground is much more than a decorative or anecdotal detail.

Spanish people have a weakness for fried eggs. They are not elegant and, being usually one of the cheapest meals available, cannot be said to enhance the social status of anyone who eats them in public. However, a Spaniard will always opt for

Still-life, Luis Meléndez (1716–80); FINE ARTS MUSEUM, SEVILLE
Good country bread was a staple that was never absent from the table. A nourishing food on its own, it also combined happily with other foods — and it helped fill the stomach.

a couple of fried eggs when at a loss for what to eat. All restaurants are ready for this emergency, usually not even bothering to list them on the menu as everyone knows that a plate of fried eggs is always available.

In Spain the ability to fry an egg has long been considered the yardstick by which culinary skills are measured, and it is therefore most derogatory to remark that someone "doesn't even know how to fry an egg."

Eggs can be fried with or without *puntilla* (crispy edges) or *abuñuelados* (encased in puffed-out skin). To make an egg with *puntilla*, the oil must be very hot before the egg is added. Then a border of toasted lace will form, enclosing small bubbles of oil. To avoid the formation of *puntillas*, the oil should not be too hot and the eggs must be removed when the white solidifies. *Abuñuelados* require a certain degree of skill as the amount of very hot oil required means that it is liable to spatter and may even catch fire.

In Spain, eggs are often fried with *chorizo* sausage, which gives them a transparent,

The present, Valeriano D. Becquer (1834–70); PRADO MUSEUM, MADRID

reddish varnish. The *morcilla* blood sausage is actually preferable, however, because its softer texture allows it to meld more effectively with the egg yolk.

Eggs may also be served with Spanish-style fried potatoes, which are thick and soft and can be squashed with a fork and mixed with the yolk to create a dish suggestive of the great Spanish potato omelet.

A painting by Velázquez, from his Seville period, *An Old Woman Frying Eggs*, features the various elements involved in egg-frying. Instead of the more usual metal skillet (frying pan), an earthenware casserole is portrayed, perhaps because it is more appropriate to the rustic nature of the scene. It is tempting to imagine that the old woman is going to make eggs with *puntillas*, because she is holding her spoon ready to sprinkle on the hot oil. This painting is an important record of egg-frying, especially as it is one of the few Spanish works of art showing the act of cooking.

The best way to find out how to make an authentic *tortilla española*, the famous Spanish potato omelet, is if you happen to get to know a down-to-earth, older Spanish woman. Then, one day, ask her to make you a *tortilla española* — you'll be amazed at the results. Failing that, try the traditional recipe given in this chapter.

BREAD

Bread has always been an extremely important element in the Spanish diet. Like rice in the East and pasta in Italy, it was traditionally the main provider of calories, and

Still-life with bread and onions, Antonio Lopez Torres (born 1902);
PRIVATE COLLECTION, MADRID

In Spain bread is usually consumed fresh, and not kept; so, most people buy it twice a day. The traditional way of tackling a loaf is to break it open with your hands, releasing the delicious, fresh-baked aromas and also preserving its lightness of texture. Bread like the one depicted here is baked to be broken apart in this way — taking a knife to it would spoil it.

Spanish people have exercised great skill in making the most of its possibilities. In another chapter we saw how it is used in *tapas* and soups, but here we are going to look at its various functions in a supporting role.

One basic way of using bread is as a plate — for example, like a shepherd using his knife to hack hunks off a loaf to accompany a few pieces of cheese. This rustic meal might have been accompanied by a few olives. As a more refined alternative, the olives smeared on bread might be replaced by olive oil.

In its use of oil Spanish cooking reveals one of its most attractive aspects — and it all starts with bread and the myriad possibilities opened up when the two are combined. Maybe it goes back to the habit the tasters had in the oil mills of using bread as a medium through which to try out the oil. Having acquired a liking for this combination, they might have sometimes added salt when they went back home or perhaps rubbed the bread with garlic before drizzling on the oil. Then, the introduction of a touch of red, from adding tomato, might have been the next step and finally, when the purse stretched far enough, some of that wonderful Spanish ham would have brought this creation to its pinnacle of perfection. And yet, even then, there was more as bread with oil could also be served in a sweet version — sprinkling on sugar was enough for some, and for those closer to nature there was honey; the more imaginative added orange juice and *aguardiente* (a liqueur).

The Miracle of St Hugo (detail), Francisco de Zurbarán (1598–1664); FINE ARTS MUSEUM, SEVILLE
This painting is a reminder that bread, beyond its practical uses, also has a sacred significance. Zurbarán was a master of genre paintings characterized by an almost ascetic simplicity of style, in which everyday objects — like the bread, unadorned on the table — become charged with a sense of mystic symbolism.

SAVORY PIES

The *empanada*, a kind of savory pie, seems very Spanish because, unlike similar recipes in other countries, the filling and bread-like dough are used in equal proportions. The basic idea behind a Spanish *empanada* always stems from bread. It's the same sort of idea suggested by the Valencian habit called *entrepan* — holding a mouthful of food between two pieces of bread. Or when a sausage is added to bread dough before baking to produce *pan preñado* (pregnant bread). Nobody would suspect that this ordinary-looking loaf contained such a surprise.

Dance of the Virgin of the Harbor (detail), Manuel R. Guzmán (nineteenth century); MUSEO ROMANTICO, MADRID

Every Spanish community or parish has its fiesta day dedicated to its own patron saint, after whom the local church is named. The Virgin Mary, under many different names, was a popular saint in Spain. Such festivals were always great occasions, when local people could leave routine cares aside for a day. Bread and wine were as much a part of that enjoyment and pleasures as they were part of the solemn, religious aspect of the day's celebrations.

The empanada gained its popularity from its suitability for taking on journeys. Its reputation was, however, marred by unscrupulous traders who took unfair advantage of the unknown nature of its filling — a subject that crops up frequently in picaresque literature. Francisco de Quevedo, the seventeenth-century satirical writer, even made a joke involving an empanada de ajusticiado, supposedly made with the flesh of an executed criminal.

This chapter would not be complete without mentioning migas (fried bread-crumbs), one of the most characteristic dishes of Spanish bread cooking. It is made from stale bread, which is either finely diced or, if the magnificent peasant bread known as hogaza is used, cut into thin slices and then softened overnight by being wrapped in a damp cloth. The following day, it is sprinkled with paprika and finally fried slowly in top-quality oil with garlic and perhaps other more unusual ingredients. The migas are ready when they have taken on a sort of old-gold color, and how crumbly it is depends on how much the mixture has been stirred and tossed around in the process.

Migas can be used to accompany all kinds of dishes, especially fried eggs, not to mention perhaps the most extraordinary concoction in European cuisine, migas with chocolate. It is difficult to conceive how chocolate could possibly blend well with paprika and garlic, but it does — and it must be recognized that the Mexicans had already combined cocoa with savory and spiced foods long before Europeans arrived in the Americas.

The basket of bread, Salvador Dali (1904–89); DALI MUSEUM, FIGUERAS
One day in the early 1930s, having just finished eating, Dali noticed "the heel of a long loaf lying on its belly, and I could not cease looking at it." This was the start of his preoccupation with what he called "the enigma of bread" and a series of Surrealist bread-projects and events. These culminated with his arrival in New York for his first visit in 1934 carrying a 8¼ foot (2.5 m) stick of bread made at his request by the ship's cook during the voyage.

75

Baked egg salmorejo

Preheat the oven to 300°F (150°C/Gas 2).

Heat the oil in a skillet (frying pan). Fry the pork fillets on both sides over medium heat. Transfer to an earthenware casserole and sprinkle with salt.

Lightly fry the sausage and ham in the same oil, then transfer to the casserole.

Sauté the onion and garlic in the same oil, then add the bay leaf. Add the flour, cook until it browns, then add the wine and broth to make a sauce which is smooth but not too thick.

Pour the sauce over the other ingredients in the casserole. Carefully break the eggs on top, then arrange the asparagus spears around them. Bake until the eggs set and serve immediately.

BAKED EGG SALMOREJO

Huevos al salmorejo   Serves 4

Eggs provide all-round nutrition and can easily take the place of a meat dish. In some regions people believe meat should accompany eggs, which is perhaps a reflection of the tradition of treating the egg as a symbol of creation. The inhabitants of Aragón are traditionally no strangers to austerity but since ancient times have flouted this condition by preparing flamboyant *salmorejos* in honor of their local produce, including both meat and eggs.

⅓ cup (3 fl oz/90 ml) olive oil
4 pork loin fillets (3½ oz/100 g each)
salt
8 oz (250 g) longaniza (cured pork sausage), diced small
2 oz (60 g) cured ham, diced
1 medium-size onion (5 oz/155 g), peeled and chopped
2 cloves garlic, finely chopped
1 bay leaf
1 teaspoon all-purpose (plain) flour
⅔ cup (5 fl oz/155 ml) dry white wine
⅔ cup (5 fl oz/155 ml) beef broth (stock)
4 eggs
4 cooked white asparagus spears (fresh, canned or frozen can be used)

SPRING VEGETABLE AND EGG CASSEROLE

Huevos con verduras   Serves 4

Hardcooked (hardboiled) eggs with vegetables go back a long way in Spanish culinary history. Endless permutations are listed in detail by several experts, such as Martínez Montiño back in the seventeenth century and Juan de Altamiras over 100 years later. The influence of the Romans and Arabs, combined with the joys of living on the shores of the Mediterranean, has produced many colorful, exciting egg recipes, such as this casserole, which is typical of Majorcan cooking.

> Take the hardboiled [hardcooked] eggs and peel them. Put them in a pot with seasoned water. Fry plenty of onion and add parsley, mint and other herbs and a hazelnut sauce, and bring to a boil. Then add some bread soaked in water and vinegar. Crush some hazelnuts with two cloves of garlic, and add oil with fried garlic to the eggs. Thin the sauce with the seasoned water: the quantity of sauce depends on the number of eggs.
>
> Juan de Altamiras, *Nuevo Arte de Cocina*, 1745

4 eggs, hardcooked (hardboiled)
1 lb (500 g) fresh peas (weight with pods)
1 lb (500 g) fresh lima (butter) or fava (broad) beans (weight with pods)
¼ cup (2 fl oz/60 ml) olive oil
2 small onions (8 oz/250 g), finely chopped
4 green onions (spring onions), sliced
4 cloves garlic
2 medium potatoes, diced
¾ cup (6 fl oz/185 ml) water
salt

Spring vegetable and egg casserole

1 pinch freshly ground pepper
1 pinch ground cinnamon
1 pinch ground cloves

Peel the eggs and slice in half lengthwise.

Shell the peas and chop the beans in their pods.

Heat the oil in a casserole and add the onions and green onions. Turn down the heat and cook until soft, then add the whole garlic cloves, unpeeled, and the beans.

Add the potatoes, stir and pour in the water. When it comes to a boil, add the peas and season with a little salt and a pinch each of pepper, cinnamon and cloves.

Cover and cook over very low heat until the vegetables are cooked (about 45 minutes).

Add the hardcooked eggs and cook for a few more minutes. Remove the garlic cloves and serve in the casserole.

An old woman frying eggs, Diego de Velázquez (1599–1660); NATIONAL GALLERY, EDINBURGH
The amount of oil used, and its temperature, is crucial in creating the characteristically Spanish fried egg. A *cazuela* (earthenware dish) like the one used here, also preserves the flavor of ingredients better than metal pans do; it is, as well, the traditional dish used for making *huevos a la flamenca*.

COUNTRY OMELET

Tortilla campera   Serves 4

Omelets in Spain — except when "French-style" — are round and large and usually have a vegetable filling, although brains, sausages or seafood may also be used. The name of this particular version might suggest that it is prepared in the great outdoors, but this would, in fact, be a little tricky. We think it is more likely a name conjured up by a restaurant to beguile the customers into trying its garden produce by luring them with the more appetizing idea of an egg dish.

2 eggplants (aubergines) (13 oz/410 g),
* peeled and diced*

salt

⅔ cup (5 fl oz/155 ml) olive oil

2 cloves garlic, peeled and finely chopped

1 red bell pepper (capsicum) (6½ oz/200 g),
* finely chopped*

2 zucchini (courgettes) (13 oz/410 g), peeled
* and finely chopped*

2 large, ripe tomatoes (8 oz/250 g), peeled
* and finely chopped*

freshly ground pepper

4 eggs

2 tablespoons (1 fl oz/30 ml) milk

Place the eggplants in a colander, sprinkle with salt and leave for 30 minutes to get rid of the bitter taste. Pat dry with paper towels.

Heat the oil in a large skillet (frying pan). Brown the garlic, then add the eggplants, followed by the red bell pepper and zucchini, stirring occasionally.

Add the tomatoes, season with salt and pepper and cook on low heat for 40 minutes.

Break the eggs into a bowl, add a little salt and pepper, then pour in the milk and beat together. Add the fried vegetables.

Heat some oil in a skillet, pour the egg and vegetable mixture in and cook the omelet on one side, then turn it out onto a plate or wide lid. Slide it back into the pan to set the other side. Serve immediately.

HAM AND CHORIZO SCRAMBLE

Duelos y quebrantos　　　　　　　　Serves 4

The literal translation of this simple and tasty Castilian dish is "grief and distress." To understand the roots of this dish, we have to go back to the daily fare of Don Quixote, as explained very clearly by Cervantes: "Three parts of his income were consumed in food — a stewpot of beef, leftover ground meat on other nights, *duelos y quebrantos* on Saturdays, lentils for Fridays and perhaps a pigeon on Sundays." The many and varied theories about the name of this dish include one by the eminent man of letters Calderón de la Barca, who says in one of his comedies:

. . . for a troubled, sad and wretched widow,
eggs and fried bacon will suffice,
and are grief and distress itself.

2 oz (60 g) streaky, fatty bacon, diced small
3½ oz (100 g) cured ham fat, diced small
3½ oz (100 g) chorizo (paprika-flavored cured pork sausage), finely chopped
6 eggs, beaten

Heat the bacon, ham fat and *chorizo* in a skillet (frying pan). When the fat starts to ooze out, add the eggs and stir over low heat until just set. Serve in an earthenware dish.

Country omelet (left); ham and chorizo scramble (right)

SPINACH TURNOVERS

Empanadillas rellenas de espinacas Serves 4–6

The term *empanada* is used for any raw or cooked filling wrapped in a dough and baked in the oven or over an open fire. These pies are mentioned in culinary documents as far back as medieval times. Individual servings are called *empanadillas* ("little pies"). There are also some delicious recipes with sweet fillings. Both sweet and savory turnovers can also be fried.

Filling:

1½ lb (750 g) spinach (English spinach), chopped

⅓ cup (3 fl oz/90 ml) olive oil

4 cloves garlic, finely chopped

6½ oz (200 g) tomatoes, peeled and chopped

3½ oz (100 g) bonito tuna in oil or boiled shrimp (prawns)

½ cup (2 oz/60 g) pine nuts

2 eggs, hardcooked (hardboiled) and finely chopped

salt

Dough:

2 cups (8 oz/250 g) all-purpose (plain) flour

¼ cup (2 fl oz/60 ml) olive oil

¼ cup (2 fl oz/60 ml) milk

a few drops lemon juice

1 tablespoon beer

½ teaspoon baking soda (bicarbonate of soda)

salt

1 egg, beaten

Boil the spinach for 10 minutes. Drain.

Heat the oil in a skillet (frying pan) and sauté the garlic on low heat, followed by the tomatoes.

While the mixture is cooking, prepare the dough. Put the flour in a bowl and add the oil, milk, lemon juice, beer, baking soda and salt. Mix by hand until the dough comes away from the sides of the bowl. Leave to rest for 20 minutes.

When the tomato mixture is almost ready, add the spinach, bonito tuna and the pine nuts. Cook for 5 minutes, then remove from the heat and add the chopped eggs and some salt.

Preheat the oven to 400°F (200°C/Gas 6).

Roll the dough out thinly. Cut into 4–5 in (10–12 cm) rounds.

Place a tablespoon of filling on each round. Fold over and seal, making a narrow rim.

Transfer the turnovers to a lightly oiled baking sheet and brush each one with beaten egg. Turn the oven down to 300°F (150°C/Gas 2) and bake the turnovers for approximately 30 minutes. Serve warm or cold.

BELL PEPPER, TOMATO AND TUNA PIE

Coca de pimiento, tomate y atún Serves 4–6

A kind of open *empanada*, these shallow, thin pies topped with vegetables or salted fish are ideal for summer evenings when calm descends on country cottages, when the cicadas bring their concert to an end and the crickets start up their song among the jasmine bushes.

Dough:

3 cups (12 oz/375 g) all-purpose (plain) flour

⅔ cup (5 fl oz/155 ml) olive oil

⅔ cup (5 fl oz/155 ml) dry white wine

salt

Filling:

⅞ cup (6½ fl oz/200 ml) olive oil

¼ cup (1 oz/30 g) pine nuts

8 oz (250 g) red or green bell peppers (capsicums), washed and chopped

2 lb (1 kg) ripe tomatoes, peeled and finely chopped

salt

1 teaspoon sugar

3½ oz (100 g) tuna in oil, flaked

Put all the dough ingredients in a bowl and mix by hand to form a smooth dough which comes away easily from the sides of the bowl. Place on a floured surface and leave to rest for 30 minutes.

Meanwhile, heat the oil in a skillet (frying pan), then remove from the heat and add the pine nuts. Toss gently over low heat, taking care not to let them burn. Remove the pine nuts and set aside. Use the same oil to fry the bell peppers. When they start to brown, add the tomatoes and fry slowly until the mixture reduces and the oil comes to the surface.

Add a little salt and the sugar.

Add the pine nuts and the tuna, mix well and cook for a further 5 minutes.

Preheat the oven to 350°F (180°C/Gas 4).

Line a baking sheet with foil and grease lightly with oil.

Put the dough on a marble slab or other smooth surface. Knead, then roll out to a rectangle and transfer to the baking sheet. Spread the filling on top and fold in the edges of the dough to form a crust.

Bake the pie for about 30 minutes. Serve warm or cold.

Mediterranean vegetable pie (back, page 84); spinach turnovers (center); bell pepper, tomato and tuna pie (front)

Selling fans and rolls, Ramón Bayeu (1746–93);
PRADO MUSEUM, MADRID
Rolls twisted into a ring (called *roscas*) provide another example of the baker's art, supporting an eighteenth-century gastronomer's observation that architecture, one of the five fine arts, had as its principal subdivision, pastry-making.

MEDITERRANEAN VEGETABLE PIE

Coca de verduras   Serves 4–6

Cocas deserve a place in mythology. Imagine eating them in summertime at the foot of a vine beside a fig tree, accompanied by a bunch of muscat grapes rinsed in fresh water from the well. The word *coca* seems to come from the Latin *coquere* (cooking), proof that it is an age-old dish going back to the days of kneading and baking. These pies differ from pizzas in that they are not usually eaten hot and never contain cheese. Apart from this, however, the list of topping ingredients is unlimited. There may be just one main ingredient, such as onion or anchovies, or several, as is the case with this vegetable *coca* from Majorca.

Topping:

1¼ lb (600 g) onions, thinly sliced lengthwise
*8 oz (250 g) green bell peppers (capsicums),
    seeded and chopped*
8 oz (250 g) firm tomatoes, chopped
⅔ cup (5 fl oz/155 ml) olive oil
salt

Dough:

2 eggs
⅓ cup (3 fl oz/90 ml) olive oil
⅓ cup (3 fl oz/90 ml) water
1 teaspoon baking soda (bicarbonate of soda)

4 cups (1 lb/500 g) all-purpose (plain) flour
salt

Put all the topping ingredients in a salad bowl and dress with the olive oil and salt.

Preheat the oven to 300°F (150°C/Gas 2).

To prepare the dough, beat the eggs and gradually add the oil followed by the water, stirring constantly. In a separate bowl, mix the baking soda with the flour, then add slowly to the egg mixture, mixing first with a fork and then with your hands to form a smooth dough.

Roll the dough out thinly to line a 12 × 16 in (30 × 40 cm) rectangular baking sheet, lightly greased with oil. Pinch around the edges to form a crust.

Spread the vegetables on the dough and pour the leftover oil from the bowl over the top. Add a little salt.

Bake for approximately 30 minutes. Serve warm or cold.

GALICIAN SAVORY PIE

Empanada gallega   Serves 6

Pies have been eaten in Galicia since time immemorial. Back in the time of the Goths, this was the dish *par excellence* in Galicia and León and is mentioned in the seventh-century *Régula Monachorum*. There are endless varieties of *empanadas*, but all reflect the different characteristics of either coastal or inland traditions.

Empanadas were typical travelers' fare, the pastry protecting the filling. Different forms appear in all culinary documents and also crop up in Spanish literature. The recipe given by Francisco Martínez Montiño in *Arte de Cocina, Pastelería, Vizcochería y Conservería* (1611) features a version using sardines which is still popular today. He rejected the use of oil in the dough, advocating instead fresh "beef lard," today more commonly known as butter.

Take fresh sardines, scale them and fry them, in such a way as not to dry them out too much, then fry a little onion in a little good oil and pour over the sardines, season with a little pepper and salt, if the sardines are not salty, and put three sardines, with a little of the fried onion on top, with the oil drained off, on each turnover, then close them in the way described before; in the dough you must not use oil, but fresh beef lard, because with oil they will not turn out well.

Francisco Martínez Montiño, *Arte de Cocina, Pastelería, Vizcochería y Conservería*, 1611

Galician savory pie

Dough:

4 cups (1 lb/500 g) all-purpose (plain) flour
½ cup (4 fl oz/125 ml) olive oil
½ cup (4 fl oz/125 ml) milk
salt

Filling:

⅓ cup (3 fl oz/90 ml) olive oil
1 large onion (6½ oz/200 g), peeled and finely chopped
1 can tomatoes (2 lb/1 kg), finely chopped
1 small can red peppers (pimientos) (8 oz/ 250 g), drained cut into strips
1 small can tuna in oil (8 oz/250 g), flaked
1 egg, beaten, for brushing the dough

Mix the flour, oil, milk and a little salt thoroughly in a large bowl. Transfer to a lightly floured surface and knead to form a smooth dough. Wrap in a clean kitchen cloth and place in the refrigerator for 30 minutes.

While the dough is resting, prepare the filling.

Heat the oil in a large skillet (frying pan) and fry the onion gently for 10 minutes. Add the tomatoes, cook for a further 10 minutes, then add the red peppers and fry for another 20 minutes.

Preheat the oven to 425°F (220°C/Gas 7).

Take the dough out of the refrigerator and divide it into 2 pieces, 1 slightly bigger than the other. Roll out the larger piece on a floured surface to a thickness of ½ in (1.5 cm) to fit a large baking sheet. Spread the filling on top, then add the tuna.

Roll out the other half of the dough, then lay it on top of the pie and press the edges together to make a crust. Brush the corners and sides with beaten egg to prevent the filling from oozing out. Prick the center of the pie, then brush all over with egg and transfer to the oven.

Bake for 15 minutes, then turn the heat down to 400°F (200°C/Gas 6) and cook for a further 30 minutes. Serve.

The gathering, Josep Berga i Foix (1837–1914); MUSEUM OF MODERN ART, MONTSERRAT, BARCELONA   Foix, a Catalan, has captured a typical outdoor celebration near Valencia of a

religious holiday. Part of the enjoyment of such occasions was the food, with its enhanced flavor from being cooked on open fires.

RICE

Rice is one of the basic foods in Spanish cuisine, especially on the Mediterranean coast. There are so many ways of preparing it that a different, equally delicious rice dish could be eaten every day of the year. Although normally served as a first course, it is sometimes used as a filling, or to make a dessert and even a drink.

In Spain, traditional rice dishes are prepared and cooked in a broth (stock) along with various ingredients. When the rice is cooked correctly, it will absorb the flavors of whatever foods it is cooked with — meat, fish, vegetables or legumes (pulses) — whether they are savory or sweet. Each grain of rice is like a tiny sponge mopping up all the flavors of the broth. The grains must, however, be cooked for exactly the right length of time, so that the texture is firm and the grains are whole and soft. When rice is overcooked, the grains open up and release the starch inside, resulting in a mushy texture and diminishing the intensity of the flavor.

When rice is used as a filling for vegetables, it is usually mixed with meat or fish and then cooked inside the vegetables, as in a dish such as *pimientos rellenos de arroz* (bell peppers [capsicums] stuffed with rice).

One of the best-known and most popular desserts in northern and central Spain is *arroz con leche*, a version of rice pudding, in which the rice is cooked with milk and sugar and flavored with cinnamon. In coastal areas, however, where rice — cooked to perfection — is served as a main course virtually every day, the locals tend to shun this kind of dessert as they generally do not appreciate rice that has lost its firm texture and has turned into a thick, creamy paste.

Rice drinks, known for their astringent properties, are made by soaking the rice in water for several hours, then straining it and flavoring the water with sugar and lemon zest (rind), or preparing it like *horchata* (a sweet drink), with sugar and cinnamon.

Spain produces 660–705 million lb (300–320 million kg) of rice per year, of which one-third is exported. Long-grain rice of the Indian variety is mostly exported to EC countries. Among the various kinds of rice grown in Spain, medium-grain is the most popular, as it is the most suitable for making traditional dishes and desserts; the grain has a higher proportion of starch than other varieties, which means it is better at absorbing flavor.

Nevertheless, nowadays long-grain rice is used for what are known as "white rice" dishes, boiled with water and salt and served to accompany other ingredients.

The Madrid Fair (detail), Manuel de la Cruz (1750–92); MUNICIPAL MUSEUM, MADRID

Olive-oil seller (nineteenth century), from the Collection of Spanish National Costumes; NATIONAL LIBRARY, MADRID
One of the distinctive street-cries of nineteenth-century Spanish towns was that of the olive-oil seller.

Romería *of the rice*, H. Anglada Camarasa (1872–1959); MUSEUM OF MODERN ART, MADRID
A *romería* was a devotional pilgrimage to a local shrine, a favorite subject for Spanish *plein-air* painters like *Camarasa*, who were known as the "1910 generation."

One of these recipes, maybe the best-known and most widespread, is *arroz a la cubana* (Cuban rice), which features fried eggs, fried tomatoes and tomato sauce This dish, and others such as rice salads, clearly have American influences.

There is some doubt as to exactly when rice was first grown in Spain. The Byzantines may have been the first to cultivate it, in the southeast of the country at the beginning of the sixth century, but it was the Arabs who introduced large-scale production. In the eighth century rice was planted on the Mediterranean coasts and particularly in the Valencia area, where the soil and climate were highly suitable for rice-growing. Near the city of Valencia and not far from the sea, there is a natural freshwater lake, called the Albufera (Arab for "little sea"), which is linked to the sea at some points. The land adjoining this lake was used to grow rice and, as there were a lot of eels in the water, it is not surprising that one of the first ways of flavoring rice was with eels.

Later, the rice-growing areas gradually spread toward other coastal areas of the eastern part of the country, particularly toward the delta of the Ebro River and then to the marshlands of the Guadalquivir River, in the south of Andalusia, and to some areas of Extremadura in the west.

Historical and gastronomic references to rice in Spain go back to the thirteenth century. In an anonymous manuscript dealing with Hispanic–Maghrebi cooking, the rice recipes are sweet, and cooked in milk. Later, the *Libre de Sent Soví* (1324) includes a recipe for rice cooked with almonds and flavored with cinnamon. Medieval and Renaissance cookbooks give recipes for *menjar blanc*, an exquisite dish made of a mixture of ground rice, chicken breast, almonds and sugar. Over the years this recipe underwent a change, with the meat being omitted so that it then became a

The crockery sellers, Francisco de Goya (1746–1828); PRADO MUSEUM, MADRID

dessert with the addition of orange-blossom water and rosewater. In *El Libre del Coch* (1520), Ruperto de Nola gives a recipe for rice baked in the oven with meat broth, which is still prepared in almost the same way today. Over the centuries historical gastronomic references to rice became more frequent, even though rice cultivation was subjected to many prohibitions and restrictions due to its links with malaria — the warm, wet conditions so necessary for rice-growing are, of course, also ideal for mosquitoes. Rice started to become a basic food in Spain in the eighteenth and nineteenth centuries, and the cookbooks from these periods feature many different ways of preparing it.

The physical features of the Spanish coastal regions vary considerably, with areas where, just a few miles inland from the coast, fields of fruit and vegetables stretch almost to the foothills of mountain ranges. With so many small areas, each with its own soil and climatic conditions, this means there is an enormous diversity of crops. All these factors influence and characterize the different ways of cooking that make up Spanish cuisine, and, of course, the ways of cooking rice.

Peasants, Jose Benlliure y Gil (1855–1937); FINE ARTS MUSEUM, GRANADA
A moment of repose for some Valencian peasants. It was people such as these who worked the rich agricultural lands around Valencia to bring in their bountiful harvests of produce for the table.

The great climatic contrasts within Spain have given rise to certain regional preferences regarding the way rice is cooked. The more liquid rice dishes, cooked in pots or deep casserole dishes, are more suitable for the autumn and winter, and the northern climate; while the dry dishes, cooked in a casserole either on top of the stove or in the oven, and particularly in shallow *paella* pans, are made more frequently in the Mediterranean regions.

The countless rice dishes that enrich Spanish Mediterranean cooking all benefit from the intuition and skill of the local inhabitants, both on the coast and inland, who draw on a wide range of culinary processes to obtain the best results. The dishes they cook use the ingredients available at different times of the year — individually or combined in different ways.

From the wide variety of fish and shellfish to be found around the coasts, tasty, basic broths are prepared, which might then be used for any one of the following dishes: *arroz a la marinera* (seafood rice), *arroz a banda* (seafood-flavored rice), *fideuá* (noodle *paella*), *caldero murciano* (Murcia seafood rice) or *arroz negro* (rice with cuttlefish ink), not to mention all the typical fishermen's recipes there are. Further away from the coast, rice is cooked with fresh garden vegetables, or with pork, poultry or game, often combined with vegetables or legumes (usually beans and chickpeas).

Lent, with its fasting and abstinence, has given rise to a broad range of austere, but nonetheless extremely tasty recipes, such as rice with Swiss chard (silverbeet), with cuttlefish and cauliflower, and with cod and vegetables.

Other, more baroque rice dishes are virtually a meal in themselves, such as *arroz al horno* (baked rice), with *cocido* broth, chickpeas and meat. Or there is *arroz con costra al estilo de Elche* (Elche-style crusty rice), which is made with pork, sausage and chicken, to which some beaten eggs are added for the last few minutes of baking to form a golden crust. *Cazuela de arroz a la malagueña* (Málaga rice casserole) is a typical dish from the south of Spain. It is made with monkfish, shrimp (prawns), clams, wild asparagus, peas and bell peppers, which are cooked with rice and *sofrito* (a well-fried tomato mixture) to a quite liquid consistency. To make *arroz a la zamorana*, a famous dish in Castile, the rice is cooked with pork and covered with slices of bacon fat. *Arroz brut*, a specialty of Majorca, is made with game; *arroz con calabaza* (rice with pumpkin) is typical of Castellon; Catalonia is famous for *arroz con conejo* (rice with rabbit) and a variety of fish and shellfish recipes to be found along its coast.

PAELLA

It would be impossible to list all the rice dishes typical of the various regions of Spain, but there is no doubt that the best-known and most representative Spanish dish is *paella*. Most importantly, a distinction must be made between everyday rice recipes cooked in a *paella* pan over a flame, and the authentic dish actually called *paella*, which is cooked outdoors over a wood fire. Unfortunately, what is served up in the majority of restaurants, both in Spain and abroad, is geared towards the tourist market and bears little relation to the authentic version. *Paella* has been discussed in countless ill-informed articles and reports about Spanish food, which list ingredients that have nothing to do with its true composition — all because of this confusion between rice dishes that happen to be cooked in a *paella* pan and the dish *paella* itself.

The genuine article is *paella valenciana* (Valencian *paella*), which is made with the following ingredients: rice, chicken, rabbit or lean pork, green beans, fresh lima (butter) beans, tomato, olive oil, paprika, saffron, land snails (or a sprig of fresh rosemary, which lends a similar flavor), water and salt. In winter, when no green or fresh fava beans are available, these ingredients are replaced with artichokes and peas. The authentic *paella* does not mix meat with fish or shellfish — a very common mistake — and it uses fresh vegetables, not frozen or canned. Ideally it should be cooked outdoors over a wood fire, because the steam when it cools, descends and impregnates the broth with subtle flavors. For the rice to cook properly, achieving the right texture, the layer should not exceed ½ inch (1.5 cm) so that the heat can spread and cook the grains evenly at the bottom and at the top of the pan. As the rice is spread out thinly, there is plenty of room for all the accompanying ingredients, whether they have been pre-cooked or are to be cooked with the rice.

Engraving, Vicente Blanco Pérez (twentieth century); PRIVATE COLLECTION
The Arabs introduced the short-grain rice used for *paella* dishes to the Valencia region and perfected the old Roman irrigation systems there. A bonus for farmers were the eels that could be fished from the irrigation channels and which were frequently used in the dish, too.

In Moslem Andalusia there were rice-based dishes, such as casseroles with fish and spices, that had a distinctly traditional and symbolic character and were served on special family occasions and during religious festivals. Centuries later — maybe in remembrance of those Moslem customs — special days and festivals were commemorated in the countryside around Valencia by preparing a big meal outdoors, cooking rice in a *paella* with seasonal vegetables and meat from the animals bred in the farmyard: chicken, rabbit or duck.

The sociological changes of the nineteenth century meant that social gatherings and outings to the countryside became more common. The dish typically eaten on these special days was originally called *arroz a la valenciana* (Valencian rice), but as it became more known came to be called *paella valenciana*.

The utensil called a *paella* (not a *paellera*) is a round, wide, shallow receptacle made of metal, with two or more handles, and a depth varying from 1½–3 in (4–7 cm). *Paella* pans are made in a great many sizes, from 8–40 in (20 cm–1 m) or more in diameter, and it is important to use the right size for the amount of rice to be cooked. The following is an approximate guide to the appropriate diameter-size of *paella* to use: for 2–3 people, 12 in (30 cm); for 4–5, 16 in (40 cm); for 6–8, 20 in (50 cm); and for 15, 26 in (65 cm).

In the 1970s some restaurants in the Valencia area started specializing in making huge *paellas* to feed from 100 to 3,000 people or even more, at conferences, parties, electoral rallies, and so on, both in Spain and abroad. The diameters of these exceptional *paellas* may vary from 3 ft 8 in to 13 ft 4 in (1.1 to 4 m). The preparation is quite a spectacle in itself.

This utensil, the *paella*, symbolically brings together the Romans, who introduced this type of pan, and the Arabs, who brought rice to Spain — and is a legacy of

The journey of Lot's family, Pedro Orrente (1580–1645); PRADO MUSEUM, MADRID

Angels' kitchen (detail), Bartolomé Murillo (1617–82); LOUVRE, PARIS Commissioned by the Franciscan monks of Seville, this painting gives an insight into an Andalusian monastery kitchen.

their joint influence. The primitive *páteras*, used for religious purposes, or the *patinas* and *patellas* the Romans used for cooking, were concave with one or two handles, according to size. This concave base gradually became less curved, to provide better heat distribution, and eventually became completely flat. The pans were always circular and of varying diameter.

The source of heat used for cooking depended on local environmental conditions. With the lack of forests around the Mediterranean, people had to adapt to using whatever combustion materials were available. In coastal areas, where rice was first grown, the only wood available was in the form of branches or small trunks — vine shoots, leftover pieces from the pruning of fruit trees. This acidic wood has the advantages of providing more heat than other kinds of wood and of maintaining the embers at a constant temperature. Cooking utensils were gradually adapted to suit this kind of wood, giving rise to the practice throughout southern Europe of frying in various kinds of skillets (frying pans). When large skillets or *paellas* were used for cooking rice, it became apparent that the diameter had to be in proportion to the quantity of ingredients, and that the sides of the receptacle had to be low enough not only to aid evaporation but also for the rice to cook evenly and absorb the aromas from the firewood.

The classic way of eating *paella* in olden times was for everyone to sit in a circle and eat straight from the pan. Thus, surrounded by chairs, the wide, round

The chicken-coop, Darío Regoyos (1857–1913); PRADO MUSEUM, MADRID
It was productive market-gardens such as this one that could provide all the necessary vegetables for a recipe such as *arroz con verduras* (rice with vegetables).

receptacle became a sort of round table. The participants, each equipped with an intricately carved boxwood spoon, would mark out exact triangles as portions for each person with a respect and courtesy that might be worthy of the Knights of the Round Table. This custom of eating from a main dish around a table is mentioned in the *Libre de Sent Sovi* (1324) as part of medieval tradition, and is still common practice in Arab countries.

There are some interesting aspects to the ritual of preparing *paella*. Around Valencia, it has long been customary for the male of the family to take charge of proceedings — men who usually never cook at home, and usually have no idea how to make anything other than *paella*. From about the mid-1960s, however, the interest in cooking *paella valenciana* has spread to other Spanish regions and now, coinciding with the rise in popularity of cooking as a weekend hobby, 90 percent of Spanish men opt for a *paella* when preparing food for a special occasion. All this would seem to suggest the operation of certain psychological factors.

The ancient rite of fire-making plays a principal role in the making of *paella*, and also has that mythical–magical component that perhaps attracts many men to take charge of the ceremony. Fire, full of ambivalent symbolism, represents purification and punishment, the power and lightness of the impalpable, attraction and rejection.

The vegetable garden, (1918)
Joan Miró (1893–1983);
NATIONAL MUSEUM COLLECTION, ESTOCOLMO

Like some kind of purifying ceremony, the four basic elements — fire, earth, water and air — are integrated. Fire, which is land-based, is the physical element which brings about the cooking process through the boiling of water. Air, which stirs up the flames of a fire, condenses the steam produced by the water, which cools and returns to the open receptacle.

Making a *paella* is a social event that takes place in the open air, away from the kitchen environment and the feminine connotations it traditionally has had. Many men are afraid that their love for cooking will be taken the wrong way, and that their virility will be brought into question. At the same time, however — and this is where vanity comes in — they want to show off their skill at making a complicated dish, which is difficult to get just right. Success is therefore much applauded and the clever chef can wallow in the praise heaped upon him.

Furthermore, the baroque nature of *paella*, together with the fact that all the ingredients are spread out and clearly visible, is in such direct contrast to the concept of hunger that it indicates the magical symbol of plenty. Another psycho–physical connotation is that rice is a carbohydrate that is absorbed slowly, producing a pleasant sensation of fullness. Thus, the psychic pleasure of making the dish and the ostentatious demonstration of ability is complemented by the physical pleasure of actually eating it, while at the same time being congratulated and proclaimed a master of the art of *paella*-making.

Summer, F. Barrera (eighteenth century); FINE ARTS MUSEUM, SEVILLE
June, July and August were the months of plenty, when the tables were loaded with a rich variety of produce from the fields, gardens and woods. The harvest was also a time of long, hard toil for the peasants, who would cook their simple meals in the open where they worked.

PAELLA VALENCIANA

Paella valenciana   Serves 4

The *paella* is the pan used to cook this legendary dish, and *valenciana* refers to the region of Spain on the shores of the Mediterranean where it originated. It is typically cooked outdoors in the countryside on a dry wood fire. The *paella* must be set at a suitable height to be surrounded by flames during the first part of the cooking, and the fire must be kept burning at the correct strength.

Generally, a good *paella* depends not so much on the quality of the ingredients as on combining all the components in the correct proportions. The five basic elements — oil, water, rice, heat and cooking receptacle — need to be balanced with an almost mathematical precision. The experience and personal touch of whoever is in charge of the cooking are also of utmost importance.

The preparation of a *paella* in the countryside is a ritualistic, festive occasion which can sometimes turn into a gastronomic debate! The relaxed, lighthearted atmosphere is punctuated with jokes and comments on the progress of the food. The experience culminates when the *paella* is deemed ready, removed from the fire and carried to the table.

Paella valenciana

*1 tomato (3½ oz/100 g), peeled and finely
    chopped*
1 teaspoon paprika
salt
12 small land snails or 1 sprig rosemary
2 pinches saffron
2½ cups (13 oz/410 g) medium-grain rice

Put the lima beans on to boil in 2 cups
(16 fl oz/500 ml) of water.

Heat the oil in an 18 in (45 cm) *paella* pan
(shallow metal pan) and fry the chicken and
rabbit chunks, turning to ensure even cooking.
Add the green beans and fry gently. Keeping
the heat low, add the tomato, then the paprika,
immediately followed by the rest of the water.
Add the lima beans with the cooking water. Add
salt and bring quickly to a boil, then turn down
the heat and continue cooking until the meat
is cooked (45–60 minutes).

Add the snails or rosemary. Check the seasoning and add the saffron. Turn up the heat
and add the rice, spreading it out as evenly as
possible. Cook quickly for the first 10 minutes,
then turn down the heat gradually for another
8–10 minutes. Taste the rice to check if it is
done. The grains should be soft but still quite
firm inside. Remove from the heat and allow
to rest for 5 minutes before serving.

Land snails have the flavor of the aromatic wild plants on
which they feed. When fresh land snails are not available, a
sprig of rosemary can be substituted. It will add a similar flavor.

*6½ oz (200 g) fresh or dried large lima
    (butter) beans, or fava (broad) beans,
    soaked overnight*
4½ cups (2 qt/2 l) water
⅔ cup (5 fl oz/155 ml) olive oil
1½ lb (750 g) chicken, in chunks
1 lb (500 g) rabbit or lean pork, in chunks
8 oz (250 g) green beans, trimmed and halved

Picking out the saffron (detail), Josep Bru (second half
nineteenth century); FINE ARTS MUSEUM, VALENCIA
Saffron is derived from the plant *Crocus sativus*. In autumn the
flowers are collected and the yellow stigmas are separated
from the flower-head. They are dried in a sieve held over the
embers of a fire. It is a very delicate operation.

Mosaic (twentieth century); LA CASA DE VALENCIA, MADRID
This Valencian ceramic depicts the traditional way to eat
paella — straight from the dish, seated round the table.

SEAFOOD RICE

Arroz a la marinera   Serves 4

The ancient Greeks were very fond of fish — their "Phocian soup" combined a number of different kinds very successfully and was the predecessor of the well-known *bouillabaisse*. This kind of rice dish is based on a substantial broth (stock), the formula for which has been passed down over the centuries. The rice should be made with fish with a lot of bones and not much flesh. These varieties are generally not very pleasant to look at but are second to none when it comes to flavor. These fish — scorpion fish, red sea bream, redfish, etc. — can usually be found in fish markets and quayside warehouses and are fortunately still very reasonably priced. Although this dish requires quite a lot of work, it is definitely worth the trouble as the results are truly splendid.

Broth (stock):

8 oz (250 g) monkfish

1 hake (or other fish) head

all-purpose (plain) flour, for coating

8 oz (250 g) small sea crayfish (Dublin Bay prawns, scampi) or shrimp (prawns)

(the 3 seafood ingredients may be replaced by 4 lb (2 kg) of other rock fish such as scorpion fish, red sea bream, redfish, etc.)

⅓ cup (3 fl oz/90 ml) olive oil

1 medium-size onion (5 oz/155 g), chopped

1 medium-size tomato (3½ oz/100 g), peeled and finely chopped

1 teaspoon paprika

8 cups (1¾ qt/1.75 l) water

salt

Rice:

1 lb (500 g) mussels

salt

4 medium-size sea crayfish (Dublin Bay prawns, scampi)

2 pinches saffron

⅓ cup (3 fl oz/90 ml) olive oil

8 oz (250 g) squid, chopped

1 clove garlic, finely chopped

1 medium-size tomato (3½ oz/100 g), peeled and finely chopped

1 teaspoon paprika

2½ cups (13 oz/410 g) medium-grain rice

To prepare the broth, coat the monkfish and hake head (or other fish) with flour. Heat the oil in a large casserole and if using crayfish or shrimp, fry them, then remove and set aside. Fry the monkfish and hake head in the same oil. Remove and reserve. Sauté the onion until it starts to brown, then add the tomato and fry gently for a few minutes.

Add the paprika, the water and a little salt and continue cooking.

Meanwhile, remove the skin and bones from the fried fish. Add these scraps to the broth and set the fish aside.

Peel the fried crayfish or shrimp and set aside. Crush the heads, shells and legs in a mortar and add to the broth.

Cover the casserole and cook the broth over medium heat for 45 minutes, then strain through a fine sieve.

To prepare the rice, first steam the mussels. Remove the empty halves of the shells and set aside the other halves. Strain the liquid produced and add to the fish broth.

Add a little salt to the crayfish, then heat up the fish broth and add the saffron.

Heat the oil in a 16 in (40 cm) *paella* pan (shallow metal pan) and fry the crayfish, then the squid (be careful, as the oil is likely to spatter), followed by the garlic and tomato. Fry gently for a few minutes, then add the paprika and the rice. Stir briskly, then add 5⅔ cups (1¼ qt/1.25 l) of the boiling fish broth. Check the seasoning.

Cook quickly for 10 minutes, then add the fish and the crayfish tails. Turn the heat down gradually over the next 8–10 minutes. Taste a few grains of rice to check that it is done. Arrange the mussels decoratively on the top.

Remove from the heat, allow to rest for 5 minutes and serve.

Seafood rice

Murcia seafood rice (fish slices with garlic sauce and fish sauce)

Murcia Seafood Rice

Caldero murciano   Serves 4

There are many different kinds of fish-flavored rice dishes to be found along the coasts of Spain. In Murcia, Alicante and Tarragona, *ñoras*, dried red bell peppers (capsicums), are used to provide flavor and color. This dish is traditionally cooked in an iron pot on board fishing-boats and should have a somewhat mushy texture.

Broth (stock) and rice:

1 lb (500 g) gray mullet
1 lb (500 g) scorpion fish
1 lb (500 g) gilthead (sea bream or sea bass)
  (or 8 oz/250 g grouper and 8 oz/250 g monkfish)
¾ cup (6½ fl oz/200 ml) olive oil
2 dried red bell peppers (capsicums)
1 head (bulb) garlic, whole and unpeeled
2 ripe tomatoes (6½ oz/200 g), peeled and
  finely chopped
1 teaspoon paprika
6¾ cups (1½ qt/1.5 l) boiling water
salt

1 small potato, peeled and boiled
saffron
2½ cups (13 oz/410 g) medium-grain rice

Garlic sauce:

1 small head (bulb) garlic
½ cup (4 fl oz/125 ml) fish broth (stock)
1 egg yolk
2 tablespoons (1 fl oz/30 ml) olive oil
salt
freshly ground pepper

Fish sauce:

1 dried red bell pepper (capsicum)
3 cloves garlic, peeled
1 tablespoon finely chopped parsley
½ cup (4 fl oz/125 ml) fish broth (stock)
2 tablespoons (1 fl oz/30 ml) olive oil
juice of 1 lemon
½ teaspoon paprika
salt

To prepare the broth, clean the fish, pat dry and drain. Remove the heads and cut the rest into slices.

Heat the oil in an iron pot (*caldero*) or a large casserole. Fry the dried bell peppers and the head of garlic. Remove and set aside.

Peel the fried garlic cloves.

Fry the fish in the same oil. Meanwhile, crush the fried bell peppers and garlic in a mortar. Pour the mixture over the fish. Cook the tomato separately in a little oil, then add to the fish. Add the paprika, the boiling water and a little salt.

Murcia seafood rice (the rice in broth)

Meal on the boat, Joaquín Sorolla (1863–1923); ROYAL ACADEMY OF SAN FERNANDO, MADRID

Cook slowly for 10 minutes, then remove the fish slices, transfer to a serving dish and keep warm. Add the whole potato to the pot. Continue cooking the broth with the rest of the ingredients for 15 minutes, then remove the potato and set aside for the sauce.

Press the broth through a fine sieve to extract all the liquid. Check the seasoning. Set aside about 1 cup (8 fl oz/250 ml) of broth for the sauces.

Pour the rest of the strained broth into the pot (about 5⅔ cups/1¼ qt/1.25 l) and add a pinch of saffron. When it comes to a boil, add the rice and cook over medium heat for 18–20 minutes.

Taste a few grains of rice to check that it is cooked — it should be neither dry nor soggy.

Remove from the heat and serve as the first course accompanied by the garlic sauce.

To make the garlic sauce, peel the head of garlic and crush in a mortar. Add half the reserved fish broth and the boiled potato and mash everything together. Add the egg yolk and blend thoroughly until smooth. Stirring all the time, drizzle in the oil drop by drop until the mixture thickens like mayonnaise. Season with salt and pepper.

To prepare the fish sauce, fry the dried bell pepper and crush in a mortar with the garlic and parsley. Add the remaining reserved fish broth, oil, lemon juice, paprika and a little salt. Blend thoroughly and serve in a sauce boat with the fish slices as a second course.

Market, Dionisio Baixeras (nineteenth century);
MUSEUM OF THE CITY'S HISTORY, BARCELONA
Such wooden barrels usually displayed salt cod. One of the
advantages of salt cod was its availability throughout the year
and, made as a casserole (*bacalao al ajoarriero*) or as salt cod
soldiers (*soldaditos de Pavía*), it was a tasty snack at any time.

RICE WITH SALT COD
AND SPINACH

Arroz con bacalao y espinacas   Serves 4

Salt cod is the main ingredient of many Lenten rice dishes.
The fish used for these dishes is not usually soaked, so
the more fleshy and less salty it is, the better. It is toasted on
a skewer or a long-handled fork over a gas flame or the griddle
of an electric stove for 5 minutes. The kitchen should be well
ventilated to get rid of the strong smell produced. The cod is
then rinsed, the skin and bones are removed and it is crumbled
or flaked into small pieces. Salt should be added only very
sparingly, if at all, before adding the rice.

5 oz (155 g) dried salt cod, unsoaked
¼ cup (2 fl oz/60 ml) olive oil
6 garlic cloves, peeled and chopped

*1 lb (500 g) spinach (English spinach),
chopped*
1 tomato (3½ oz/100 g), peeled and chopped
1 teaspoon paprika
4 cups (1 qt/1 l) water
1 pinch saffron
salt
1⅓ cups (6½ oz/200 g) medium-grain rice

Toast the unsoaked cod over a naked flame or
an electric griddle. Rinse, remove the skin and
bones and break the flesh into pieces.

Heat the oil in a heatproof casserole. Fry the
garlic, followed by the spinach and then the
tomato. When the water yielded by the spinach
has evaporated, add the paprika, then pour in
the water. Add the saffron and a little salt. Cook,
covered, for 10 minutes.

Check the seasoning. Add the rice, stir and
cook, uncovered, over medium heat for 16–18
minutes.

Taste a few grains of rice to check that it is
cooked. Dish out and allow to rest on the plates
for a minute before eating.

NOODLE PAELLA

Fideuá   Serves 4

Fideuá was originally a fishermen's stew from the coast
of Gandía (birthplace of the famous medieval poet and
writer Ausiàs March), but its fame has now spread much farther
afield. Every spring an international competition is held to find
the tastiest *fideuás*. The basis of the broth (stock) is very similar
to that of *arroz a banda*, and the noodles absorb all the fish
flavors with excellent results.

Broth (stock):
¾ cup (6½ fl oz/200 ml) olive oil
*1 medium-size onion (5 oz/155 g), peeled and
chopped*
*1 medium-size tomato (3½ oz/100 g),
chopped*
1 teaspoon paprika
11¼ cups (2½ qt/2.5 l) water, approximately
*4 lb (2 kg) fish (redfish, monkfish, scorpion
fish or other)*
½ in (1 cm) fresh red chili pepper
1 black peppercorn
salt

Noodle paella:
*13 oz (410 g) small sea crayfish (Dublin Bay
prawns, scampi) or shrimp (prawns)*
salt

Rice with salt cod and spinach (left); noodle paella (right)

2 cloves garlic, peeled

1 tablespoon finely chopped parsley

2 tablespoons (1 fl oz/30 ml) lemon juice

⅓ cup (3 fl oz/90 ml) olive oil

8 oz (250 g) monkfish or grouper, chopped

3½ oz (100 g) cuttlefish or squid, cleaned and chopped

1 tomato (3½ oz/100 g), peeled and finely chopped

1 teaspoon paprika

13 oz (410 g) short-cut flat noodles

To prepare the broth, heat the oil in a large heatproof casserole and gently fry the onion, followed by the tomato. Add the paprika and the water, then add the fish, chili pepper, peppercorn and a little salt. Cook, covered, over low heat for 30 minutes.

Strain the broth through a sieve and keep hot.

Wash and drain the crayfish or shrimp and add a little salt.

Crush the garlic with the parsley in a mortar, then add the lemon juice.

Heat the oil in a 16 in (40 cm) *paella* pan (shallow metal pan), then fry the crayfish or shrimp until golden. Remove from the pan and set aside. Fry the monkfish or grouper, followed by the cuttlefish or squid (taking care, as the oil might spatter) and then the tomato. Add the paprika and the fish broth. Add salt if necessary.

When it comes to a boil, add the noodles and spread out evenly. Add the crayfish or shrimp and the parsley mixture. Cook over medium heat for 15–17 minutes.

Taste the noodles. If they are cooked, remove from the heat, allow to rest for 5 minutes and serve.

Country meal, tiles (nineteenth century);
NATIONAL MUSEUM OF CERAMICS, VALENCIA

BELL PEPPERS STUFFED WITH RICE

Pimientos rellenos de arroz   Serves 4

Bell peppers (capsicums) were brought from America and are an important ingredient in the cuisines of all the countries surrounding the Mediterranean. In this recipe the rice is lightly fried before being used to fill the fleshy red bell pepper, and takes on a slightly sweet but intense taste while baking slowly in the oven.

4 large red bell peppers (capsicums) (about 5 oz/155 g each)
⅓ cup (3 fl oz/90 ml) olive oil
1 medium-size onion (5 oz/155 g), finely chopped
8 oz (250 g) lean pork, ground (minced)
8 oz (250 g) ripe tomatoes, finely chopped
salt
1 pinch oregano
1 teaspoon sugar
1⅓ cups (6½ oz/200 g) medium-grain rice

Preheat the oven to 400°F (200°C/Gas 6).

Wash and drain the bell peppers. Trim off the tops to use as lids, then remove the seeds. Place in a deep ovenproof earthenware casserole.

Heat the oil in a skillet (frying pan) and fry the onion. When it starts to brown, add the minced pork, stir, then add the tomatoes, a little salt, the oregano and the sugar. Fry slowly for 15 minutes.

Check the seasoning. Add the rice, stir and, when it comes to a boil, remove from the heat and use to stuff the peppers. Put the tops back on and spear with cocktail sticks or toothpicks.

Stand the bell peppers vertically in a baking dish, packed close together. Bake for about 1½ hours, checking on them from time to time. Cover with foil if the bell peppers are getting too brown. Remove the lids and taste a few grains of rice to check that it is cooked.

Transfer to a platter, cut in half vertically and serve.

Bell peppers stuffed with rice

Seafood-flavored rice with potatoes and onions

SEAFOOD-FLAVORED RICE WITH POTATOES AND ONIONS

Arroz a banda   Serves 4

This remarkably simple Mediterranean recipe has survived over a number of centuries. Fishermen and sailors used to share a pan of *arroz a banda* while sitting on the decks of the old brigantines, sheltered from the blazing sun by the shade of the sails.

A banda means "separately." In this dish the rice is eaten first, and the fish, potatoes and onions are cooked as a second course. *All-i-oli* or *salmorreta* sauce is used to dress the fish, which loses some of its flavor in the cooking process.

2 lb (1 kg) mixed white fish, for example 8 oz (250 g) monkfish, 1 lb (500 g) scorpion fish, 8 oz (250 g) redfish or grouper

⅔ cup (5 fl oz/155 ml) olive oil

4 medium-size onions (1 lb/500 g), peeled but left whole

4 medium-size potatoes (1 lb/500 g), peeled but left whole

1½ teaspoons paprika

6¾ cups (1½ qt/1.5 l) water

salt

8 oz (250 g) small cuttlefish or squid, cleaned and chopped

2 cloves garlic, peeled and finely chopped

1 tomato (3½ oz/100 g), peeled and finely chopped

2 pinches saffron

2½ cups (13 oz/410 g) medium-grain rice

All-i-oli (see page 207 for instructions):

2 or 3 cloves garlic

1 egg yolk

1 cup (8 fl oz/250 ml) olive oil

salt

lemon juice

Clean the fish, rinse and drain.

Heat ¼ cup (2 fl oz/60 ml) of the oil in a large pan or casserole. Fry the onions and potatoes, left whole, turning to cook evenly. Add ½ teaspoon of the paprika and the water. Add a little salt, cover and cook over medium heat for about 30 minutes.

When the potatoes and onions are almost ready, add the fish, turn the heat down and cook for 10–15 minutes. Remove from the heat and keep covered.

Heat the remaining oil in a 16 in (40 cm) *paella* pan (shallow metal pan). Fry the cuttlefish or squid, then add the garlic and tomato.

Add the remaining paprika, followed immediately by 5¾ cups (1¼ qt/1.25 l) of the broth from cooking the fish. Add the saffron. Check the seasoning.

When it comes to a boil, add the rice. Spread it out evenly and boil quickly for 10 minutes, then gradually turn the heat down over the next 8–10 minutes.

Taste a few grains of rice to check that it is cooked. Remove from the heat, allow to rest for a few minutes and serve.

Remove the bones from the fish and serve as the second course, accompanied by the potatoes, onions and a small amount of broth. Serve the *all-i-oli* (or other seafood sauce if preferred) separately.

Valencian fisherwoman, Joaquín Sorolla (1863–1923); PRIVATE COLLECTION
Sorolla's beach scenes are considered to be among his best work. The early morning sight of baskets of fish being carried along the strand to the village was more common formerly, when boats used to be pulled up on the sand.

HEARTY BAKED RICE

Arroz al horno   Serves 4

Some of the oldest recipes in historical documents on eating habits in Spain involve cooking rice in a heavy meat broth (stock). These dishes are traditionally prepared on Mondays to make use of the broth and leftovers from Sunday's *cocido* (see page 60). The women used to carry their pans of rice to be cooked in the village oven, chatting about the events of the weekend on the way. The intense flavor of the broth and great variety of ingredients make *arroz al horno* a very tasty and attractive dish.

Pick all the stones and dirt out of the rice. Wash in two or three changes of cold water, then in hot water, and when it is well rinsed, put it to dry on a wooden block in the sun or in the warmth of the fire, and when it is dry, pick over it again, in such a way that it is very clean, then take a very clean casserole. Add some thick meat broth [stock] and heat it up; when it starts to boil, put two or three strands of saffron to it, enough to turn the broth yellow, and when the broth is good and yellow, put the rice in little by little, stirring with a stick or a ladle; when the rice is in the casserole, add as much broth as you think is enough for it to cook and no more; taste to find out if it needs some salt, and when it is nice and thick, put it in the oven to bake. A short time before it is ready, take it out of the oven and add to it a few yolks of whole eggs, fresh ones, then return it to the oven to finish cooking; it is cooked when you see that the rice has formed a nice crust on the top: afterward put it in bowls; and in each one put one or two of the egg yolks which are on top of the rice; and in case the oven is not ready, put the casserole on the coal fire and fill the iron covering with embers; in this way it will taste as if it were baked in the oven, and maybe even better because it is closer at hand to watch over; this is how to make good rice.

Ruperto de Nola, *Libre del Coch*, 1520

Farmer's wife (detail), Joan Miró (1893–1983); PRIVATE COLLECTION
Despite living most of his life in France, Miró never forgot that he was Catalan. Perhaps the ingredients of this still-life represent a nostalgia for typical Catalan food.

2¼ *cups (18 fl oz/520 ml)* cocido *broth (stock) (see page 60) (or other meat broth, although flavor will not be as good)*

¼ *cup (2 fl oz/60 ml) olive oil*

1 head (bulb) garlic

1 medium-size potato (5 oz/155 g), in ½ in (1 cm) slices

3 small tomatoes (10 oz/315 g), 2 halved, 1 peeled and finely chopped

2 onion-flavored blood sausages (black pudding (8 oz/250 g)

1 teaspoon paprika

1¾ *cups (10 oz/315 g) medium-grain rice*

4 oz (125 g) chickpeas, cooked

6½ *oz (200 g) beef from the* cocido *(or other cooked beef), boned and chopped*

3½ *oz (100 g) pork fat, chopped*

salt

Heat the broth.

Preheat the oven to 400°F (200°C/Gas 6).

Heat the oil in a 14 in (35 cm) shallow, heatproof earthenware casserole and fry the head of garlic whole, along with the potato, followed by the halved tomatoes, blood sausages and finally the chopped tomato. Add the paprika, followed immediately by the rice. Stir quickly, then add the hot broth. Add the chickpeas, beef and pork fat. Distribute the ingredients so that the garlic is in the middle surrounded by the potato and tomato. Check the seasoning.

When it starts to bubble, transfer the casserole to a hot oven and bake for 15–18 minutes. Taste a few grains of rice to check that it is done.

Remove from the oven and serve immediately from the casserole.

Hearty baked rice

Baked rice with currants and chickpeas (left); rice with vegetables (right)

BAKED RICE WITH CURRANTS AND CHICKPEAS

Arroz con pasas y garbanzos   Serves 4

While coastal areas have seafood risottos based on fish broth (stock), inland villages use *cocido* broth as a basis for countless rice dishes.

A head (bulb) of garlic, familiarly called a partridge, is placed in the center of the dish.

5 oz (155 g) currants
⅓ cup (3 fl oz/90 ml) olive oil
1 head (bulb) garlic, rinsed and dried
1 tomato (3½ oz/100 g), peeled and finely chopped
1 teaspoon paprika
6½ oz (200 g) chickpeas, cooked
3⅓ cups (27 fl oz/750 ml) cocido (see page 60) or meat broth (stock), hot

salt
2½ cups (13 oz/410 g) medium-grain rice

Soak the currants in warm water for 3–4 hours. Drain.

Preheat the oven to 400°F (200°C/Gas 6).

Heat the oil in a 14 in (35 cm) shallow casserole. When it is hot, add the head of garlic and half the currants and fry gently. Add the tomato and then the paprika. Stir, then add the chickpeas and broth.

Check the seasoning. When the broth comes to a boil, add the rice and spread out evenly. The head of garlic should be in the center. Sprinkle the remaining currants on top, then bake for 15–18 minutes.

Taste a few grains to check that the rice is cooked, then remove from the oven and serve immediately straight from the casserole.

RICE WITH VEGETABLES

Arroz con verduras   Serves 4

The exuberance of the *huertas* (market gardens) of Spain is displayed in its full glory in this recipe, which combines a wonderful variety of delicate flavors.

Rice dishes with vegetables and pulses require extra oil because the ingredients are lightly fried beforehand. It is therefore handy to have a little oil in reserve — heated previously with a clove of garlic — to add to the mixture if it gets too dry.

2 medium-size fresh artichokes (6½ oz/200 g)

juice of 1 lemon

1¼ cups (10 fl oz/315 ml) olive oil

1 medium-size eggplant (aubergine), peeled and diced small

4 oz (125 g) green beans, trimmed and chopped

4 oz (125 g) spinach (English spinach), washed and chopped

1 tomato (3½ oz/100 g), peeled and finely chopped

3 cloves garlic, peeled and finely chopped

1 teaspoon paprika

13½ cups (3 qt/3 l) water

3½ oz (100 g) fresh peas, shelled

3½ oz (100 g) fava (broad) beans, shelled

3½ oz (100 g) fresh lima (butter) beans, shelled

salt

1 pinch saffron

2½ cups (13 oz/410 g) medium-grain rice

Remove the tough outer leaves of the artichokes, trim the ends and divide into quarters. Place in a dish, add the lemon juice and cover with water.

Heat the oil in an 18 in (45 cm) *paella* pan (shallow metal pan) and fry the eggplant, then remove and set aside. Fry the green beans, followed by the spinach and artichokes, then the tomato and garlic.

When everything is done, add the paprika and water.

When it comes to a boil, add the peas, both types of beans, eggplant, a little salt and the saffron. Cook for 35–40 minutes.

Check the seasoning.

Add the rice, spreading it out evenly.

Cook over high heat for 10 minutes, then gradually turn the heat down over the next 8–10 minutes. Taste a few grains of rice to check that it is cooked. Remove from the heat, leave for 5 minutes, then serve.

Merienda *in San Isidro*, Lucas Villamil (1824–70); MUSEO ROMANTICO, MADRID
San Isidro was a meadow on the outskirts of Madrid, beside the Manzanares river. People liked to stroll and picnic there, like these women, who are taking their *merienda* (the late afternoon snack).

RICE WITH BULLFIGHTERS' CAPES

Arroz con capitas de torero   Serves 4

Rice with cod always used to be served on Good Friday, the last day of Lent. This dish was originally very frugal, with the sole addition of chickpeas, but later came to be decorated with strips of baked red bell pepper (capsicum), which became known popularly as cows' lips because of their fleshy, flattened appearance. The bell peppers are cut into little triangles, which, set against the rice, are reminiscent of red capes in the bullring.

4 oz (125 g) chickpeas, soaked overnight
6 cups (1½ qt/1.5 l) water
1 large red bell pepper (capsicum)
5 oz (155 g) dried salt cod, unsoaked
1 pinch saffron
salt
⅓ cup (3 fl oz/90 ml) olive oil
1 tomato (3½ oz/100 g), peeled and finely chopped
1 head (bulb) garlic, finely chopped
1 teaspoon paprika
2½ cups (13 oz/410 g) medium-grain rice

Preheat the oven to 350°F (180°C/Gas 4).

Boil the chickpeas in the water.

Wash and dry the bell pepper, then bake for 30 minutes, turning after 15 minutes. Remove from the oven and set aside, covered.

Toast the unsoaked cod over a naked flame or electric griddle. Rinse, remove the skin and bones, then crumble the flesh into small pieces.

Peel the bell pepper, remove the seeds and cut into quarters.

Check on the chickpeas, adding the saffron and a little salt. If they are done, strain the broth and keep hot. Set the chickpeas aside.

Heat the oil in a heatproof casserole. Fry the tomato and garlic, add the cod and stir thoroughly.

Add the paprika, followed by the rice. Stir, then add 4 cups (1 qt/1 l) of broth and the chickpeas. Spread the rice out evenly. When it comes to a boil, check the seasoning and add salt if necessary. Cook uncovered over medium heat for 17–20 minutes. Add the pieces of baked bell pepper, arranged with the peaks upward to resemble bullfighters' capes, about halfway through the cooking time.

Taste the rice and, when it is cooked, remove from the heat and serve.

BAKED RICE WITH CUTTLEFISH AND CAULIFLOWER

Arroz con sepia y coliflor al horno   Serves 4

The creativity and imagination of Mediterranean people are reflected in all art forms, as shown by the perfect combination of ingredients from both land and sea in this tasty dish in which cinnamon provides a touch of Arab flavor. Although traditionally served during Lent, it is by no means a spartan meal.

Rice with bullfighters' capes (left); baked rice with cuttlefish and cauliflower (right)

¾ cup (6½ fl oz/200 ml) olive oil

8 oz (250 g) whole small cuttlefish, cleaned

2 cloves garlic, peeled and finely chopped

1 tomato (3½ oz/100 g), peeled and finely chopped

1 teaspoon paprika

5 cups (1¼ qt/1.25 l) water

1 pinch saffron

salt

10 oz (315 g) cauliflower florets, washed and drained

2½ cups (13 oz/410 g) medium-grain rice

1 pinch ground cinnamon

Preheat the oven to 400°F (200°C/Gas 6).

Heat the oil in a heatproof casserole and sauté the cuttlefish until golden on both sides, followed by the garlic and then the tomato. Cook for a few minutes, then quickly stir in the paprika. Add the water, saffron and a little salt. Cook for 20 minutes.

Add the cauliflower and check the seasoning. Stir in the rice and spread out evenly. When the water comes back to a boil, transfer to the oven and bake for 15–18 minutes.

Taste to check that the rice is cooked and sprinkle on the cinnamon. Serve immediately.

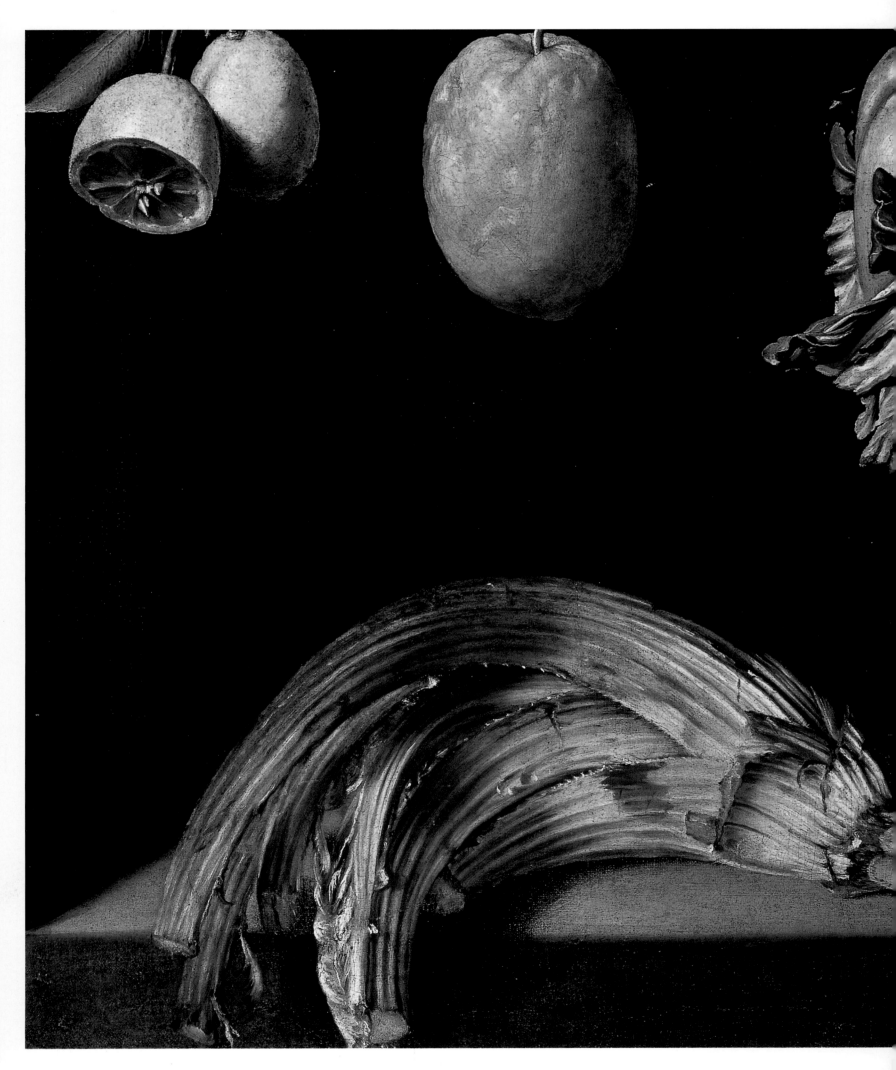

Still-life, Alejandro de Loarte (early seventeenth century); PRIVATE COLLECTION, MADRID   Before the introduction of New World produce, Spanish cooks used ingredients such as

VEGETABLES

these — cabbage, carrot, cardoon, endive — in traditional salads, which could be additionally flavored with herbs or fruit or orange juice.

VEGETABLES

The most important thing to understand about the use of vegetables in Spanish cooking is that they are considered to constitute a complete dish in themselves, unlike in other countries where they are used as a side-dish or decoration. In Spain a vegetable dish as a first course is almost obligatory, both at home and in restaurants.

Vegetables have, however, had a checkered history in the development of Spanish cuisine. Their role as a food has been held both in high regard and in contempt at different times in the past. There was a time, too, when the consumption of vegetables was associated with poverty and illness.

The plentiful supply of vegetables and the high cost of meat has often generated a certain contempt towards vegetables and an exaggeratedly high regard for meat. These attitudes crop up constantly throughout Spanish literature when the economic standing of literary characters is suggested by their eating habits. Financially destitute characters eat vegetables, while improved circumstances are reflected by the serving of meat.

Nowadays we are much more knowledgeable about the beneficial effects of eating vegetables in helping to prevent illness. But in the past the role of vegetables in health-care used to be more as a remedy for those who were already sick.

The requirements of Lent and other fast-days provided people with yet another reason to be negative about vegetables. The obligation to eat vegetables at such times meant that people had to devise all sorts of imaginative ways to make up for the absence of meat and only served to increase their distaste for vegetables. To this day, a person with a wan complexion and hangdog expression is often called "chard face," and in former times the term "Friday face" was common.

Even though there have been periods when negative attitudes towards vegetables tended to prevail, overall, vegetables have retained a consistently important place in Spanish cuisine since the time of the Muslim occupation of Spain. The Arabs took a much more positive approach towards fruit and vegetables generally, and understood their importance in diet.

They also saw the opportunities for cultivation presented by the rich soil and mild climate of Spain, and irrigated the most appropriate areas using their great hydrological skills.

Still-life, B. Palencia (1894–1980); PRIVATE COLLECTION, MADRID
The vivid exchange of color produced by different combinations of fresh fruit and vegetables is as important for the cook in creating recipes as it is for the artist. Such an arrangement also brings light, color and aroma into the kitchen just as a vase of flowers does for the living rooms.

Children's alphabet primer of street-sellers of Madrid (nineteenth century); MUNICIPAL MUSEUM, MADRID

For ordinary, working families living in the larger towns, street-sellers were often the main source of fresh produce. Some of the sellers shown here carried produce suitable for the *cocido* or for other soups: olives (A), hens and chickens (G), fava (broad) beans and peas (H), fish (P), tomatoes and bell peppers (capsicums) (T).

Arab cuisine did not separate vegetables and meat, but instead harmoniously combined them on the plate and at the table. The Arabs appreciated the beauty of the vegetables in Spain, and their ability to convey that appreciation struck a chord with the Spaniards.

An Arab writer, Ben Sara, sang the praises of the eggplant (aubergine) in the thirteenth century: "It is a fruit with a spherical shape, with an agreeable taste, fed by the abundant water in all gardens. Girded by the covering of its petiole, it looks like a red lamb's heart in the claws of a vulture."

Traditionally, each vegetable appeared at its due time throughout the year and was eaten according to its seasonal availability. This may have been restrictive in some ways but it also meant that there was a continual unfolding of new delights as each vegetable, in turn, came into season. Until recently, it would have been unthinkable to eat a *pisto* (vegetable stew), based on hothouse bell peppers (capsicums), tomatoes and zucchini (courgettes), in the middle of winter, or eggplant fritters out of season. Now round-the-year cultivation has become the norm. Despite this, however, it is still better to consider vegetables in their proper, and more natural, seasonal context.

After the gastronomic excesses of the winter, when large quanties of meat, fat and high-calorie foods are consumed, spring is a welcome relief when it arrives with its broad selection of healthy vegetables. But first it may be necessary to clean out the system. The first crop of artichokes heralds the end of wintertime, and this vegetable is wonderful for cleansing the liver. Artichokes can be cooked to perfection in just a little water with some olive oil, adding lemon and aromatic herbs according to individual taste. If this proves too austere for some tastes, the artichokes can be fried in batter or used as an omelet filling. When springtime is in full swing it is time to venture into the countryside and make an artichoke *paella* before those vegetables disappear once more.

Fava (broad) beans provide a good mineral stimulus. Pythagoras may have had something against beans but these, when they are still small and tender, are sweet and delicious. Young fava beans are at their best eaten raw, but this is only possible immediately after picking. Fava beans can be used in salads or in all sorts of vegetable medleys, but they really come into their own in a dish with ham known as *cazuela granadina* (Granada casserole) — dancing up and down to the flamenco rhythms of the sizzling oil.

Still-life, J. L. Enguidanos (1760–1812);
ROYAL ACADEMY OF SAN FERNANDO, MADRID
Fava (broad) beans and artichokes have been cultivated in Spain for a very long time and may have been introduced by the Romans. Both vegetables have been consistently popular ingredients in many dishes. Artichoke hearts, with their curiously stimulating taste sensation, are eaten also as a salad or *tapas*. Fava beans are used both fresh and dried.

Still-life, Luis Meléndez (1716–80);
PRADO MUSEUM, MADRID

Long, thick, green-tipped asparagus is another springtime vegetable with cleansing properties. Asparagus was one vegetable that used to be regarded as a highly prestigious food, since it was very scarce and eaten only by the well-to-do. A steady increase in demand has, however, led to its being grown on a much greater scale. Nevertheless, white asparagus is still expensive, and this often means that people ignore the excellence of green asparagus, its much tastier, more versatile and much cheaper cousin. White asparagus with mayonnaise is delicious, but there are few other ways of serving it. Green asparagus can be prepared in lots of different ways, the best-known of which is with scrambled eggs. In Spain green asparagus spears are called *trigueros*, and originally only grew wild. People had to go out and search for them, and would return home happily clutching their green bundles of slim *trigueros*.

In springtime the family of liliaceous plants offers a vast array of delights, and the food on broilers (grills) throughout Catalonia gleams with its seasoning of garlic cloves, green onions (spring onions) and leeks. And, before spring draws to a close, in the most remote areas of Spain aficionados of wild herbs are out gathering their crops of golden thistles, chickweed, salsify, sorrel, dandelion and other magical plants.

The freshness of spring gives way to the summer sun, and the juiciest fruits appear to bring us much needed refreshment. The heat is so intense in much of the country that any kind of life outside the coolest, shadiest part of the house is considered well nigh impossible. Nothing can lure the locals outdoors while the sun is high in the sky. It is easy in such heat to imagine that even the tap-water may dry up and that it will never again be possible to replenish the last stocks of food in the refrigerator. Nevertheless, the reserves of water in the subsoil aid the sprouting of the most tender, enormous zucchini, the firmest eggplants, and green beans that dangle off their stalks like gypsies' earrings. It is impossible to work in any normal way in summer. So manual labor is treated, instead, as if it were a festival, carried out under the cool, generous shade of white mulberry trees, accompanied by the murmur of the water channels and enlivened by the dazzling reds of tomatoes and bell peppers.

And we do not leave behind this festival mood, when venturing from the house, we stick close to the high walls, under the shade of the smallest roof, until we reach the first tree. We are no longer afraid of the sun, which evokes nothing more than a mocking smile as the rays filtering through the leaves light up the jug of ruby-red *sangria* that stands waiting for us to drink it.

Many dishes of *pisto* later, summer eventually begins to draw to a close. The first drops of rain release the most surprising aromas from the earth, preparing us for the wild mushrooms to come, especially in Catalonia. Catalonians love to broil almost any food, mushrooms included; but there are some mushrooms that are not suitable for broiling. The most plentiful variety, *Lactarius deliciosus*, should be cooked on a slate that has been liberally rubbed with garlic and oil. It is indeed a shame that the use of wild mushrooms is so restricted in Spanish cuisine. Away from the humid area in the north, their rarity arouses such suspicion and fear that very few varieties are used. One of the most popular is the delicately purplish *seta de cardo* (oyster mushroom, *Pleurotus eryngii*) of central Spain that sybarites enjoy in autumn.

This is also the time of year for picking legumes (pulses). Some lucky people get to eat certain varieties fresh, as is the case of *pocha* beans. A good supply of lentils, beans and chickpeas is dried and stored up for the rest of the year. Following a good soaking overnight, all these varieties recover the qualities they had when young and fresh.

The cold weather in winter is a good excuse for eating more, and sausages are added to the vegetables and legumes in the cooking pot.

How wise Mother Nature is to hold all the different cabbages in reserve until now, when they are most needed. Cabbages — true medicinal food — include the strongly flavored white, chalky cauliflower, and green and red cabbages. As a contrast to their rough strength, there is also the delicate, velvety, mouthwatering flavor of cardoon, offset by almond sauce, or crushed fried bread or a coating of egg batter. Potatoes, turnips and carrots, too, are available right through winter.

A Valencian woman (nineteenth century), from the Collection of Spanish National Costumes; NATIONAL LIBRARY, MADRID The Valencian region was famous for its rich soils and the extensive level of cultivation in its fertile market gardens developed by the Moors, and worked by these Valencian women, who were noted for their beauty and their unusual silver jewelry, particularly their earrings. The diverse range of crops produced here included rice, wheat, oranges, lemons, dates, carob, flax, mulberries (for silk production), as well as the *chufas* (tiger nuts), from which that typical Valencian drink, *horchata*, is made.

CATALAN FRAGRANT PEA CASSEROLE

Guisantes a la catalana   Serves 4

Peas used to be seen as marking the arrival of spring. Mint appears about the same time, providing an ideal accompaniment. The use of muscatel and pork fat pays homage to the seasons left behind and serves as a reminder that the evenings can still be quite cool.

⅓ cup (3 fl oz/90 ml) olive oil

6½ oz (200 g) streaky, fatty bacon, diced small

4 green onions (spring onions), finely chopped

8 garlic cloves, finely chopped

4 lb (2 kg) fresh peas (unshelled weight), shelled

4 sprigs fresh mint and 4 sprigs oregano, tied together

2 tablespoons (1 fl oz/30 ml) dry anisette liqueur or grappa

2 tablespoons (1 fl oz/30 ml) muscatel or other sweet white wine

a few drops peppermint liqueur

salt

Heat the oil in a heatproof casserole and fry the bacon. When it starts to brown, add the green onions and garlic shoots. Fry over medium heat until the mixture starts to brown.

Add the peas and herbs and fry gently for a couple of minutes.

Add the anisette, muscatel, peppermint liqueur and a little salt. Cover the casserole, putting baking parchment (paper) under the lid, and cook very gently for 30–45 minutes, shaking the casserole occasionally to prevent sticking.

Add a little water if it looks dry. Serve from the casserole.

Catalan fragrant pea casserole

Spinach with raisins and pine nuts

SPINACH WITH RAISINS AND PINE NUTS

Espinacas con pasas y piñones   Serves 4

T his delicious dish is made with the first young spinach of the season and is a good example of the creative and imaginative talents of the Catalan people when combining tastes, textures and colors. It may be included among a variety of appetizers, be served as a first course or even be used as a filling for turnovers or *coca* pies.

1 cup (8 fl oz/250 ml) water
2 lb (1 kg) spinach (English spinach), washed and chopped
salt

3 tablespoons (1½ fl oz/45 ml) olive oil
3½ oz (100 g) cured ham, diced small
3 tablespoons pine nuts
3 tablespoons seedless raisins, soaked in warm water
freshly ground pepper

Heat the water in a heatproof casserole. When it comes to a boil, add the spinach and a little salt. Cook over high heat for 10 minutes. Drain.

Heat the oil in a skillet (frying pan), add the diced ham, stir briskly, then add the pine nuts, stirring constantly. Drain the raisins and add to the pan.

Add the cooked spinach and mix everything thoroughly. Check the seasoning, and add a little pepper if desired. Serve.

127

Tudela vegetable medley (top); cauliflower in garlic and paprika sauce (left); stuffed peppers (right)

TUDELA VEGETABLE MEDLEY

Menestra de Tudela   Serves 4–6

The gastronomy of the Ribera del Ebro is closely linked to the produce of its gardens and fields and therefore varies greatly from season to season. In springtime vegetable medleys are the crowning glory of local cuisine.

This dish may also include nonvegetable ingredients, although they are not essential. The most usual are cured ham or lamb, which are really added only to give a taste of the other gastronomic delights of the region.

16 artichokes (3 lb/1.5 kg)
13 oz (410 g) fresh peas (unshelled weight)
*8 oz (250 g) green beans, trimmed and
    chopped*
*4 Swiss chard (silverbeet) leaves, washed and
    chopped*
salt
2 eggs, beaten

¼ cup all-purpose (plain) flour
olive oil
4 oz (125 g) cured ham, diced small
*6½ oz (200 g) Pamplona chorizo (paprika-
    flavored cured pork sausage), sliced*
3 cloves garlic, peeled and chopped
¾ cup (6½ fl oz/200 ml) dry white wine
12 white asparagus spears (canned)

Remove the tough outer leaves of the artichokes and trim the ends. Shell the peas.

Boil the artichokes and peas in one pan and the green beans and Swiss chard in another for 30 minutes in salted water.

Drain the vegetables separately. Reserve the water from the artichokes and peas. Cut the artichokes into quarters, dip into the beaten egg and flour, then deep-fry. Do the same with the Swiss chard leaves. Transfer the vegetables to a large heatproof casserole and add the peas and green beans.

In some of the same oil, fry the ham, *chorizo* and then the garlic, but do not allow to brown.

Add a little flour, stir, then add the white wine and a little of the artichoke cooking water.

Pour into the casserole, add a little salt, cover with the asparagus spears and cook over low heat for 10 minutes. Serve in the casserole.

CAULIFLOWER IN GARLIC AND PAPRIKA SAUCE

Coliflor con ajos y pimentón   Serves 4

The produce of the lush fruit and vegetable gardens of Murcia is all of the highest quality. Cabbage from Murcia is included in a sixteenth-century painting, *Retrato de la Lozana Andaluza*, showing the popular foods of the time in Andalusia.

Paprika — ground red pepper — is well known throughout the world and is used in Murcia to put an individual stamp on the dishes made with the delicious local produce. The ingredients are handpicked just before cooking and turned into simple dishes which highlight their freshness.

The juice can be drained off and is excellent for dunking bread. An omelet can be made with the cauliflower, or it can be served with fried eggs or charcoal-grilled chops to make a nutritious but light meal.

1½ lb (750 g) cauliflower, in florets
1 teaspoon lemon juice or white wine vinegar
¼ cup (2 fl oz/60 ml) olive oil
2 thick slices French bread (2 oz/60 g)
2 teaspoons paprika
1⅔ cups (13 fl oz/410 ml) water for cooking
salt
1½ tablespoons finely chopped parsley
2 cloves garlic, peeled
2 teaspoons pine nuts

Rinse the cauliflower and put in a bowl of water with the lemon juice or vinegar.

Heat the oil in a heatproof casserole and fry the slices of bread. Remove and set aside.

Turn down the heat and add the paprika. Stir, then quickly pour in the water. Turn the heat back up. When the water comes to a boil, add the cauliflower florets and a little salt. Cook, uncovered, over medium heat for 20–30 minutes.

Crush the parsley, garlic, the slices of fried bread and the pine nuts in a mortar.

When everything is mixed thoroughly, add a little of the cooking water from the cauliflower,

stir, then pour into the casserole. Check the seasoning. Cook for a further 5 minutes and serve.

STUFFED PEPPERS

Pimientos rellenos   Serves 4

Piquillo red peppers — small, sweet and pointed at one end — are one of the wonderful vegetables grown on the riverbanks of Navarre. They are marketed precooked and have an excellent flavor. *Piquillo* peppers can now be enjoyed all year round and no larder is complete without a can or jar of this specialty.

8 small red peppers (pimientos)
6½ oz (200 g) ground (minced) pork
3½ oz (100 g) ground (minced) beef
1 tablespoon finely chopped parsley
2 cloves garlic, finely chopped
⅔ cup (5 oz/155 ml) olive oil
3 tablespoons all-purpose (plain) flour, plus flour for coating
¼ cup (2 fl oz/60 ml) milk
nutmeg
salt
2 eggs, beaten
olive oil, for deep-frying
⅓ cup (3 fl oz/90 ml) dry white wine
¼ cup (2 fl oz/60 ml) tomato sauce (purée)

Toast the peppers in the broiler (grill) or in the oven, then peel, trim the stalks and remove the seeds, taking care to keep them whole.

To prepare the filling, mix the pork and beef and season with the parsley and garlic. Sauté in a small amount of oil in a skillet (frying pan) and add 2 tablespoons of flour, the milk, a little ground nutmeg and salt.

Stuff the peppers with this mixture and spear with cocktail sticks or toothpicks. Dip into the flour and beaten egg. Fry first in plenty of very hot oil, then turn down the heat and cook until golden.

Transfer to a heatproof casserole as they are ready and remove the sticks.

Prepare a sauce using a little of the same oil, adding 1 tablespoon of flour, the white wine, tomato sauce and a little water. Strain the mixture through a fine sieve and pour over the peppers. Heat through in the casserole for a few minutes over moderate heat and then serve piping hot.

POTATO AND SALT COD CASSEROLE

Patatas con bacalao   Serves 4

Potatoes and salt cod were traditionally combined to make a tasty meal for meatless days or during Lent, when Spanish larders were never without a stock of almonds and pine nuts, as well as a string of garlic and salt cod hanging from a nail. These dietary limitations are no longer observed, but potato and salt cod casserole is still a typical homemade dish and is served in taverns and simple restaurants.

8 oz (250 g) dried salt cod, soaked overnight
⅓ cup (3 fl oz/90 ml) olive oil
1 tomato (3½ oz/100 g), peeled and finely chopped
4 medium-size potatoes (1 lb/500 g), peeled and chopped
1 teaspoon paprika
1 tablespoon finely chopped parsley
2 cloves garlic, peeled
2 teaspoons pine nuts
12 almonds
salt

Drain the cod and break into small pieces.

Heat the oil in a heatproof casserole, add the cod and stir, then add the tomato and cook gently for 5 minutes. Add the potatoes and fry for a further 5 minutes, turning to cook evenly. Add the paprika and stir again.

Cover with water, put a lid on and cook over low heat for 30–45 minutes (depending on the quality of the potatoes).

Crush the parsley, garlic, pine nuts and almonds in a mortar. Stir this mixture into the casserole. Check the seasoning, cook for a further 5 minutes and serve.

St Diego giving food to the poor, Bartolomé Murillo (1617–82); ROYAL ACADEMY OF SAN FERNANDO

Potato and salt cod casserole (top); potato casserole (bottom)

POTATO CASSEROLE

Patatas a la importancia   Serves 4

This is a marvelous everyday dish, sometimes said to be "widowed" because it contains no fish or meat. The batter creates an attractive appearance which justifies the name of *a la importancia* ("of importance"). Unfortunately this dish is becoming less and less common, which is a great shame, as it is quite delicious and is always enjoyed.

olive oil, for deep-frying

4 large potatoes (1 lb 10 oz/800 g), peeled and cut into ½ in (1 cm) slices

2 eggs, beaten

all-purpose (plain) flour for coating

4 cloves garlic, finely chopped

2 small onions (6½ oz/200 g), finely chopped

4 small tomatoes (12 oz/375 g), peeled and finely chopped

1 teaspoon sugar

1⅔ cups (13 fl oz/410 ml) beef broth (stock)

salt

Heat the oil in a skillet (frying pan). Dip the potato slices into the beaten egg and flour, then fry until golden on both sides. Transfer to a heatproof casserole, leaving a little oil in the pan. Fry the garlic and onion, then add the chopped tomato and cook over low heat until it reduces a little. Add the sugar.

Add ½ tablespoon of flour, stir, then pour over the potatoes. Add the broth and a little salt. Cover and cook over low heat for 30–45 minutes. Serve.

131

WILD ASPARAGUS SCRAMBLE

Espárragos esparragados   Serves 4

In certain parts of Spain the search for green asparagus is regarded almost as a sport, requiring sharp observation and a somewhat reckless spirit, as finding it is no easy task. But in Granada the wild plant has become successfully acclimatized and grows on a huge scale on the plains. This nutritious and very beautiful vegetable appeared in the sepulchral paintings of ancient Egypt, while the Greeks valued its diuretic and pain-killing qualities. It has featured in Spanish recipes throughout the ages. The fourteenth-century Catalan book *Libre de Sent Sovi* includes a recipe which is definitely a predecessor of the current version of *espárragos esparragados*. *Libro del Arte de Cocina* (1599) by Diego Granado and *Nuevo Arte de Cocina* (1745) by Juan de Altamiras both mention wild asparagus and suggest different ways of preparing it.

For this recipe, the best asparagus is the dark green, sharp-tasting variety which grows in mountainous areas. There is also a sweeter light green variety called *trigueros*.

> If you want to prepare dressed asparagus, this is how it is done. Take the tender part of the asparagus spears and cook them well. When they are cooked, remove them from the water and chop them up very small, then fry them in a casserole with a lot of oil. Chop up a small, scalded onion and fry it. When it is fried, put to it a little syrup or honey.
>
> Make the sauce like this. Take some toasted bread, soaked in vinegar and good spices, and wet it with a little water or broth [stock]. When the asparagus are fried, put the sauce to them as it says above and cook everything together, stirring all the time with the spoon until you take it off the heat.
>
> Anonymous, *Libre de Sent Sovi*, fourteenth century

Wild asparagus scramble

1 bunch wild green asparagus (or white ribs of Swiss chard/silverbeet, cut into strips) (8 oz/250 g)

3 tablespoons (1½ fl oz/45 ml) olive oil

4 cloves garlic, peeled

1 thick slice French bread (1 oz/30 g)

1 teaspoon paprika

salt

1 tablespoon (½ fl oz/15 ml) white wine vinegar

3 eggs

Wash the asparagus and snap off the woody stems. Break into pieces.

Heat the oil in a heatproof casserole and fry the garlic and bread. Remove and set aside.

Sauté the asparagus in the same oil.

Crush the garlic and bread in a mortar, or purée in a blender, adding a small amount of water. Add this mixture and the paprika to the asparagus and stir. Add a little more water, a small amount of salt and the vinegar.

Cover and cook over medium heat for approximately 30 minutes (some liquid should be left).

Before serving, beat the eggs, add to the casserole and stir to scramble with the asparagus.

ANDALUSIAN STUFFED ZUCCHINI

Calabacines rellenos al estilo Andalucia   Serves 4

This dish is very popular in Andalusia and is typical of Seville because of the finely chopped ingredients in the filling. Other vegetables can be used instead of zucchini (courgettes). It is excellent as part of a varied supper for a festive occasion.

¾ cup (6½ fl oz/200 ml) olive oil

1 onion, finely chopped

whole outerlayers only of 4 onions, to cap the zucchini (courgettes)

3½ oz (100 g) ground (minced) pork

salt

⅓ cup (2 oz/60 g) green olives, pitted and finely chopped

⅓ cup (2 oz/60 g) seeded raisins

2 eggs, hardcooked (hardboiled)

4 zucchini (courgettes), peeled and cut in half horizontally

all-purpose (plain) flour for coating

2 eggs, beaten

Sauce:

1 onion, finely chopped

Andalusian stuffed zucchini

3 tablespoons (1½ fl oz/45 ml) olive oil

1 tablespoon all-purpose (plain) flour

3 tablespoons (1½ fl oz/45 ml) dry white wine

1 cup (8 fl oz/250 ml) beef broth (stock)

salt

2 tablespoons ground almonds

Heat 3 tablespoons (1½ fl oz/45 ml) of oil in a skillet (frying pan) and gently fry half the finely chopped onion. When it colors, add the ground pork, season with salt and brown. Remove from the heat and add the olives, raisins and chopped hardcooked eggs.

Scoop out the zucchini flesh from one end only, then stuff with the pork mixture. Top each piece with a cap made from the outer layer of a whole onion. Coat with flour and beaten egg, then fry in the rest of the oil, which should be very hot. Transfer to a heatproof casserole and set aside.

Make the sauce by frying the chopped onion in the olive oil. When it starts to brown, add the flour, stir, then add the white wine and broth. Cook for a few minutes, stirring all the time, and add salt if necessary. Strain through a fine sieve and pour over the zucchini.

Put the casserole on the heat, add the almonds and cook slowly for 20–30 minutes until the zucchini are soft. Transfer carefully to a serving platter and pour the sauce over the top.

CRISPY FRIED EGGPLANT WITH CHEESE

Berenjenas con queso   Serves 4

There are records of eggplant (aubergine) being used in Spain back in the Muslim period in the thirteenth century. The Fadálat al Jiwán manuscript and the *cento* dealing with Hispanic–Maghrebi cooking of that time both include recipes using it. The writer and sailor Baltasar de Alcázar bestowed the following praise on it in the sixteenth century: "Three things have my heart imprisoned, the beautiful lady Inés, ham, and eggplant with cheese." Ruperto de Nola, in his *Libre del Coch* (1529), confirms the Andalusian origins of the dish by calling it "Moorish Eggplant." The goat's cheese should ideally come from the Ronda Mountains in Andalusia.

> Hull the eggplants and cut into four quarters; cut off the peel and put them on to cook; when they are well cooked, take them off the stove, and then press them between two wooden blocks to get rid of all the water, then chop them up with a knife, and put them into the pot and fry them very well with good bacon fat or with oil which is sweet, because the Moors do not eat bacon, and when they are well fried, cook them in a pot with good thick broth; and the meat fat, and finely grated cheese, and ground cilantro [coriander] with everything, and then stir them as if they were squash, and when they are almost cooked, put the yolks of beaten eggs to them as if they were squash.
>
> Ruperto de Nola, *Libre del Coch*, 1529

2 lb (1 kg) eggplants (aubergines), peeled
  and halved lengthwise
⅓ cup (3 fl oz/90 ml) olive oil
1 medium-size onion (5 oz/155 g), finely chopped
1 teaspoon dried mint
4 eggs (2 beaten)
½ cup (2 oz/60 g) dry breadcrumbs
2 oz (60 g) goat's cheese, grated
salt
1 pinch ground pepper
1 pinch ground cloves
1 pinch ground cinnamon
1 pinch ground nutmeg
⅓ cup (2 oz/60 g) sugar
olive oil, for deep-frying
½ cup (2 oz/60 g) all-purpose (plain) flour
1 teaspoon dried mint leaves

Cook the eggplants in boiling salted water for 10 minutes. Drain, then chop 2 up very finely and set aside. Scoop out a walnut-size hollow in the others (reserving the scooped-out flesh). Heat the oil in a skillet (frying pan) and sauté the chopped onion until it starts to brown. Add the chopped eggplant and the scooped-out flesh from the others, along with the mint and the 2 whole eggs.

Stir constantly over low heat to prevent sticking. When a smooth mixture has formed, add the breadcrumbs and grated cheese. Season with salt and the spices, then add a teaspoon of sugar. Stir and remove from the heat.

Heat plenty of oil for deep-frying.

Fill the hollows in the eggplants with the cheese mixture, dip into beaten egg and flour, then fry 1 at a time. Transfer to a serving dish as they are ready and sprinkle with sugar and cinnamon before serving.

FAVA BEAN CASSEROLE

Cazuela de habas   Serves 4

Fava (broad) beans are one of the best things about the local cuisine in Granada. When they are shelled, their fresh green color seems to bring the surrounding fertile land right into the kitchen. In this casserole, fava beans are combined with other vegetables and given a Moorish touch with the addition of a mixture of ingredients crushed in a mortar, which accentuates the contrasting flavors and aromas. Topped with eggs and accompanied by some crusty bread, this makes an excellent springtime dish. It is said to have exceptional properties and goes back to the time of Pythagoras and the ancient Greek dietitians.

8 artichokes (1 lb 10 oz/800 g)
4 lb (2 kg) fresh fava (broad) beans
  (unshelled weight)
⅓ cup (3 fl oz/90 ml) olive oil
1 thick slice French bread (1 oz/30 g)
3 green onions (spring onions), finely chopped
1 clove garlic, finely chopped
2 ripe tomatoes (8 oz/250 g), peeled and
  finely chopped
3 sprigs mint, 3 sprigs flat-leaf (Italian) parsley
  and 1 bay leaf, tied together
salt
1 pinch cumin
1 pinch saffron
3 black peppercorns
4 eggs

Crispy fried eggplant with cheese (left); fava bean casserole (right)

Remove the tough outer leaves of the artichokes, trim off the top halves and cut the bases in half.

Shell the beans and cook in a small amount of boiling water for 10 minutes.

Heat the oil in a skillet (frying pan) and fry the bread. Remove and set aside. Fry the green onions in the same oil, then add the garlic. When it starts to brown, add the chopped tomatoes and cook over low heat.

Drain the beans and place in a heatproof casserole. Pour in the tomato mixture. Add the artichokes and the bunch of herbs and enough water just to cover. Add a little salt, cover, then cook over low heat for about 40 minutes.

Meanwhile, crush the cumin, saffron, peppercorns and fried bread in a mortar. Dilute with a little of the cooking liquid, then add the mixture to the casserole. The sauce should be quite thick.

At the end of 40 minutes, check the seasoning, then break the eggs into a cup 1 at a time and arrange on top of the beans. Allow to set, then serve in the casserole.

Stuffed eggplant (left); stuffed onions (right)

STUFFED EGGPLANT

Berenjenas rellenas   Serves 4

The Arabs wrote about eggplant (aubergine) from the East in the ninth century and were responsible for bringing the vegetable to Spain. It is mentioned in the Catalan *Libre de Sent Sovi*, written in the fourteenth century. The Balearic Islands in the Mediterranean grow perhaps the best eggplant in the world (or so the locals claim), and this recipe is just one tasty example of how it can be combined with other vegetables or meat.

8 long, small eggplants (aubergines), peeled
4 cloves garlic (3 finely chopped, 1 left whole)
3 tablespoons finely chopped parsley
6½ oz (200 g) lean pork, ground (minced)
1 egg, separated (eggwhite beaten)
salt
dry breadcrumbs, for coating
1 cup (8 fl oz/250 ml) olive oil

4 black peppercorns
2 tomatoes (6½ oz/200 g), peeled and finely chopped
1 teaspoon paprika

Slice the eggplants in half lengthwise and scoop out the centers.

Mix the garlic and 1 tablespoon of the parsley with the ground pork, then add the egg yolk and a little salt. Fill the eggplants with this mixture, then dip into the beaten eggwhite and breadcrumbs.

Heat the oil in a skillet (frying pan), then fry the eggplant halves on both sides, transferring them to a casserole as they are ready.

In a mortar, crush the whole clove of garlic, 2 tablespoons of parsley and the peppercorns.

Pour off nearly all the oil used to fry the eggplants, leaving just enough to cover the base

136

of the pan, then add the tomatoes and fry lightly. Add the mixture from the mortar, a little paprika and a small amount of water. Stir, then pour over the eggplants. Add enough water just to cover. Add a little salt, cover and cook over low heat for 15 minutes. Serve with tomato sauce.

STUFFED ONIONS

Cebollas rellenas   Serves 4

Like some other vegetables, onions can be used as an edible container. The different regions of Spain provide an endless variety of fillings.

The glorious custom of preparing a large baking dish with stuffed vegetables — such as green or red bell peppers (capsicums), potatoes, onions, zucchini (courgettes) and tomatoes — unfortunately seems to be dying out. *El Libro Anónimo de un Gatrónomo Jubilado* defines ground (minced) meat stuffing as an "article of general use." This book deals with making use of leftovers in a typically thrifty nineteenth-century way. Stuffed onions are, however, a great traditional dish in their own right, not just as a way of using up surplus food. In *Nuevo Arte de Cocina* (1745), Juan de Altamiras provides a meatless version, flavored with cheese, which uses spices but has a mild flavor typical of the time.

Tilework (eighteenth century); DECORATIVE ARTS MUSEUM, MADRID

> You remove the heart of the Onions, leaving the outer layers whole; then you cook the hearts with water and salt, and chopped, put them in the skillet [frying pan] with oil or beef lard, adding parsley, mint, lettuce hearts, which must be cooked if they are not tender, with water and salt; you cut it up, and stir it into the skillet with the onion, add some beaten eggs, and stir everything together until it cooked: turn it out onto a board and chop again very finely; you add cheese, breadcrumbs, raw eggs, and season it with all the spices; and if you want to make it sweet, then do not put spices to it, nor cheese: then you fill the Onions, if you have some chickpea broth [stock], boil it and put a sauce of pine nuts or hazelnuts to them.
>
> Juan de Altamiras, *Nuevo Arte de Cocina*, 1745

8 medium-size onions (approximately 5 oz/ 155 g each)

salt

5 oz (155 g) ground (minced) meat (pork and beef)

1 cup (3½ oz/100 g) coarse fresh breadcrumbs soaked in ⅓ cup (3 fl oz/90 ml) hot milk

1 tablespoon finely chopped parsley

2 cloves garlic, peeled and finely chopped

1 teaspoon dry white wine

2 eggs, beaten
all-purpose (plain) flour for coating
olive oil, for deep-frying
⅓ cup (3 fl oz/90 ml) beef broth (stock), hot

Preheat the oven to 350°F (180°C/Gas 4).

Peel the onions and slice off the tops and bases. Heat plenty of water in a pan with a little salt. When it comes to a boil, add the onions and cook for 15 minutes. Drain, reserving the cooking water.

Put the ground meat, breadcrumbs, parsley, garlic, white wine, eggs and a little salt in a bowl (keep a little beaten egg for coating) and mix thoroughly.

Scoop out the centers of the onions, then fill with the meat mixture.

Brush the exposed filling with the rest of the egg, then coat the whole onion with flour. Heat the oil in a deep skillet (frying pan) and fry the onions 2 at a time.

Grease a baking dish with a little oil and transfer the onions from the skillet. The filling end should face upward. Pour the hot broth into the dish to half cover the onions. If necessary, add a little of the onion cooking water.

Bake for approximately 30 minutes, or until the onions are soft and golden, basting occasionally with the broth. Serve in the baking dish.

Mediterranean vegetable casserole

MEDITERRANEAN VEGETABLE CASSEROLE

Tumbet   Serves 4

The dark purple, almost cylindrical "Moorish" variety of eggplant (aubergine) which is grown in Spain is an extremely popular vegetable. According to the Balearic peasants, "the island soil makes them sweet," while the fishermen claim that "the sea air removes the bitterness," and there is no doubt that Moorish eggplants do have a wonderfully sweet taste. The locals explain that "you have to make them weep away their bitterness by cutting them in half and covering them with salt, then soothing their sorrow with cool water."

There is a wide range of recipes for eggplant in the Balearic Islands, but *tumbet* is the most important. This dish is wonderful when freshly made, but is also delicious when left to stand and then eaten at room temperature. It can be served on its own as a main course or as an accompaniment to fish, meat or eggs. *Tumbet* is a magnificent example of how well the flavor of the ancient eggplant contrasts with other foods coming from the New World.

1 lb (500 g) eggplants (aubergines), cut into ¼ in (0.5 cm) slices

salt

2¼ cups (18 fl oz/500 ml) olive oil

1 lb (500 g) potatoes, cut into ¼ in (0.5 cm) slices

1 lb (500 g) green bell peppers (capsicums), seeded and chopped

3 cloves garlic, peeled

2 lb (1 kg) ripe tomatoes, peeled and finely chopped

Place the eggplant slices in a colander, sprinkle with salt and leave for 1 hour.

Dry off the water yielded by the eggplant with paper towels.

Heat the oil in a skillet (frying pan), then fry the potato slices over low heat until soft but not golden. Transfer to a heatproof casserole as the slices are done. Fry the eggplant in the same oil and arrange them on top of the potatoes. Fry the bell peppers in the same oil over low heat. Drain the oil thoroughly from the bell peppers, then arrange on top of the eggplant and add a little salt. Leave enough oil in the skillet to cover the base of the pan. Fry the garlic cloves, then add the tomatoes and cook over medium heat for 20–30 minutes, stirring frequently. When the oil starts to come to the surface, add a little salt and strain the tomato sauce through a fine sieve. Pour over the vegetables.

Preheat the oven to 350°F (180°C/Gas 4).

Sprinkle a little of the used oil over the vegetables and tomato sauce. Transfer to the oven and bake for 10 minutes. Serve hot, warm or cold.

VALENCIAN BOILED VEGETABLES

Hervido valenciano Serves 4

It seems incredible that such an apparently simple dish can express the serenity of the Mediterranean, the appreciation of nature and the shared eating experience. Everyone loves *hervido valenciano*. It easily becomes a habit that, once acquired, is hard to break. In the Valencia region it makes a perfect everyday supper dish, served with a good dash of olive oil and sometimes vinegar, too.

Some people vary the classic recipe by adding zucchini (courgettes), eggplants (aubergines) and carrots. The vegetables are cooked whole and served piping hot and steaming. A cruet with extra virgin olive oil and vinegar should always be on the table for people to help themselves.

Valencian boiled vegetables

1¼ lb (600 g) onions, peeled

2¼ cups (18 fl oz/500 ml) water

salt

1 lb (500 g) potatoes, peeled

1 lb (500 g) green beans, trimmed

extra virgin olive oil

white wine vinegar

Make a cross-shaped incision at both ends of the onions.

Heat the water in a heatproof casserole. When it comes to a boil, add a little salt, the onions and potatoes, then cover and cook over low heat for 20 minutes.

Add the green beans, cover and cook for a further 20 – 30 minutes (depending on the thickness).

Transfer to a serving dish and serve with oil and vinegar on the side for all to help themselves.

Maize fields in Guipuzcoa, Dario Regoyos (1857–1913);
SPANISH MUSEUM OF CONTEMPORARY ART, MADRID

Guipuzcoa is one of the Basque provinces, where maize (corn) is grown extensively. Maize is, of course, a comparatively recent addition from the New World to such local produce as chestnuts, pears, apples, beans, turnips, clover and cattle. The Basque countryside was distinctive for its hedges, said by the fourteenth-century English poet, Chaucer, to be "as thicke as a castel wall," traditionally used to separate properties.

MADRID RED CABBAGE

Lombarda a la madrileña   Serves 4

Red cabbage came originally from southern Europe. The many wholesome properties of the cabbage family have been known and appreciated since Roman times. The Inquisition doctor Juan Sorapán de Rieros described several varieties of red cabbage back in 1572, and their decorative value in salads was highly valued during the Renaissance. This is a winter recipe, traditionally prepared at slaughter time, and also served as a garnish for Madrid roasts.

2 lb (1 kg) red cabbage
salt
¾ cup (6½ fl oz/200 ml) olive oil
3 cloves garlic, peeled
½ cup (2 oz/60 g) pine nuts
⅓ cup (2 oz/60 g) seedless raisins, soaked in
    water for 30 minutes
4 black peppercorns
1 clove
1 pinch ground cinnamon

Remove the outer leaves of the red cabbage and discard. Cut the cabbage into quarters, cut out the woody stem and chop the rest into thin strips.

Boil in plenty of salted water. Drain and transfer to a heatproof casserole.

Heat the oil in a skillet (frying pan) and fry the garlic cloves. Remove and set aside. Fry the pine nuts in the same oil. When they start to brown, transfer to the casserole with the red cabbage.

Drain the raisins and add to the casserole.

Crush the fried garlic with the peppercorns and the clove in a mortar. Mix in 1 tablespoon of water and add to the casserole. Season with a little salt and add the cinnamon. Heat through in the casserole on top of the stove, stirring to mix all the ingredients. Serve hot.

VEGETABLE PARCEL

Pastel de verduras   Serves 4–6

Like cuisines across the world, Spanish cuisine has various versions of vegetable pies. When we fancy eating lots of vegetables at once, we can choose between a mixed vegetable platter or some kind of pie. This latter alternative has the added advantages that it is good at any temperature and is ideal for picnics in the country, as it is easily transportable.

6–8 outer cabbage leaves, washed
1 lb (500 g) leeks, finely chopped
6½ oz (200 g) green beans, trimmed and
    halved
3 tablespoons (1½ fl oz/45 ml) olive oil
8 oz (250 g) button mushrooms
    (champignons), washed and chopped
6 eggs, beaten
salt
freshly ground pepper

Cook the cabbage leaves in boiling water until the green part is soft (the stalks will be removed later, so they do not need to be soft). When the leaves are ready, dip into cold water to halt the cooking process, then transfer to a flat surface and dry thoroughly on layers of paper towels.

Boil the leeks and green beans separately for 10 minutes. Drain and set aside.

Heat 2 tablespoons of oil in a skillet (frying pan) and sauté the mushrooms.

Preheat the oven to 400°F (200°C/Gas 6).

Grease a 12 × 4 in (30 × 10 cm) rectangular pan (or individual pans) with 1 tablespoon of oil. Snip the stalks off the cabbage leaves and discard. Lay the leaves in the pan, overlapping the edges. Put in a layer of leeks, then a layer of mushrooms and a layer of green beans. Season the beaten eggs with salt and pepper, then pour over the vegetables, piercing with a knife to increase absorption.

Fold the overlapping leaves over the top to form a parcel, then cover with aluminum foil. Transfer to the oven and bake for 45–60 minutes.

Remove from the pan and serve with tomato sauce or a light mayonnaise.

Madrid red cabbage (left); vegetable parcel (right)

SUMMER VEGETABLE MEDLEY

Pisto manchego   Serves 4–6

There are many varieties of *pisto*, but the ingredients are lightly fried and sweated in all the different versions. As well as a variety of vegetables, these dishes may include scrambled eggs, tuna in brine or sausages. *Pisto* has always been popular in Madrid and is found on the menu of many basic restaurants.

¾ cup (6½ fl oz/200 ml) olive oil

3 cloves garlic, finely chopped

2 large onions (16 oz/500 g), finely chopped

3 red or green bell peppers (capsicums) (1 lb/ 500 g), chopped

2 eggplants (aubergines), peeled and chopped into small chunks

13 oz (410 g) zucchini (courgettes), peeled and chopped into small chunks

1 lb 4 oz (600 g) tomatoes, peeled and finely chopped

Summer vegetable medley (left); zucchini and onion casserole (right)

ZUCCHINI AND ONION CASSEROLE

Zarangollo   Serves 4

A great variety of simple, traditional dishes is made with the extraordinary produce of the *huertas* of Murcia, picked from the gardens immediately before cooking. If the broth (stock) is strained off — delicious soaked up on hunks of bread — the vegetables can be used to make a chunky, round omelet, or maybe served with fried eggs, or charcoal-grilled chops.

¾ cup (6½ fl oz/200 ml) olive oil
1 lb (500 g) onions, thinly sliced
3 lb (1.5 kg) zucchini (courgettes), peeled and
   cut into small chunks
salt
1 teaspoon oregano

Heat the oil in a heatproof casserole and add the onion. Turn the heat down, cover and cook very slowly. When the onion starts to soften, add the zucchini, mix well, cover and cook over low heat for a further 20–30 minutes.

Add a little salt and the oregano. Cook for another 10 minutes and serve.

Tilework (eighteenth century); NATIONAL MUSEUM OF CERAMICS, VALENCIA

salt
1 pinch sugar

Heat the oil in a large skillet (frying pan) and fry the garlic and onion over low heat. When it starts to brown, add the bell peppers and eggplants and fry gently until the mixture begins to soften. Add the zucchini and tomatoes and cook until the liquid evaporates, stirring frequently. Add salt and a pinch of sugar at the end. Serve.

Still-life of fish, crockery and greens, Thomas Yepes (1600–74); NASEIRO COLLECTION, MADRID With such a variety of seafood available, the cook might well combine them in

...he pot with a *sofrito* of green (spring) onions and garlic.

FISH AND SHELLFISH

Spaniards can be somewhat equivocal about fish as food: it is often regarded as a poor alternative to meat but also treated with a kind of reverence, in part because of its cost, and is consumed like some ritual food. There are a number of reasons for this, which mainly have to do with the nature of the Spanish fishing industry and its market in Spain.

In terms of both its consumption of fish and the size of its fishing fleet Spain occupies second place in the world, despite being a relatively small country. Its fishing fleet is second only to the Japanese.

Spain consists of a peninsula and two very different archipelagos situated in very different seas — the Balearics and the Canary Islands in, respectively, the Mediterranean Sea and the Atlantic Ocean. With much of its mainland surrounded by sea, Spain has an extremely broad variety of marine environments. In the Bay of Biscay and the Atlantic Ocean on the northern seaboard, which connect Spain with northern Europe, there are colder waters with strong tides, rough seas and steep cliffs. In the south, the Atlantic gets progressively warmer towards the equatorial waters around the Canary Islands. The Pillars of Hercules provide the gateway for the Atlantic waters to flow into the Mediterranean Sea. The whole of the Levante region of Spain is bathed by the waters of the Mediterranean, from the Pyrenees to the tip of Tarifa.

In ancient times important fisheries were set up to take advantage of the well-stocked sea around Gibraltar. The migratory habits of fish through this gateway into the Mediterranean were well known to the Phoenicians, Greeks and Romans, who established fishing stations to catch and salt the fish and make them into sauce. These same activities have continued at many of the same locations until the present.

With so many parts of Spain involved in the fishing industry, there is therefore a fishing economy that supplies a wide market stretching all the way inland to the center. This fishing economy established the basis for a cuisine of fresh fish in Spain. But it also meant that, however cheap and readily available it might be close to the coasts, the further inland towards the center the fish had to travel, the more costly it became. Consequently, fresh fish was all the more prized. And because people tend to accord special status to something that is hard to obtain and also extremely costly, in the center fresh fish was often treated as though it were some kind of consecrated food.

Fish-hawker, Leoncio Talavera (nineteenth century); MALAGA TOWN-HALL
In the old parts of port towns and in villages within sight or smell of the sea, one of the eagerly anticipated morning sounds would be the cries of the fish-hawkers. Loaded with fresh produce, they would call out the catch of the day as they went their rounds.

Tilework from the Municipal Market in Manises, Valencia (nineteenth century). In addition to the range of fish on sale in this section of the market, other essential ingredients can be found for the Valencian *arroz a la marinera*, such as cuttlefish, octopus and mussels.

Before the invention of the railway, some incredible methods were employed to transport fish around the country. Originally, portable saltwater tanks were used, but many of the fish died in transit. As a solution, they were transported already dead but kept as fresh as possible: snow wells were set up along the routes to implement this system.

However, for the inhabitants of many inland villages dried salt cod and sardines in brine were the traditional fare when it came to seafood and even today, despite the widespread availability of fresh fish, it is still preferred. The taste for this kind of fish developed over the centuries of strict imposition by the Catholic Church of the forty-day Lent period, as well as many other fasting days, when meat was forbidden.

Spanish people have always known how to take advantage of all the fresh-water and salt-water produce their rivers and seas abound with. In the past Spaniards who traveled to farflung countries were amazed to discover that the local inhabitants often did not take advantage of the stocks of shellfish in their waters, as they had no idea how tasty it was. In the Atlantic off the coasts of Ireland and the United States, voyagers came across great banks of top-quality eels (*angulas*), which in Madrid would have been worth their weight in gold. The habit of eating species such as the cephalopods has spread from the Mediterranean to other parts of the world.

In Spain the Mediterranean marshes contain eels, which were a favorite delicacy in Roman times and continue to be. Cephalopods are caught almost everywhere, although each area has its specialty, such as the *chipirón* squid from the Bay of Biscay and the Mediterranean cuttlefish.

Spain nowadays, is as polluted as any other developed country, so the rivers no longer produce good fish. Trout is now bred on fish farms, with either white or salmon-pink flesh.

Hake is the most famous white fish of the Bay of Biscay and a very typical feature of Basque, Asturian and Galician cuisine. The price has varied over the years, fluctuating with fashion and the size of the catches. These days it is more expensive than salmon, which used to be caught only in Asturias but now is imported by air on a large scale from Norway. The same goes for porgy (sea bream), which used to be a very popular weekly dish in Madrid, and is now reserved for the Christmas festivities.

Grouper is the king of the white fish in the Mediterranean. Its flesh is juicy, with a lot of flavor and it has an extraordinary texture — something commented on in an old proverb: "*De la mar el mero y de la tierra el carnero*" (grouper from the sea and mutton from the land). Fish of the sole family are not very plentiful, and are therefore considered more as luxury items. The only one eaten on an everyday basis is John Dory, which can be very fleshy, and is spongier and lighter than sole and turbot.

Andalusian fried fish, although apparently such a simple dish, can be exceptional provided the quality of the oil and the texture of the flour is right. A lot of oil must be used so that no flavor is lost and the temperature is kept high. Andalusians, well aware of the skills involved, like to show off their expertise by frying the fish in front of everyone.

Worthy of special mention is the *chanquete*, a type of goby. This tiniest of fish mixes perfectly with flour and oil. When cooked, it resembles a kind of jade-colored coral and, when eaten, produces indescribable tactile and taste experiences.

Although there is an abundant supply of blue fish around the coasts of Spain, these varieties are more subject to seasonal factors than other fish and they deteriorate quickly. However, they are ideal for preserving, which overcomes these drawbacks. There has recently been a change of attitude towards blue fish since the discovery that, despite their high fat content, far from increasing cholesterol levels, eating them actually helps remove cholesterol from the body.

Blue fish require careful cooking to compensate for their strong flavors and tendency to dryness. They are usually cooked in casseroles on top of the stove or baked in the oven. This kind of fish combines very well with onions, tomatoes and bell peppers (capsicums), such as in *bonito a la riojana*, a dish restaurants always serve. Adherents of a new style of cuisine have taken a great interest in promoting blue fish to make the most of the plentiful supplies and overcome the old concerns about their fat content. In this style of cooking the bones are removed and molds are used to create unusual shapes, and it can be accompanied by almost anything.

Sardines are very common around Spain. On the coast they are eaten grilled (barbecued), just after being caught when they are really fresh. Cooking them outdoors has the added advantage of dispersing the intense smell of the fish as it cooks.

In the north, white fish are cooked in casseroles with great emphasis on the quality of the sauces. Success sometimes depends on the ability of the cook and the movement applied to the casserole at crucial moments during the preparation, as is the case with hake *pil-pil*. On other occasions the important factor is the alcohol used in the sauce; the recipe for *merluza asturiana* uses cider, for instance.

Bowl decorated with a woman holding fish, thirteenth–fourteenth-century pottery from Paterna: CERAMICS MUSEUM, BARCELONA

Still-life: a slice of salmon, a lemon and cooking vessels, Luis Meléndez (1716–80); PRADO MUSEUM, MADRID
When this was painted, salmon abounded on the Biscayan coasts of Spain — in the Basque, Asturian and Galician regions. It was so plentiful that locals used to complain of having it too frequently, which is not a problem nowadays as it has long since been fished out.

In the Levante, fish is charcoal grilled in its own juice or *a la marinera*, which is how the fishermen used to prepare it on board their boats. In Murcia, sea bass is completely covered with kosher (coarse) salt and baked in the oven. This method ensures that none of the juices is lost, and once the fish is cooked, the salt casing is simply cracked open to remove the fish.

Pescadito frito (fried pieces of fish) is a typically Spanish dish that makes excellent use of the olive oil from the south. A great variety of different fish is used, but preferably small kinds — the smallest oily fish group, the *boquerón* (fresh anchovy), is ideal. *Boquerón* is often served in a fan-shaped cluster formed by attaching the tails with the help of a little flour.

A steep coastline and rough waters such as in the Galician estuaries provide an ideal habitat for various kinds of shellfish. The only thing more that is required is a creative imagination that can see in these little creatures, so exotic and disconcerting in appearance, the gastronomic delights they promise. In the places where such creatures are found the local people not only are aware of the potential each one has as food but they put this knowledge to good use in the creation of a shellfish cuisine. The weakness for shellfish that people have in Spain created a demand for specialist establishments called *marisquerías* to sell it. Over the Christmas period in 1991, approximately 26.5 million lb (12 million kg) of shellfish were eaten in Madrid alone.

The most highly esteemed of the crustaceans, and the best-known internationally,

Activities of the Andalusian fishermen: salting the fish, Georgius Hoefnagle, published *Civitatis Orbis Terrarum*, Georgius Braun (1599);
HISTORICAL ARCHIVE OF THE CITY, BARCELONA
The catching and salting of the blue-fin tuna — the *almadraba* — had been carried out in Andalusia since antiquity using precisely the same methods as depicted here. Each year in May–June vast shoals of tuna, arriving on their spawning run, were driven into nets, hauled out, cut up, salted and barreled. Salted tuna was popular throughout the Mediterranean and in classical times was used as the base for *garum*, the highly prized, pungent sauce that accompanied practically all Roman food.

Still-life leo, Jaime Mercadé (1887–1967); PRIVATE COLLECTION, MADRID
This painting is of the *langosta* (spiny lobster). The *bogavante* (lobster) is slightly longer and has two large claws. In Spain the *langostas* of Minorca are famous and there are a number of Catalonian recipes for both types of lobster — a well-known one typically uses a sauce of which the basis is chocolate.

is the spiny lobster. Galicia has the best lobsters in the world, as the characteristics of the sea there are ideal. Shrimp (prawns) are best in the Mediterranean. Among the mollusks, clams from the Bay of Biscay are absolutely first-class; mussels are bred artificially in Galicia with excellent results, and supply a wide market with top quality mussels at a very reasonable price.

It would be impossible to list all the different varieties, so only some of the most interesting are mentioned here. Tiny *quisquilla* shrimp are eaten in paper cornets and have a barely discernible, salty, fishy taste. The sweet flesh of the aristocratic and very popular crayfish (Dublin Bay prawn, scampi) contrasts very well with the bitter taste of beer. The best meat of the monstrous spider crab is served in the shell with an exotic wine sauce. In the inland rivers of the mountain ranges crabs are caught to be served at local summer festivals.

Some species look so strange that only the locals appreciate them — for example, the goose barnacle, which is found on very rocky cliffs. Collecting it is an extremely hazardous business, and many people have died in the attempt. The Mediterranean sea urchin is really only for the initiated, who dare to eat it alive *in situ* with just a little lemon squeezed over it.

Baked stuffed crab

BAKED STUFFED CRAB

Txangurro al horno   Serves 4

T he *centollo* — spider or spiny crab — is described by
Alan Davidson in his book *North Atlantic Seafood* as an
animal capable of disguising and hiding itself by using saliva
to stick algae onto its shell. This ruse does not, however, fool
the skillful shellfishermen of Galicia and the Basque country,
who are well aware of the high price people are prepared to
pay for this delicacy whether at local markets or in bars and
restaurants. The shells are used to serve the crabmeat in.

*4 spider (spiny) crabs, weighing about 1½ lb
    (750 g) each*
salt
¾ cup (6½ fl oz/200 ml) olive oil
*1 medium-size onion (5 oz/155 g), finely
    chopped*
1 clove garlic
½ cup (4 fl oz/125 ml) dry white wine
*1⅔ cups (13 fl oz/410 ml) tomato sauce
    (purée)*
1 pinch tarragon
freshly ground pepper
2 teaspoons dry breadcrumbs
2 teaspoons finely chopped parsley
2 tablespoons (1 oz/30 g) butter

Wash the crabs and boil in sea water, or water
with plenty of salt added, for 15 minutes after
it comes to a boil. Remove and allow to cool.

Remove the legs, split them in half and scoop
out the meat from inside. Open the crabs, remove

the meat, chop finely and set aside. Drain the
liquid from inside the shells into a cup and
scrape around with a spoon to get out all the
paste inside. Add to the meat from the legs.

Wash and dry the shells.

Heat the oil in a skillet (frying pan) and sauté
the onion with the garlic until it starts to brown.
Add the white wine and tomato sauce and cook
for a few minutes, then add the liquid from the
shells. Allow to reduce for a few minutes, then
add the crabmeat, tarragon, pepper and salt.
Cook for a few more minutes. Fill the shells
with this mixture and smooth over the surfaces.

Mix the breadcrumbs with the parsley and
sprinkle over the top. Dot with butter and brown
in the oven. Serve in individual portions in crab
shells.

GALICIAN HAKE

Merluza a la gallega   Serves 4

I t has been said that nowhere in Spain is the eating experience
enjoyed as intensely as in the province of Galicia, where
both land and sea form an integral part of the way of life. The
French writer Alexandre Dumas was not the only traveler to
appreciate its merits. All dishes called *a la gallega* feature top-
quality olive oil, bright red paprika and salt.

½ onion
1¼ lb (650 g) potatoes, sliced
*3 cloves garlic, peeled (1 left whole and 2
    sliced lengthwise)*
3 sprigs flat-leaf (Italian) parsley
salt
3⅓ cups (27 fl oz/750 ml) water
4 hake (or cod) steaks, 8 oz (250 g) each
3½ oz (100 g) fresh peas, shelled
¾ cup (6½ fl oz/200 ml) olive oil
2 teaspoons sweet paprika

Heat the onion, potatoes, whole garlic clove,
parsley and salt with the water in a heatproof
casserole. After about 15 minutes add the hake
and the peas, then cook over low heat for another
15 minutes.

Remove the hake, peas and potatoes from the
broth, transfer to a serving platter and keep
warm.

Heat the oil in a skillet (frying pan) and fry
the sliced garlic until golden. Add the paprika,
then quickly take the pan off the heat and pour
the contents over the fish and potatoes. Serve
immediately.

Galician hake

The sardine-dealers, Joaquín Sorolla (1863–1923); AMAT COLLECTION
Along the Mediterranean coast in summer, sardines were fished at night, and in the afternoon when the boats returned, villagers would be waiting to buy them. Fresh from the boat, the sardines would be cooked *a la brasa* (a method of broiling/grilling without using oil or fat), usually on pine-wood cinders.

CATALAN SEAFOOD STEW

Zarzuela de pescado   Serves 4–6

Zarzuela is a Spanish musical genre which is a combination of theatrical operetta and comedy of manners with a bit of sentimental drama thrown in. This eclectic mixture is perhaps the reason behind the name of one of the favorite dishes of Catalonia, *zarzuela de pescado*, which consists of a variety of fish and shellfish cooked in a shallow, wide earthenware casserole. The selection of fish varies according to personal taste and economic possibilities. This is a very popular choice at the quayside restaurants in Barcelona.

13 oz (410 g) monkfish, in 4 slices
13 oz (410 g) grouper or sea bass, in 4 slices
13 oz (410 g) hake, in 4 slices
1 lb (500 g) squid, cut into thin rings
salt
freshly ground pepper
¾ cup (6½ fl oz/200 ml) olive oil
6 almonds
4 sea crayfish (Dublin Bay prawns, scampi)
10 oz (315 g) onion, finely chopped
4 large shrimp (prawns)
3 medium-size tomatoes, peeled and finely chopped
⅓ cup (3 fl oz/90 ml) dry white wine
2 tablespoons (2 fl oz/60 ml) Cognac
1⅔ cups (13 fl oz/410 ml) fish broth (stock)
2 cloves garlic, finely chopped
1 tablespoon finely chopped parsley
2 cookies (milk arrowroot type)
16 mussels, steamed

Preheat the oven to 400°F (200°C/Gas 6).

Season the fish and squid with salt and pepper.

Heat the oil in a skillet (frying pan), fry the almonds, then remove and set aside. Fry the crayfish and shrimp, then transfer to a large, shallow heatproof casserole. Fry the squid (be careful, as the oil might spatter) and transfer to the casserole when it starts to brown.

Fry the white fish and transfer to the casserole. Then fry the onion and add the tomatoes when it starts to brown. Cook over high heat, then add the white wine and Cognac and allow to reduce almost completely. Add the fish broth and a little salt to the pan. Boil for 2–3 minutes, then transfer to the casserole.

Crush the garlic with the parsley in a mortar, followed by the almonds.

Add the cookies and crush to form a smooth paste. Add a little broth from the casserole, then pour the mixture over the fish and shellfish. Add the mussels. Check the seasoning.

Cook, covered, on top of the stove over low heat for 10 minutes, then transfer to the oven for 5 minutes. Serve piping hot.

FISH ROMESCO

Romesco de pescado   Serves 4

The coastline of Tarragona has the honor of being the birthplace of *romesco*, a term which refers to both a sauce and a basis for stews. It is not only found along the coast, however, but also throughout the inland areas of this region. The main ingredient is *pebrot de romesco* — a red pepper of the *Capsicum annuum* variety, which is exceptionally sweet, flavorsome and mild. This luxurious dish forms part of the mythical legends of the Tarragona coast.

¾ cup (6½ fl oz/200 ml) olive oil
13 oz (410 g) crabs, washed and drained
2 ripe tomatoes (6½ oz/200 g), peeled and finely chopped
1 medium-size onion (5 oz/155 g), finely chopped
8 cloves garlic, finely chopped
2 cups (16 fl oz/500 ml) water
1 small slice bread (½ oz/15 g)
2 dried peppers (Capsicum annuum variety)
16 almonds
8 hazelnuts
4 small cuttlefish, cleaned and chopped
4 small slices hake
4 small slices monkfish or swordfish
8 large shrimp (prawns)
salt

Heat a little oil in a skillet (frying pan) and fry the crabs. Remove and set aside. Fry the tomatoes, onion and half the garlic in the same oil for 15 minutes over low heat.

Heat the water in a large pot. Mash the crabs a little in a mortar and add to the pot, followed by the tomato mixture. Cover and cook over medium heat for 25 minutes.

Catalan seafood stew (top); fish romesco (bottom)

Strain off the broth and set aside. Heat the rest of the oil in a skillet and fry the following ingredients separately: the bread, dried peppers (taking care not to burn them), almonds and hazelnuts, and finally the rest of the garlic. Transfer each ingredient to a mortar as it is cooked, and mash to form a smooth paste.

Strain the oil into a large heatproof casserole, then lightly fry the cuttlefish followed by the mixture from the mortar. Add a little broth from the crabs, and cook the cuttlefish for a further 15 minutes.

Add the rest of the fish and the shrimp. Check the seasoning. Pour in the rest of the broth and cook over very low heat for 10 minutes.

Serve in the casserole.

LOBSTER STEW

Caldereta de langosta   Serves 4

The lobsters are exquisite on all the Balearic Islands, but Minorca definitely has the best. The Minorcans cook their lobsters separately, then combine them with onion, garlic and olive oil or — as in this case — a tomato mixture which is diluted then reduced with a concentrated fish base. *Caldereta de langosta* is always a success and has the effect of making everyone so gregarious that the after-dinner conversation is likely to go on for hours.

2 medium-size spiny rock lobsters (about 2 lb/ 1 kg each)
sea salt
¾ cup (6½ fl oz/200 ml) olive oil
2 medium-size onions (10 oz/315 g), chopped
2 cloves garlic, finely chopped
2 medium-size ripe tomatoes (8 oz/250 g), peeled and chopped
4 cups (1 qt/1 l) fish broth (stock)
2 tablespoons finely chopped parsley
2 bay leaves
freshly ground pepper

Cook the lobsters for 8–10 minutes in boiling water with sea salt. Remove and allow to cool a little, then chop up and set aside.

Heat the oil in a large heatproof casserole and fry the onion over low heat. When it starts to brown, add the garlic and tomatoes, and allow to reduce over low heat almost to the consistency of a purée.

Add the lobster pieces, fish broth, parsley and bay leaves. Cook over high heat for 10 minutes.

Season with salt and a little pepper (the broth also provides flavor). Lower the heat and cook over medium heat for another 20 minutes. Serve in the casserole.

Fisherfolk, Salvador Maella (1739–1819); PRADO MUSEUM, MADRID
Especially on the Mediterranean coast much of the fishing activity has always been carried out from small boats either in fishing grounds not too distant from the coast or at the shoreline itself, using beach seine-nets, as in this painting.

Lobster stew (left); jumbo shrimp in sauce (right)

JUMBO SHRIMP IN SAUCE

Langostinos en salsa   Serves 4

*L*angostinos (jumbo shrimp/king prawns) are very good cooked in a sauce for special occasions. In this recipe their exquisite flavor is heightened by the addition of ham and vegetables.

¾ cup (6½ fl oz/200 ml) olive oil

1 medium-size onion (5 oz/155 g), finely chopped

3 cloves garlic (1 finely chopped and 2 sliced lengthwise)

1 lb (500 g) tomatoes, peeled and chopped

16 jumbo shrimp (king prawns)

1 bay leaf

salt

5 oz (155 g) cured ham with the fat on, chopped small

Heat half the oil in a skillet (frying pan) and fry the onion and the finely chopped clove of garlic. When it starts to brown, add the tomatoes and cook gently until the mixture thickens. Set aside.

Peel the raw shrimp, leaving the heads on. Cook the shells in a little water with the bay leaf and a little salt. Cook for 3 minutes after the water comes to a boil, then strain and set the broth aside.

Heat the rest of the oil in a heatproof casserole and fry the sliced garlic. As soon as it starts to brown, add the ham and shrimp. Mix carefully so as not to break the heads, then add the tomato sauce and the broth from the shells. When the liquid comes to a boil, cook for exactly 3 minutes and serve.

Stuffed squid

STUFFED SQUID

Calamares rellenos   Serves 4

The people of the Balearic Islands are by nature self-confident. They are proud of their traditions, which include some highly unusual culinary characteristics with numerous ancient and medieval elements. Only a few of their specialties stray to mainland Spain, which gives some indication of how far away the islands are in spirit.

In 1886 Père d'Alcántara Peyna provided valuable accounts of the somewhat intricate but always original and exquisite, Balearic cuisine.

4 medium-size or 8 small squid
1 teaspoon finely chopped parsley
2 tablespoons pine nuts
2 tablespoons (1 fl oz/30 ml) olive oil
1 tablespoon lard
1 small onion (4 oz/125 g), finely chopped
3 cloves garlic, finely chopped
2 tablespoons currants
salt

Sauce:
⅓ cup (3 fl oz/90 ml) olive oil
all-purpose (plain) flour for coating
6½ oz (200 g) onion, finely chopped
3 cloves garlic, finely chopped
1 lb (500 g) ripe tomatoes, finely chopped
salt
1 teaspoon sugar

Clean and gut the squid, taking care not to break the sacs. Chop the tentacles finely.

Crush the parsley with the pine nuts in a mortar.

Heat the oil and lard in a heatproof casserole and fry the onion and garlic for 5 minutes. When it starts to brown, add the finely chopped tentacles, currants, and pine nuts and parsley. Add a little salt and fry gently over low heat for 5 minutes. Stuff the squid with this mixture (use a small amount or they will burst) and fasten with cocktail sticks or toothpicks at the edges.

To make the sauce, heat the oil in a large skillet (frying pan).

Dip the squid into flour, then fry. Remove and set aside.

Fry the onion and garlic in the same oil. When it starts to brown, add the tomatoes, a little salt and the sugar. Fry over low heat for 5 minutes. Add the squid (and any leftover filling) and cook over low heat for 30–45 minutes. Remove the sticks before serving.

SQUID WITH FAVA BEANS

Calamares con habas   Serves 4

The squid caught off the mountainous coast of Santander are known locally as *rabas*. This dish seems to have been created to celebrate the close relationship between land and sea. Both the fishing waters and the agricultural land are extremely fertile, and the cows produce marvelous meat and delicious cheeses, which unfortunately are largely unknown outside the region.

⅓ cup (3 fl oz/90 ml) olive oil
4 cloves garlic, peeled and crushed whole
4 thick slices French bread (4 oz/125 g)
1 large onion (6½ oz/200 g), finely chopped

Squid with fava beans

Mixed fish grill

1 teaspoon paprika
2 lb (1 kg) squid, cleaned and sliced
1 tablespoon finely chopped parsley
1 pinch cumin
2 teaspoons white wine vinegar
1 lb (500 g) fava (broad) beans, shelled
salt

Heat the oil in a heatproof casserole, fry the garlic and remove. Fry the slices of bread in the same oil and remove. Then brown the onion over low heat. Add the paprika and squid and stir. Add a little water, cover and cook over low heat for approximately 1 hour.

Meanwhile, crush the parsley in a mortar with the cumin, then add the garlic and bread and blend thoroughly. Add 1 teaspoon of water and the vinegar and mash with the pestle to form a smooth paste.

When the squid is cooked, add the fava beans, the mixture from the mortar and a little water. Add a little salt, cook for another 30 minutes and serve.

MIXED FISH GRILL

Parrillada de pescado   Serves 4

The thought of the different tastes, textures and colors of expertly barbecued, freshly caught fish, mollusks and crustaceans will always have people licking their lips in anticipation. The best results are achieved using natural firewood with sprigs of fennel or other aromatic herbs to add to the flavor of the fish. Sometimes the ingredients are marinated for a few hours beforehand. When the fish is ready — never too dry — it is sprinkled with a dressing of garlic, parsley, salt, oil and lemon.

4 medium-size squid, cleaned and sliced
4 small cuttlefish, chopped
4 slices (13 oz/410 g) monkfish or swordfish
4 small sole
4 fleshy shrimp (prawns)
4 jumbo shrimp (king prawns)
4 sea crayfish (Dublin Bay prawns, scampi)
16 mussels
salt
freshly ground pepper
¾ cup (6½ fl oz/200 ml) olive oil
1 teaspoon finely chopped parsley
2 cloves garlic, finely chopped
*romesco sauce (see page 208) or mayonnaise
   as an accompaniment*

Wash the shellfish and fish, drain and season with salt and a little pepper. Sprinkle with plenty of oil.

Heat the griddle or broiler (grill) a little and cook the cuttlefish and squid for 15 minutes, the monkfish, shrimp and crayfish for 10 minutes (5 minutes each side) and the sole for 5–8 minutes.

Open the mussels on the griddle or by steaming.

Mix the parsley and garlic with a little oil. As the fish cook, remove from the griddle or broiler and add this mixture before arranging on a platter.

Serve with romesco sauce or mayonnaise.

Fish in a fruit-bowl beside the pool, Perez Villalta (twentieth century); PRIVATE COLLECTION, MADRID

CATALAN CRAYFISH

Cigalas a la catalana   Serves 4

It is always difficult to decide whether the bright blue Mediterranean Sea is a reflection of the sky or vice versa. There is, however, no doubt about the fact that it always arouses passionate emotions. The crayfish caught in these waters are an experience never to be forgotten. This version, *a la catalana*, with its characteristic crushed sauce mixture called a *picada*, is a good example of the creative inspiration of the traditional culinary culture.

⅓ cup (3 fl oz/90 ml) olive oil
2 lb (1 kg) sea crayfish (Dublin Bay prawns, scampi)
6½ oz (200 g) onion, finely chopped
8 oz (250 g) ripe tomatoes, finely chopped

Sauce:

1 tablespoon finely chopped parsley
2 cloves garlic, peeled
24 almonds, toasted
1 oz (30 g) bread, crusts removed and soaked in water and drained
1 teaspoon unsweetened (plain) chocolate, grated
1 pinch ground cinnamon
salt

Heat the oil in a heatproof casserole and fry the crayfish over low heat. Remove and set aside. Fry the onion gently in the same oil until it starts to brown. Add the tomatoes and continue cooking until the juice has evaporated and a thick mixture begins to form.

To make the sauce, crush the parsley, garlic, almonds and bread in a mortar. Add the chocolate and cinnamon and blend thoroughly to a smooth paste. Add a little water, then mix with the tomato mixture. Add a bit more water and a little salt to the casserole, put the crayfish back in and cook for 15 minutes, or until the sauce thickens. Serve hot.

MONKFISH IN MATELOT SAUCE

Rape a la marinera   Serves 4

This tasty sailors' dish is more complicated than the usual shipboard recipes and has two important secrets: the cooking time, and the fact that the sauce is added in two parts. Monkfish takes a bit longer to cook than other varieties, and the sauce makes it more succulent. A bit of the sauce is kept back to be added at the end of the cooking procedure, as this heightens the flavor of both ingredients and seasonings.

2 lb (1 kg) monkfish, thinly sliced
⅓ cup (3 fl oz/90 ml) olive oil
6½ oz (200 g) onion, finely chopped
10 oz (315 g) ripe tomatoes, peeled and finely chopped
1 tablespoon finely chopped parsley
1 teaspoon paprika
3 cloves garlic, peeled
⅓ cup (2 oz/60 g) almonds, toasted
2 tablespoons (1 oz/30 g) pine nuts
1 thick slice French bread (1 oz/30 g), fried
½ cup (4 fl oz/125 ml) water
salt

Catalan crayfish (top); monkfish in matelot sauce (bottom)

Wash the monkfish and allow to drain.

Heat the oil in a heatproof casserole or skillet (frying pan) and sauté the onion. When it starts to soften, add the tomatoes and fry gently to form a thick mixture. Add the parsley and paprika, stir, then remove from the heat.

Crush the garlic cloves in a mortar with the almonds, pine nuts and fried bread. Add the tomato mixture and mash to blend thoroughly, then add the water.

Pour half this mixture into a shallow heatproof casserole and lay the monkfish slices on top. Season with salt, cover, then cook over low heat for 15 minutes. Turn the fish over, add the rest of the sauce mixture and a little water if necessary. Check the seasoning and cook, uncovered, for another 15 minutes. Serve.

161

Gilthead baked in salt (top); baked porgy (bottom)

GILTHEAD BAKED IN SALT

Dorada a la sal   Serves 4–6

For centuries saltworks proliferated around the Mediterranean coastline, taking advantage of the amount of salt and the high evaporation rate caused by the warm climate. The Mediterranean's long history as a source of salt is shown in numerous accounts of the region.

The waters off Cartagena in Murcia provide a particularly rich supply of gilthead. The traditional cooking method is to lay the fish — without gutting — in an earthenware casserole, then pack salt all around it. It should be as fresh as possible, straight from the sea. The fish is then baked and turns out wonderfully white, sweet and juicy. It is eaten hot with plenty of oil and garlic.

1 gilthead (sea bream or sea bass) (about 3 lb/1.5 kg)
3 lb (1.5 kg) kosher (coarse) salt
12 small potatoes (1 lb 4 oz/600 g), steamed
mayonnaise or all-i-oli *(see page 207) as accompaniment*

Preheat the oven to 400°F (200°C/Gas 6).

Scale the fish, but do not gut it. Wash with sea water, if possible, or salted water. Drain and dry.

Put a layer of salt in a baking dish, place the fish on top, then cover completely with the rest of the salt.

Bake for 40 minutes, or until the salt is a dark golden color.

Remove from the oven, break the salt crust and remove completely. Serve accompanied by the potatoes and mayonnaise or *all-i-oli*.

BAKED PORGY

Besugo al horno   Serves 4

Although Madrid lies inland, hundreds of miles from the coast, one of its most symbolic foods is porgy (sea bream). Professor Joaquín de Entreambasagauas, the Spanish literary critic and author of *Gastronomía Madrileña* (1971), has claimed that this fish really comes into its own in Madrid, where it is baked in the oven, resulting in a crisp, toasted skin and firm, succulent flesh.

Baked porgy is a traditional dish for festive occasions. It became a typical choice for Christmas Eve back in the days when it was still obligatory to abstain from meat at Christmastime.

In *Nuevo Arte de Cocina* (1745), Juan de Altamiras gives a thorough description of how to roast porgy, which shows how little the recipe has changed over the years. He also offers the rather unusual advice that the fish should be painted with olive oil while it is cooked, just as one would paint a picture.

> This is the best fish in the countries of Aragón: after cleaning and scaling it well, wash and dry it with a clean cloth; lay it in an ample pot on a few bay leaves; some more on top; and when the pieces are half-baked, have ready a casserole, minced garlic, pepper, parsley, salt, sour juice of lemon or lime, and scatter it with a handful of feathers or parsley here and there.
>
> Juan de Altamiras, *Nuevo Arte de Cocina*, 1745

1 porgy (sea bream), weighing 3 lb (1.5 kg)
⅓ cup (3 fl oz/90 ml) olive oil
salt
1 large onion (6½ oz/200 g), thinly sliced
1 lb (500 g) ripe tomatoes, thinly sliced
5 cloves garlic, crushed in a mortar
2 bay leaves, torn into small pieces
freshly ground pepper
¾ cup (6½ fl oz/200 ml) dry white wine
1 lemon, thinly sliced

Preheat the oven to 325°F (170°C/Gas 3).

Clean and scale the porgy, then brush with oil and sprinkle on a little salt.

Grease a baking dish with half the oil and add the onion. Put the tomatoes on top, then the crushed garlic, followed by the torn bay leaves. Add salt and pepper.

Place the fish on top and sprinkle with the rest of the oil and the white wine. Cover with the lemon slices.

Bake for 35–45 minutes, basting frequently. Serve in the baking dish.

LARDED TUNA

Atún mechado   Serves 4

This is one of the classic Andalusian fish dishes. The possible dryness of the tuna is offset by threading it with strips of pork fat and sometimes ham as well. It is then seasoned and cooked over an open fire or in the oven and served either hot or cold. People always exclaim that it tastes like beef. It is an ideal dish to take to the countryside or for the long, lazy family lunches on the beach which are so popular in Andalusia.

1 lb (500 g) tuna
6 cloves garlic, peeled
6 black peppercorns
3½ oz (100 g) fresh pork fat, diced
8 oz (250 g) lard
2¼ cups (18 fl oz/500 ml) dry white wine
salt

Wash the tuna, remove the skin and soak in cold water for 30 minutes.

Crush the garlic and peppercorns in a mortar.

Make small holes in the tuna, then fill with the pieces of fat and the garlic and pepper mixture.

Melt the lard in a heatproof casserole or pan, then gently fry the tuna. Add the white wine and a little salt. Cover and cook for 20–30 minutes.

Cut into slices and serve warm or cold with the cooking liquid.

Larded tuna

Still-life: porgy (sea-bream) and oranges, Luis Meléndez (1716–80); PRADO MUSEUM, MADRID
This combination of ingredients is found frequently in recipes along the southern coast, from Valencia to Andalucia.

SALT COD WITH ONION

Bacalao con cebolla   Serves 4

Salt cod has formed the basis of everyday meals in inland areas for a great many generations, as it is inexpensive and can be prepared in lots of different ways. Cooks know which part of the cod is most suitable for any particular dish. The thicker cuts are for frying, then using in stews, while the less fleshy bits with more skin — rich in gelatin and fat — are used to provide texture in simpler dishes, such as this recipe with onion. In *Nuevo Arte de Cocina* (1745), by Juan de Altamiras, there is a recipe called "codfish in another way," using *abadejo*, the poor relation of the family of gadids, which was traditionally used as an alternative to *bacalao* during Lent. Altamiras adds a little tomato juice when serving the dish, which is the first written evidence of using tomatoes as an ingredient.

> Take the portions and put them on to boil, and at the same time put plenty of onion on to fry; crush cloves of garlic in the mortar, with pepper, and put some water to some saffron, then put it in the skillet [frying pan] with the onion, seasoned with salt; put it in a casserole on the stove, and when you are going to serve it, put some of the onion on the plates on top of the Codfish, with a little tomato juice, or verjuice, whatever the season brings, and a handful of parsley.
>
> Juan de Altamiras, *Nuevo Arte de Cocina*, 1745

2 lb (1 kg) fleshy dried salt cod (soaked for 48 hours in 3 changes of water), in pieces
½ cup (2 oz/60 g) all-purpose (plain) flour

1 cup (8 fl oz/250 ml) olive oil
2 lb (1 kg) onions, cut into thin segments
salt
2 teaspoons paprika
2 tablespoons finely chopped parsley

Drain the cod and dry thoroughly with paper towels or a cloth.

Coat with flour and fry lightly for a few minutes on each side, then place in a heatproof casserole.

Fry the onions over medium heat in the same oil. Do not allow to brown too much. Add a little salt, then the paprika, stir with a wooden spoon and add to the cod.

Add a little water to the pan, then pour into the casserole. Cook over low heat for 25 minutes. Turn the pieces of fish over halfway through the cooking time.

Check the seasoning, sprinkle with parsley and serve hot in the casserole.

MAJORCAN GROUPER

Mero a la mallorquina   Serves 4

Grouper is one of the largest edible fish, sometimes weighing more than 100 lb (50 kg). It is found in warm, rocky parts of the Atlantic as well as in the Mediterranean and has very tasty white flesh. Although it does not feature widely in the classic recipe books, it has been known since ancient times. This fish can be prepared in many different ways — broiled (grilled), barbecued, baked or used in stews — and is guaranteed to make everyone's mouth water when it is put on the table.

1 lb (500 g) potatoes, thinly sliced
salt
¾ cup (6½ fl oz/200 ml) olive oil
2 lb (1 kg) grouper (or sea bass), in slices
1 tablespoon lemon juice
3 cloves garlic, peeled and finely chopped
4 green onions (spring onions), finely chopped
1 lb (500 g) green bell peppers (capsicums), chopped
6½ oz (200 g) tomatoes, peeled and finely chopped
8 oz (250 g) spinach (English spinach), shredded
⅓ cup (2 oz/60 g) raisins
⅓ cup (2 oz/60 g) pine nuts
1 bay leaf
1 teaspoon paprika
⅓ cup (3 fl oz/90 ml) dry white wine
white pepper
2 teaspoons finely chopped parsley

Preheat the oven to 300°F (150°C/Gas 2).

Put the potatoes in a shallow, heatproof casserole, season with salt and sprinkle with a little oil. Lay the fish slices on top and season with salt and lemon juice.

Heat the rest of the oil in a skillet (frying pan) and sauté the garlic, green onions, green bell peppers and then the tomatoes. Fry gently for a few minutes, then add the spinach, raisins, pine nuts and bay leaf. Cook for a few more minutes.

Add the paprika, then the wine and allow to reduce.

Season with salt and pepper, then pour over the fish. Sprinkle with parsley.

Bake for 20 minutes, basting occasionally. Serve.

Salt cod with onion (left); Majorcan grouper (right)

165

BONITO CASSEROLE

Marmitako   Serves 4

The Basques have a great seafaring tradition. They also like eating well and are renowned as good cooks. *Marmitako* is the most popular dish among fishermen during the bonito season from October to June. It can be cooked perfectly even in a small oven on board, amid the swaying of the boat and the splashing of waves against the gunwale. On land the best accompaniment to *marmitako* is undoubtedly a good *txacoli* cider from Guetaria, served well chilled.

2 lb (1 kg) bonito tuna
¾ cup (6½ fl oz/200 ml) olive oil
2 small onions (6½ oz/200 g), finely chopped
2 green bell peppers (capsicums), seeded and
   chopped
1 lb (500 g) potatoes, cut into chunks
salt
4 dried red bell peppers (capsicums), soaked
   for 12 hours

Remove the skin and bones of the bonito, then cut into chunks.

Heat the oil in a heatproof casserole and fry the onions and green bell peppers over low heat until they start to soften. Add the potatoes, fry gently, then add enough water to cover. Cook for 30 minutes.

Sauté the bonito in a small amount of oil in a skillet (frying pan). Transfer to the casserole, add a little salt and cook for 10 minutes. Purée the dried red bell peppers and add to the casserole. Check the seasoning, then remove from the heat and allow to rest for a few minutes. Serve hot.

MARINATED SARDINES

Escabeche de sardinas   Serves 4–6

Although inexpensive, sardines are very highly esteemed in Spain. In olden times they were known as sea beef, casting doubt over whether they could be included on abstinence menus. At the beginning of the seventeenth century the Duke of Medina Sidonia gave King Philip IV 1,400 barrels of pickled fish, among other foods, at the Coto De Ocaña. Juan de Altamiras's eighteenth-century recipe uses the age-old *escabeche* pickling technique.

Bonito casserole

Marinated sardines

This is an Arabic term for the long-term preservation of foods, meats and fish, which involves first frying the food, then marinating it in oil, vinegar, spices and herbs. The technique was described in the first century by Apicius in *De Re Coquinaria*. This is, therefore, one of the most authentic ancient recipes.

> Fry the fish without flour, and make the marinade in the following way: take bay leaves, crushed cloves of garlic, strong vinegar, thyme, fennel, oregano, some small pieces of orange; boil all these things together, and add to it the cold fish, and if there is not enough salt, add it in the correct proportion.
>
> Juan de Altamiras, *Nuevo Arte de Cocina*, 1745

2 lb (1 kg) sardines
6 cloves garlic, peeled and finely chopped
2 bay leaves
salt
freshly ground pepper
1 cup (8 fl oz/250 ml) olive oil
1 cup (8 fl oz/250 ml) vinegar

Clean and gut the sardines, removing the heads and scales.

Place in layers in a heatproof casserole, with the garlic and bay leaves in between. Season with salt and pepper, then pour in the oil, making sure it is well absorbed. Add enough vinegar to cover the sardines, then cover and cook over low heat for 30 minutes. Allow to cool before serving.

The flavor improves if the dish is prepared 24–48 hours in advance.

167

HAKE IN GREEN SAUCE

Merluza en salsa verde   Serves 4

In the fifteenth century the Basques ventured all the way to Newfoundland to fish for whales, so not surprisingly they have never had any problem catching excellent hake.

In the north, fish are cooked in a simple, balanced and healthy way. Hake in Green Sauce is a classic and very elegant dish and should never be degraded by the use of frozen substitutes. When buying hake at the market, look for fish with firm flesh that have been caught using hooks, not nets.

4 hake steaks (or cod fillets), weighing about
6½ oz (200 g) each and ¾ in (3 cm) thick
all-purpose (plain) flour for coating
⅔ cup (5 fl oz/155 ml) olive oil
4 cloves garlic, finely chopped
salt

2 tablespoons finely chopped parsley
⅓ cup (3 fl oz/90 ml) fish broth (stock)

Coat the pieces of fish with flour.

Heat the oil with the garlic in a heatproof casserole large enough to hold the hake comfortably. Take care not to let the garlic burn. When it starts to turn golden and float in the oil, remove the casserole from the heat and immediately arrange the pieces of fish in it. Sprinkle with salt and the chopped parsley. Add the broth and cook again over low heat.

When a whitish liquid starts to come out of the hake, start shaking the casserole continuously, without removing from the heat, for the sauce to thicken.

Keep doing this until the fish turns white, at which point it is ready to serve.

Merienda *(afternoon snack) in San Isidro*, Lucas Villamil (1824–70); MUSEO ROMANTICO, MADRID
The festival of San Isidro, the patron saint of Madrid, was held on 15 May each year on San Isidro meadow. It was a day for spending outdoors, strolling through the tented booths erected for the festival, dancing, cooking *buñuelos de San Isidro* (cream-filled fritters) and eating one's fill.

Hake in green sauce

The Seville Fair, (1882) Andrés Cortés y Aguilar; FINE ARTS MUSEUM, BILBAO

MEAT, POULTRY AND GAME

Meat is the most highly valued food in most societies. In Spain, too, this has traditionally been the case — partly because meat has always been scarce owing to the dry climate, and partly because in the past meat intake was believed to be essential for health and strength. A Spanish saying sums up this attitude neatly: "As we eat, so we grow." More recently, however, this traditional respect for the value of meat has undergone change in Spain, as a result of new nutritional tendencies together with increasing concern about the abuses practiced in the artificial fattening of livestock.

The twentieth century offers a wide and varied range of outlets for those who wish to pursue a hedonistic lifestyle. But for many centuries in the past the main — perhaps only — occasion for people to really indulge themselves was the banquet, where their enjoyment found its expression in the consumption of meat and wine.

The most ostentatious part of the medieval banquet was the roast. In palaces whole cows were roasted and served to the accompaniment of much pomp and ceremony, in part playing on the enormity of the beast and the prospect of devouring it. But, to be eaten, the roast had first of all to be carved — and this, too, was treated with great ceremony, sometimes being carried out by the master himself. Later, however, it became customary to have the task performed by a special servant, who would be highly skilled in the wielding of the various knives and other implements involved. This custom is described in a large fifteenth-century book, devoted to this subject, *Arte Cisoria* by Don Enrique de Villena.

The literature of the Spanish Golden Age, in the sixteenth and seventeenth centuries, clearly shows the importance of meat in Spanish eating. The writers, chroniclers and narrators who made Spanish literature famous worldwide undertook the complex task of documenting the customs, menus and banquets of their time, featuring quantities and varieties of meats that, nowadays, we would find amazing. Martínez Montiño, for instance, in his *Arte de Cocina, Pastelería, Vizcochería y Conservería* (1611), gives

Poultry Stall, (1626) Alejandro de Loarte; PRIVATE COLLECTION, AVILA
Birds of all kinds, domesticated and hunted, have consistently featured in Spanish cooking. Chicken, perhaps the most common, was cooked in any number of combinations. But game birds were also readily available — and of course the eggs of all these birds were consumed. This poultry stall also sells turkey, one of the earliest imports from the New World, which quickly displaced the peacock as the favored Christmas fare.

The Last Supper, Jaime Serra
(fourteenth–fifteenth century);
ART MUSEUM OF CATALONIA, BARCELONA
Rabbits, being so plentiful and easily
snared or shot, made a good, inexpensive
meal when roasted over a fire. Walter
Starkie, tramping through Basque country
in the 1920s, joined a rural family for
such a meal, and commented: "I
preferred that simple meal of roast rabbit
and onions to the most gorgeous meal
the Ritz Hotel could offer me." However,
it is unlikely to have been on the menu
for the Last Supper, and significantly
Judas Iscariot is the only one who seems
tempted by it.

a description of an aristocratic Christmas banquet. Let us take a look here just at
the meat courses.

The banquet began with roast turkeys with gravy, Savoyard parcels of veal, roast
pigeon, partridge with lemon sauce, sausages with more partridges, roast baby lambs
and chickens. The second course followed with roast capons, duck with quince sauce,
chicken with stuffed curly endive (chicory) lettuces, roast beef with arugula (rocket)
sauce, veal sweetbreads and livers, hare pies and various kinds of bird cooked German-
style. The third course included chickens stuffed with fried bread, roast veal udders,
a stew made with minced poultry, stewed pigeon, roast and larded goat kid, turkey
pies, rabbits with capers, pig's trotter turnovers, wood pigeons with black sauce and
poultry blancmange. And those were only the meat dishes. As well, there were other
foods on the menu, and desserts.

Climatic conditions determine where some types of livestock can be raised in
Spain. Cattle, which require humid areas, are restricted to Galicia and a narrow strip
across the north of Spain, and various mountain valleys elsewhere around the country.
Sheep graze around the central dry area, and all other animals used for meat (pigs,
fowl and game) are found throughout Spain.

Since cattle need green grazing land, which is in short supply and are, therefore,
the scarcest form of livestock in Spain, beef is correspondingly expensive. An interesting
consequence is that veal is greatly valued and very popular. Another influential factor
is that cattle are difficult to raise to adulthood and are often slaughtered quite young.
Veal is also very easy to cook. For all these reasons, a steak of young beef — a
prestigious meal that is quick and simple to prepare — has for quite a few years
now been a practical dietary solution: for meat lovers, it provides essential protein;
for those obsessed with their figures, a broiled (grilled) steak is the perfect option.

The scarcity of beef has brought prestige even to such small areas of production as the Avila region. For a great many years, saddle of Avila young beef was the main meat course served at official meals at the Royal Palace.

In complete contrast to this kind of meat there is bull, which Spaniards have, of necessity, become experts at cooking. After the bullfights, it would have been wasteful not to make use of the meat in a country where this commodity is so scarce. Formerly, eating this sort of meat was looked down upon, to such an extent that some Spanish people were often suspicious of the stewpots of certain establishments following a bullfight. On the other hand, great gourmets nowadays take pride in being able to obtain bull meat from the few butchers who deal with it. It is considered very special, as privileged as the lives the animals led before they met their tragic end.

The dry terrain providing concentrated, aromatic grazing land is ideal for sheep. Spain has a curious and very old droving system called *mesta*, which consists of a complex set of regulations to enable flocks to move freely through the country. Spain's merino sheep were the ancestors of the best wool flocks in the West, which spread via England all the way to Australia.

These dry pasture lands give lamb a particular taste that comes from grazing on specific aromatic herbs. Eating lamb is a great tradition in Spain and the meat

Still-life of cardoon, (1625) Alejandro de Loarte;
PRIVATE COLLECTION
The cardoon — whose stems and stalks were eaten, often as a salad — was then a favorite subject for still-lifes. But nowadays these pork products are more likely to attract our attention. The sheer inventiveness in finding culinary uses for each part of the pig has always assured its special place in Spanish cooking — *jamón* (cured ham) being the pinnacle of this achievement. As the Duc de St Simon remarked: "It is not possible to eat anything else so exquisite."

Book of Hours (Anonymous, fifteenth century); NATIONAL LIBRARY, MADRID
One of the scenes depicted here shows us the medieval method of slaughtering a boar. The other vignettes on this page of the devotional book give us some idea of the prized large game hunted in the middle ages. The Pyrenees was home to various types of mountain goat, also found in the Sierras, and to bears, whose range stretched along the mountainous northern region.

is classified according to the lamb's age and the time of year it was born. Sucking lamb is approximately 3 weeks old and is lean and very tender. Paschal lamb is between 5 and 7 months old, and born around Christmas time; it is also called *pastenco*, as it feeds on the pasture land in springtime.

Hunting has always been an important source of meat, both from the necessity of obtaining meat and because Spaniards are very keen on hunting as a sport. In former times there was a plentiful supply of large game, and hunting was a very popular activity among Spain's monarchs. King Charles III (1716–88) was well known for whiling away his afternoons hunting all the year round — a routine varied only for certain festivals.

Small game, however, is what has brought international fame to the devotees of this sport. The Romans called Spain "the country of rabbits," but myxomatosis has decimated the rabbit population. Other species of small game — just as famous — remain, such as the Spanish red partridge, which has the best meat of all the partridge family. Quails are smaller but are more widely available and have given rise to some interesting older recipes that are very representative of the Spanish way of cooking. There are, for example, the interesting recipes of Catalan medieval cooking included in the *Libre de Sent Soví* (1324), those by Ruperto de Nola in *El Libre del Coch* (1520), and by Martínez Montiño in *Arte de Cocina, Pastelería, Vizcochería y Conservería* (1611), which features all sorts of birds with instructions for roasting, stewing, frying and preparing them in sauces, and for filling *empanada* pies.

Poultry used to be regarded as prestigious, and in the eighteenth-century recipe book by Juan Altamiras, *Nuevo Arte de Cocina* (1745), it is given an important position. Chickens also used to be a fundamental element in soups and invalid meals. Not so long ago chicken was a dish for important occasions, such as dinner on Christmas Eve. It was traditonal to buy a chicken alive and kill it at home. But nowadays these birds come last on the list of the kinds of meat eaten in Spain, as a result of the over-industrialization of poultry production. It is interesting to observe that this decline in poultry's prestige has occurred over no more than a single generation.

Pork has always been the main standby for the meat requirements of Spanish people. Pigs are easy to keep and feed, and so can always be found around rural dwellings. Newly born sucking pigs have always been highly esteemed. Juan Altamiras gives a touching recipe for *lechoncito de leche con arroz* (sucking pig with rice), and Martinez Montiño quotes a sucking pig sauce, made with the liver of the roast pig mashed with almonds, bread and garlic — all toasted — with spices, sugar and a little lemon.

Spaniards themselves are surprised by their capacity to make the most of every part of the pig. So numerous are the specialties that have been created from it that Spanish people can be said to have achieved, with their use of the pig, the heights of food craftsmanship. And it all starts from the slaughter of the animal, which has been turned into a great festival in many villages. Beforehand, the ordinary animals, kept in sties, are fed on the leftovers from family meals. The thoroughbred Iberian pig, on the other hand, which is found only in particular areas, enjoys life in the open air and eats only acorns — never any kind of artificial feed — which ensures that its meat is aromatic and slightly sweet, even after undergoing a salt-curing process.

In the villages the bloody act of slaughter has been turned into a form of enter-

Still-life, Luis Meléndez (1716–80);
With the skillet (frying pan) in view, it seems that this meat might be destined for a *huevos fritos con jamon* (fried eggs with cured ham).

tainment which originated from the necessity of killing the animal for food, but also encompasses the poetic sense of imagination with which the participants visualize the countless products to be created out of its carcass. Everything starts with the clarion call of the pig screaming as its throat is cut; it draws to a close when everyone involved in this group effort goes home with coveted trophies to commemorate their participation.

Pork is used to make a great variety of sausages, which are processed to last a long time using natural methods such as drying, salting, the addition of spices, and smoke- or cold-curing. Each region boasts its own shapes, textures and aromas. It is the avoidance of the use of artificial preservatives that explains why each product has it own particular flavor, typical of the specific technique employed in the area

Hunting scene, Andrés Cortés y Aguilar (nineteenth century); PRIVATE COLLECTION Hunting for big game was generally the preserve of the wealthy and the nobility, who often kept well-stocked parks for that purpose. But small game was available to all who could shoot it down, or trap it.

where it has been made. The best Spanish sausages are not exported; only mass-produced varieties, which have lost the more individual characteristics, are sent overseas.

A sweet paprika will produce a very different sausage from a spicy paprika. Pepper, which is used in a very limited way, provides a more international flavor, while the biggest surprises are evoked by the Arab custom of adding onion, cinnamon, the zest (rind) of citrus fruit, aniseed, pine nuts and even sugar.

Chorizo is by far the best-known sausage of this type. It is neither very fresh nor very cured, neither very spicy nor very sweet and contains a particular kind of paprika (*pimenton*) that gives it the characteristic "*chorizo* red" color. It is useful for providing color, fat and flavor in stews and can be eaten raw with bread or fried.

The most highly valued Spanish food, which is regarded with the same veneration that caviar commands in some countries, is ham. Simply saying "ham" is, however, somewhat misleading, and it is necessary to be more precise when ordering ham, because of the various kinds available. The name *jamón serrano* guarantees that the ham has not been cooked; *jamón ibérico* is from the thoroughbred Iberian pig, which has been fattened on acorns; *pata negra*, which means "black leg," refers to a characteristic of the best breed. Unfortunately, the most reliable guarantee that you are getting the genuine article is the exorbitant price.

Top-quality ham is carved in a very unusual way and is usually eaten just as it is, on its own. This is perhaps the only remaining example of the art of carving in Spain. Faced with a whole ham, people are often unsure quite how to deal with this expensive food, since they never know whether to eat a lot or a little. Whether bread should be eaten with it is also a moot point. The only point on which everyone — or, at least, all drinkers — agrees is the Spanish saying that "a good fatty ham needs a good swig of wine."

In general, meat in Spain is cooked in its own juices. Making a sauce separately and adding it later is not normal practice. Gelatinous varieties of cooked meat are used to enrich hotpots.

Of all cooking methods for meat, roasting is the one with the greatest tradition. Spanish people apply this procedure with special veneration to lamb and sucking pig. The central region of Spain has special ovens for this purpose. This in turn gave rise to unpretentious restaurants known as *mesones* (inns) that specialize in local roasts and were frequently the locations for chivalrous and picaresque adventures in Spanish literature.

Trick board, (1755) Pedro de Acosta;
ROYAL ACADEMY OF SAN FERNANDO, MADRID
This painting, which draws from the still-life genre with its depiction of various foods and food-related items hanging up, goes further in introducing items not normally found in such paintings. It is reminiscent of a theater backdrop, which may explain the curious assemblage and its title.

LAMB STEW

Caldereta de cordero   Serves 4–6

L amb played a decisive role in the Spanish diet for the Jews, Muslims and Christians who for centuries existed alongside one another on Hispanic territory. This stew was originally prepared outdoors by shepherds in the countryside and nowadays is eaten throughout Spain with regional variations.

⅔ cup (5 fl oz/155 ml) olive oil
4 cloves garlic, peeled
3 lb (1.5 kg) lamb (or kid), chopped
6½ oz (200 g) lamb's (or kid's) liver, in one
  piece
2 dried red bell peppers (capsicums)
2 bay leaves
water
1 tablespoon paprika
8 black peppercorns
salt

Heat the oil in a heatproof casserole and fry the garlic cloves. Remove and set aside. Fry the lamb pieces and the liver in the same oil (be careful, as the oil might spatter).

When the liver browns, remove and set aside. Add the dried bell peppers, bay leaf and paprika to the casserole and stir. Add enough water to cover the meat and cook over low heat for 45 minutes.

In a mortar or a blender, crush the peppercorns, fried garlic and liver, adding a little of the cooking broth if necessary. Add to the casserole, check the seasoning and cook until the meat is very tender. Serve piping hot.

Lamb stew

Lamb chops with garlic sauce

LAMB CHOPS WITH GARLIC SAUCE

Chuletas de cordero al ajo cabañil Serves 4

Garlic is an important ingredient in the colorful cuisine of the Murcia area of Spain. Apart from the potatoes, which were added at a much later date, this is a typically medieval recipe featuring spices, oil and vinegar. The sauce is mixed in the mortar — ideally using a variety of garlic with particularly hard cloves — and requires thorough pounding by hand to create the special flavor which characterizes this dish in Murcia.

1¼ cups (10 fl oz/315 ml) olive oil
2 lb (1 kg) potatoes, thinly sliced
1 head (bulb) garlic, peeled
¼ cup (2 fl oz/60 ml) white wine vinegar
¼ cup (2 fl oz/60 ml) water
2 lb (1 kg) lamb chops

1 teaspoon sugar
salt
freshly ground pepper

Heat half the oil in a skillet (frying pan) and sauté the potatoes over low heat.

Crush the garlic in a mortar, then add the vinegar and water and mix thoroughly.

Heat the rest of the oil in another skillet. When it is very hot, add the chops and fry over high heat until golden brown.

Pour half the mixture from the mortar over the potatoes and the other half over the chops. Add ½ teaspoon of sugar to each skillet, then season with salt and pepper and cook for another 10 minutes over low heat.

Tip the potatoes out onto a serving dish, arrange the chops on top, then pour on the sauce. Serve immediately.

Spring, (detail) Francisco Barrera (1638);
PRIVATE COLLECTION, SEVILLE
Everything, as the Bible says, has its time and season; meat, too, takes its place with the garden produce of spring. Lamb in this decorous display seems to take pride of place, reflecting the fact that it was more prized than beef at that time. Don Quixote's proof of his poverty was that he ate beef more often than mutton.

LAMB AND RED BELL PEPPER STEW

Cordero al chilindrón   Serves 4

There is also a card game called *chilindrón*. No one knows which came first or whether there is any relation between the game and the recipe. Lamb, chicken, rabbit and pigeon can all be prepared *al chilindrón*. This stew is a typical dish on Sundays or special occasions in Aragón, usually accompanied by generous amounts of the delicious local wines.

*2 lb (1 kg) lamb shoulder, cut into even-size
    chunks*
*5 cloves garlic (4 finely chopped and 1
    peeled)*
⅓ cup (3 fl oz/90 ml) olive oil
3½ oz (100 g) cured ham, chopped
8 oz (250 g) carrots, sliced
*2 tomatoes (8 oz/250 g), peeled and finely
    chopped*
1 red bell pepper (capsicum), chopped
1 sprig parsley
⅓ cup (3 fl oz/90 ml) dry white wine
salt
8 oz (250 g) fresh peas, shelled

Season the lamb chunks with the chopped garlic and leave for 30 minutes.

Heat the oil in a large skillet (frying pan) and sauté the ham for a few seconds, then remove and transfer to a heatproof casserole. Fry the lamb chunks in the same oil until golden, then transfer to the casserole on top of the ham. Sauté the carrots, tomatoes and bell pepper in the same oil.

Meanwhile, crush the other clove of garlic in a mortar with the parsley and dilute with the wine. Add to the skillet. Pour this mixture into the casserole with the lamb, season with salt, cover and cook over high heat, shaking frequently to prevent sticking. Stir occasionally, taking care that the drops on the inside of the lid fall back onto the meat. Halfway through the cooking (about 20 minutes) add the peas. Serve in the casserole.

ROAST LAMB

Cordero asado   Serves 4

Each region of Spain considers its lamb to be the best. In olden times shepherds used to walk to Extremadura every year with their flocks, leaving behind them both their villages and their sweethearts.

A bread oven is best for roasting lamb, and casseroles were traditionally taken to the communal oven in the village. In some places it is still possible to come across the local women coming and going carrying their appetizing burdens. Household ovens never produce such good results as does a really hot ceramic oven.

Lamb can be roasted in either pork lard or olive oil, and red wine is usually used to cut down the fattiness.

½ lamb (6 lb/3 kg), in 1 piece
2 cloves garlic, peeled
3½ oz (100 g) lard
salt
¾ cup (6½ fl oz/200 ml) water
1 bay leaf

Preheat the oven to 275°F (140°C/Gas 1).

Rub the lamb with the garlic, grease with the lard and season with salt.

Roast for 45 minutes, basting occasionally.

Turn the meat over, then pour on the water and add the bay leaf. Roast for another 45 minutes. Toward the end of the cooking time, turn the temperature up and cook until the meat is golden and crispy. Serve.

Roast lamb (top); lamb and red bell pepper stew (bottom)

Moorish casserole (left); meatball stew (right)

MOORISH CASSEROLE

Ajillo moruno   Serves 4–6

This casserole is an example of the many dishes devised by people of limited means who had to make use of the cheapest part of the animal if they wanted to eat meat at all. These inspired preparations led to the creation of some extremely tasty dishes, including quite a variety of pâtés and hashes.

⅓ cup (3 fl oz/90 ml) olive oil
12 almonds
1 thick slice French bread (1 oz/30 g)
1½ lb (750 g) beef or liver, chopped
3 cloves garlic, peeled
4 black peppercorns
1 piece whole cinnamon
1 clove

1 pinch cumin seeds
1 teaspoon paprika
2¼ cups (16 fl oz/500 ml) water
salt

Heat the oil in a heatproof casserole and fry the almonds and the bread. Remove and set aside.

Fry the chunks of meat in the same oil.

Meanwhile, crush the garlic, peppercorns, cinnamon, clove and cumin seeds in a mortar. Add the almonds and bread. Dilute with a small amount of water.

When the meat has turned golden, add the paprika and stir, then add the mixture from the mortar, the water and a little salt.

Cover and cook over low heat for about 1 hour, or until the meat is tender. Serve.

184

MEATBALL STEW

Albóndigas de carne   Serves 4

Meatballs, called *albóndigas* or *albóndiguillas*, are little balls of ground (minced) meat — although "fishballs" are also made — bound with egg. The culinary texts of Al-Andalus describe them as "very nutritious, easily digested, fortifying and good for underweight people, the elderly and for those with weak stomachs." In the eighteenth century rather unusual meatballs were made to welcome unexpected guests, using "breast of fowl, codfish, sturgeon or frogs." *Albóndigas* are still very popular and are a common feature on the menus of cheap restaurants and taverns and as a *tapa* in bars. In Spanish homes there is also an alternative version called a *filete ruso*, which is gradually being ousted by the ubiquitous hamburger.

> This dish is delicious and easily digested. Take red and tender meat, with the tendons removed, and grind [mince] it, as described before for meatballs: put it in a large dish and add some of the juice of minced onion and a little oil, pepper, macerated flour, dry cilantro [coriander], cumin and saffron; add eggs, enough to bind the mixture, and stir until it all mixes into one piece, as if it were a hunk of meat, and put it aside; then take a clean pot and put in it the oil, vinegar, a little flour and garlic and the quantity necessary of aromatic condiments and put it on the Fire. When it has boiled and the meatballs have cooked in it, leave it for a while, and when it has finished cooking, take the pot from the embers and thicken it with beaten egg, saffron and pepper; leave it all to set, and then color this dish in its way or in the way you prefer.
>
> Anonymous manuscript from the thirteenth century about Hispanic–Maghrebi cookery

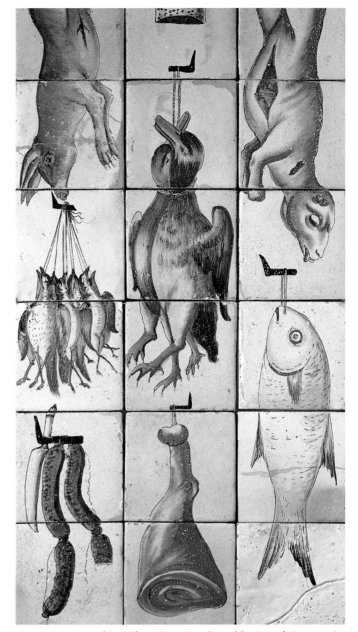

Fish and game, (detail) ceiling tiles from Manises (nineteenth century); CERAMICS MUSEUM, BARCELONA

Sauce:

¼ cup (2 fl oz/60 ml) olive oil

3½ oz (100 g) onion, finely chopped

1 carrot, thinly sliced

2 teaspoons all-purpose (plain) flour

3⅓ cups (27 fl oz/750 ml) beef broth (stock)

2 tablespoons (2 fl oz/60 ml) tomato sauce (purée)

⅓ cup (3 fl oz/90 ml) dry white wine

salt

Meatballs:

3½ oz (100 g) bread, crusts removed

⅓ cup (3 fl oz/90 ml) milk

8 oz (250 g) pork, ground (minced)

8 oz (250 g) beef, ground (minced)

1 tablespoon finely chopped parsley

2 cloves garlic, finely chopped

salt

2 eggs

all-purpose (plain) flour, for coating

olive oil, for frying

First, prepare the sauce by heating the oil in a heatproof casserole and frying the onion and carrot over low heat for 10 minutes. Add the flour. When it browns, add the broth, tomato sauce and white wine. Season with salt and cook over low heat for 20 minutes.

To make the meatballs, soak the bread in the milk, then press out the excess and mix with the meat, parsley and garlic. Season with salt, add the eggs and mix well to form a paste. Shape the meatballs with your hands, coat lightly with flour and transfer to a floured surface.

Heat the oil in a skillet (frying pan). Fry the meatballs a few at a time and transfer to a heatproof dish as they are cooked.

Put the sauce in a blender and purée. Pour over the meatballs. Cook for 30 minutes over low heat.

BEEF WITH GREEN OLIVES

Ternera con olivas verdes Serves 4–6

The inhabitants of modern-day Aragón have forgotten neither their traditional dishes nor the varied menus of yesteryear. Large portions of good food are available at low prices. There has always been a great spirit of service, generosity and altruism in the region and these qualities are clearly reflected in the local cooking. The cuisine is highly dependent on seasonal produce, as shown by this recipe, which takes advantage of the wonderful olives which grow in great abundance in the region and are also turned into excellent oil. This dish is typically served at banquets and festive meals.

⅓ cup (3 fl oz/90 ml) olive oil
1½ lb (750 g) beef, cut into small, thin steaks
1 small onion, finely chopped
1 green bell pepper (capsicum), chopped
2 tablespoons all-purpose (plain) flour
2¼ cups (16 fl oz/500 ml) water
¾ cup (6½ fl oz/200 ml) rancio wine or any
  dry red wine
salt
6½ oz (200 g) green olives, pitted

Heat the oil in a skillet (frying pan) and sauté the steaks. Transfer to a heatproof casserole.

Fry the onion and bell pepper in the same oil until golden. Add the flour, stir, then add to the casserole with the meat.

Add the water, wine and a little salt and cook over low heat for 1 hour.

Add the olives and cook for another 30 minutes. Serve in the casserole.

ROAST PORK WITH ALMONDS

Lomo de cerdo con almendras Serves 4

Preceded perhaps by a light soup, this dish makes a magnificent main course. It can be served with roast or creamed potatoes, and a curly endive salad, the bitter tang of which perfectly offsets this substantial roast.

1¾ lb (800 g) boned pork loin, in 1 piece
salt
freshly ground pepper
8 oz (250 g) almonds, peeled and toasted
⅓ cup (3 fl oz/90 ml) olive oil
¼ cup (2 oz/60 g) lard
3 tablespoons (2½ fl oz/75 ml) Cognac
2¼ cups (16 fl oz/500 ml) milk
1 lb (500 g) button mushrooms
  (champignons), washed and chopped

Still-life, Luis Meléndez (1716–80); PRADO MUSEUM, MADRID

Beef with green olives (left); roast pork with almonds (right)

Preheat the oven to 350°F (180°C/Gas 4).

Trim the fat off the pork loin, then make a series of ¾ in (2 cm) diagonal incisions without cutting right through. Season with salt and pepper.

Crush the almonds in a mortar or food processor to form a fine paste, then use to fill the cuts in the meat. Pack the mixture tightly to prevent it from oozing out. Tie up the pork loin securely with string.

Put ¼ cup (2 fl oz/60 ml) of the oil and the lard, in a baking dish, add the pork and

roast for approximately 40 minutes.

Remove from the oven and spoon off some of the fat. Pour the Cognac over the meat and put it back in the oven for another 5 minutes.

Add the milk and cook for a further 20 minutes, or until the meat is cooked.

Remove from the dish and allow to cool. Cut the pork into slices and return to the dish.

Sauté the mushrooms in the remaining oil, then add a little salt and cook until the liquid evaporates. Serve the pork hot, surrounded by the mushrooms.

Stewed round of beef

STEWED ROUND OF BEEF

Redondo de ternera   Serves 4

All Spanish women cook round of beef; of that there can be no doubt. It is the first "proper" recipe young brides learn to cook to surprise the in-laws the first time they visit.

This recipe is always a good idea for a lunch out in the country and is also a good choice if you want to have something a bit special handy in the refrigerator, as it can be served with all sorts of garnishes and accompaniments.

2 lb (1 kg) round roast of beef
salt
⅓ cup (3 fl oz/90 ml) olive oil
2 medium-size onions (10 oz/315 g), chopped
2 cloves garlic, peeled
2 medium-size carrots, scrubbed and sliced
2 small tomatoes (6½ oz/200 g), halved

¼ cup (2 fl oz/60 ml) Cognac
1⅔ cups (13 fl oz/410 ml) water, approximately
2 bay leaves
1 small piece lemon zest (rind)

Tie up the beef with string and season. Heat the oil in a heatproof casserole and brown the meat on all sides over medium heat. Remove and set aside.

Fry the onions and garlic gently in the same oil, followed by the carrots and then the tomatoes.

Add the Cognac, water, bay leaves and lemon zest, then put the meat back in. Add a little salt, cover and cook over low heat for 1–1½ hours.

Put the sauce through a food mill or purée in the blender.

Carve the meat into slices and serve accompanied by the sauce.

188

HAM WITH TOMATO SAUCE

Magras con tomate   Serves 4

For the Aragonese people there is no possible substitute for this dish; only the real thing will do. When special occasions are celebrated with *magras con tomate*, the ham is of the best possible quality.

1 cup (8 fl oz/250 ml) milk

4 slices (3½ oz/100 g each) tender serrano ham *(salt-cured and unsmoked, similar to mild prosciutto)*

4 thin slices round (cob-style), peasant-style bread

1 egg, beaten

1 lb (500 g) ripe tomatoes

½ cup (4 fl oz/125 ml) olive oil

¾ teaspoon sugar

salt

1 tablespoon white wine vinegar

2 tablespoons (1 fl oz/30 ml) dry white wine

Warm the milk and soak the ham slices for 15–20 minutes (or less if the ham is very salty). Remove, drain and dry well.

Dip the slices of bread into the milk and then into the beaten egg. Set aside.

Now prepare the tomato sauce by chopping the tomatoes and mixing with ¼ cup (2 fl oz/60 ml) of the oil, ¼ teaspoon of the sugar, and a little salt. Cook until a thick purée forms, then use to coat the base of a heatproof casserole.

Heat the remaining oil slightly in a large skillet (frying pan). Quickly sauté the ham slices, then remove from the pan. Fry the slices of bread in the same oil, then transfer to paper towels. Add the remaining sugar to the pan, taking care not to let it burn, then add the vinegar and wine and cook for a few minutes.

Lay the bread slices side by side on top of the tomato sauce in the casserole. Place a slice of ham on each one, sprinkle with the contents of the skillet and serve.

Ham with tomato sauce

189

PORK CHOPS IN CIDER

Chuletas de cerdo a la sidra   Serves 4

There are two ancient customs in the north of Spain which take place from December onward: slaughtering and the tasting of the new cider, or apple wine. This dish is closely linked to both rituals. The authentic flavor can be achieved only with cider which complies with the following ten commandments.

1. It should be dry.
2. It should be slightly tart.
3. It should be smooth.
4. It should be clear.
5. It should smell of apples.
6. It should be the color of straw.
7. It should fizz a little when poured.
8. It should have just the right amount of body.
9. It should be served in quantities of between 13 and 16 cc.
10. It should not oxidize on immediate contact with air.

Pork chops in cider

¼ cup (2 fl oz/60 ml) olive oil
3 cloves garlic, finely chopped
1 onion (6½ oz/200 g), finely chopped
6½ oz (200 g) button mushrooms (champignons), sliced and sprinkled with the juice of 1 lemon
4 pork chops (each 6½ oz/200 g)
1⅔ cups (13 fl oz/410 ml) cider
¼ cup (1 oz/30 g) grated Parmesan cheese
¼ cup (1 oz/30 g) dry breadcrumbs
salt
freshly ground pepper
1 tablespoon finely chopped parsley

Preheat the oven to 400°F (200°C/Gas 6).

Heat the oil in a skillet (frying pan) and sauté the garlic and onion. Add the mushrooms and continue frying gently. Transfer to a baking dish, lay the chops on top and pour in the cider.

Mix the grated Parmesan with the breadcrumbs and sprinkle over the chops. Season lightly with salt and pepper. Drizzle some oil over the top and bake for 45 minutes.

Remove from the oven and sprinkle with the parsley. Serve hot.

STUFFED PORK LOIN

Lomo de cerdo relleno   Serves 4

There are exquisite ways of preparing the different cuts of pork to be found throughout Spain. One of the greatest, however, has to be the meat of an animal raised on acorns in the pastures of Extremadura and cooked with the special expertise of the local chefs.

1¾ lb (800 g) pork loin, in 1 piece
cup (6½ fl oz/200 ml) milk
3½ oz (100 g) fresh breadcrumbs
6½ oz (200 g) sausage meat
3½ oz (100 g) beef liver, ground (minced)
1 onion (5 oz/155 g), finely chopped
1 tablespoon finely chopped parsley
1 egg, beaten
salt
freshly ground pepper
⅓ cup (3 fl oz/90 ml) olive oil
1⅔ cups (13 fl oz/410 ml) dry white wine

Trim the fat off the pork, slice open lengthwise and flatten with a pestle.

To make the filling, heat the milk and add

Stuffed pork loin

the breadcrumbs. Continue heating until a spongy mixture forms, then drain and put in a bowl. Add the sausage meat, ground liver, onion and parsley. Add the beaten egg and some salt and pepper.

Spoon the filling onto the meat, roll up firmly and tie with string.

Heat the oil in a heatproof casserole and brown the meat all over. Add the white wine and a little salt and pepper, then cook over low heat for 1¼ hours.

When the meat is done, remove the string and cut into slices. Arrange on a serving dish and pour the sauce over the top.

Marinated turkey

century onward, turkey came to be regarded as a somewhat fancy, inaccessible food, with the reputation previously confined to royal turkey of being symbolic of lavish banquets. The splendid common turkey made an impressive centerpiece at many a formal dinner, nevertheless, and later became immensely popular on a more domestic level, too. Surrounded by all manner of sauces, stuffings, compotes and jellies, it could easily be made to look even more splendid.

In the time of Cervantes, Philip IV's chef Francisco Martinez Montiño gave the first list of Christmas banquets in *Arte de Cocina, Pastelería, Vizcochería y Conservería* (1611), and said that "among other foods . . . roast turkeys with their gravy were served . . ."

The marinade detracts from the elegance of the dish but heightens its exquisite flavor and makes it last longer.

1 onion (5 oz/155 g), peeled and halved
4 cloves
1½ lb (750 g) turkey breast, thinly sliced
1 large carrot, scraped and sliced
3 sprigs thyme
1 bay leaf
1 tablespoon black peppercorns
1 head (bulb) garlic
1 cup (8 fl oz/250 ml) olive oil
1 cup (8 fl oz/250 ml) white wine vinegar
1 cup (8 fl oz/250 ml) chicken broth (stock)
⅛ teaspoon salt

Spear the onion halves with the cloves, then put them in a heatproof casserole with the turkey slices, carrot, thyme, bay leaf, peppercorns and the head of garlic. Add the oil, vinegar, broth and salt. Cover and cook over low heat for about 2 hours.

Cool and allow to stand for 48 hours in the refrigerator. Bring to room temperature before serving.

CHICKEN IN OLOROSO SHERRY SAUCE

Pollo al jerez Oloroso   Serves 4

Wine plays an important part in Spanish cooking. In Andalusia the various kinds of wines from the Jerez region are the favorites, including *Fino, Manzanilla, Amontillado, Oloroso, Palo cortado, Crema* and other sweet wines. *Fino* is the lightest, driest and most delicate and is excellent for flavoring consommés and sauces. For dishes with more body, the dark *Oloroso* is more appropriate, with its powerful aroma and higher alcohol content. Chicken in *Oloroso* Sherry Sauce is the perfect dish for guests or family celebrations. It can be served with potatoes, vegetables or rice, according to individual preference.

MARINATED TURKEY

Escabeche de pavo   Serves 4

Turkey came originally from Mexico and arrived in Spain at the beginning of the sixteenth century, when it quickly gained acceptance. Birds started to be raised and soon appeared in the markets. *Libro del Arte de Cocina* (1599) by Diego Granado features one of the oldest recipes known. From the seventeenth

Open the chicken or capon to draw it. When it is cleaned, brown it in a casserole, with lard or bacon fat. When it is golden, leave it in the casserole, adding salt and a little water, for it to cook, and turn it from time to time. Make a concoction of cloves of garlic, parsley, cloves, cinnamon and saffron, all minced and mixed in a little oil. Some 7 minutes before taking the chicken to the table, baste it with this concoction, making it look like a batter. And now you can put it on the table. Accompanied by a salad of radishes, it is a very tasty meal for those without appetite.

Fray Sever de Olot, *Libre del Arte de Cocina*, 1787

1 chicken (2 lb/1 kg)
2 cloves garlic, peeled
⅓ cup (3 fl oz/90 ml) olive oil
1 lb (500 g) onions, finely chopped
6½ oz (200 g) carrots, scraped and sliced
1⅔ cups (13 fl oz/410 ml) Oloroso sherry
salt

freshly ground pepper
10 oz (315 g) button mushrooms
(champignons), chopped

Rub the chicken inside and out with the garlic, then place in a large heatproof casserole with the oil. Fry gently until it starts to brown, turning occasionally. Add the onions and carrots and fry over low heat for 15 minutes. Add the sherry and cook over high heat for 3 minutes to burn off the alcohol, then add a little salt and pepper. Cover and cook for 45 minutes over low heat, turning 2 or 3 times.

Sauté the mushrooms in a little oil and set aside.

When the chicken is cooked, cut into quarters and arrange on a serving dish. Purée the sauce in a blender or food processor and pour over the chicken. Decorate with the mushrooms and serve.

Chicken in Oloroso sherry sauce

BABY GOOSE WITH PEARS

Oca con peras   Serves 4

This recipe includes some of the leading characteristics of Catalan cuisine: mixing fruit, vegetables and fowl, using pork lard, seasoning with tomatoes and finishing off the dish with a finely chopped mixture of cookies, almonds and garlic to strengthen the contrast of flavors.

1 baby goose, 3 lb (1.5 kg), chopped
salt
3½ oz (100 g) lard
1 medium-size onion (5 oz/155 g), chopped
2 tomatoes (8 oz/250 g), chopped
3⅓ cups (27 fl oz/750 ml) hot water
8 small, hard pears (1¾ lb/800 g), peeled
2 cloves garlic
⅓ cup (2 oz/60 g) almonds
1 plain cookie (milk arrowroot type)

Baby goose with pears

Season the pieces of goose with a little salt. Melt the lard in a heatproof casserole. When it starts to heat up, add the meat and fry until golden. Remove and set aside.

Fry the onion lightly in this fat. When it starts to brown, add the tomato and cook over medium heat for a few moments before adding the pieces of goose. Add the hot water and cook, covered, over medium heat for 30–45 minutes (the exact time will depend on how tender the meat is).

Add the pears and continue cooking over low heat.

Meanwhile, crush the garlic in a mortar with the almonds and the cookie to form a smooth paste.

Spoon off a ladle of the broth and add to the mortar to dilute the mixture, then pour into the casserole.

Check the seasoning and add salt if necessary. Cook for a few more minutes.

Arrange the pieces of goose in the center of a platter with the pears. Pour the sauce over the top and serve immediately.

CHICKEN IN ALMOND SAUCE

Gallina en pepitoria   Serves 4

This is an ancient dish of Castilian origin and was described in the Hispanic–Arab culinary documents of Al-Andalus back in the thirteenth century and later by Diego Granado (1599), Martínez Montiño (1611) and Juan de Altamiras (1745). It is not known which version is the most authentic, but all are similar. The dish used to be served with chopped chicken livers and quartered hardcooked (hardboiled) eggs and was surrounded by triangular croûtons. In *Arte de Cocina, Pastelería, Vizcochería y Conservería* (1611), Martínez Montiño advises serving the dish like this, although his recipe also reflects the medieval taste for vinegar and spices, which he claims should be pepper, cloves, almonds, ginger and saffron. This heavy seasoning is, however, no longer added.

⅓ cup (3 fl oz/90 ml) olive oil
1 thick slice bread (1 oz/30 g)
10 almonds
2 cloves garlic, peeled
1 chicken, approximately 3 lb (1.5 kg), chopped
1 medium-size onion, finely chopped
2¾ cups (22 fl oz/600 ml) water
1 teaspoon lemon juice
salt
1 pinch ground cinnamon

Chicken in almond sauce

1 pinch ground cloves
1 pinch saffron
1 pinch cumin seeds
2 egg yolks, hardcooked (hardboiled)

Heat the oil in a heatproof casserole and fry the bread, almonds and garlic. Remove and set aside. Sauté the pieces of chicken in the same oil, then remove and set aside. Fry the onion in the same oil until soft, then put the chicken back in, cover with water and add the lemon juice, salt, cinnamon and cloves. Cover and cook over low heat for 45–60 minutes, depending on how tender the chicken is.

Meanwhile, crush the saffron, cumin seeds, fried bread, garlic and almonds in a mortar. Add the hardcooked egg yolks and dilute with a little of the cooking water.

When the chicken is almost cooked, check the seasoning and add the mixture from the mortar. Do not allow to boil vigorously, as the sauce might separate. It should be quite thick.

Stewed partridge with chocolate

STEWED PARTRIDGE WITH CHOCOLATE

Perdices estofadas al chocolate   Serves 4

Professor Martínez Llopis, historian of Spanish gastronomy, reckoned that this dish has an anachronistic colonial air about it, possibly influenced by Mexico when it was governed by Spanish viceroys and people used to eat *mole de guajolote poblano*, which featured chocolate as a luxury ingredient. There is some doubt as to the fate of the dish over the years, but in 1901 a leading gourmet who used the pseudonym "Mari la Mesonera" was surprised to find it being served in Navarre. It can still be found on the menus of certain restaurants.

¾ cup (6½ fl oz/200 ml) olive oil

2 partridges (each 8 oz/250 g), cleaned and
  flamed (to ensure no feathers remain)

2 tablespoons white wine vinegar

2 bay leaves

2 cloves garlic, finely chopped

freshly ground pepper

1 lb (500 g) very small onions, peeled and left
  whole

salt

3½ oz (100 g) semisweet chocolate

Heat the oil in a heatproof casserole and sauté the partridges. Add the vinegar, bay leaves, garlic

and pepper. Cook for 10 minutes. Add the onions with enough water to cover, then add a little salt, cover and cook over low heat for about 1 hour, turning occasionally.

Melt the chocolate with a little of the broth from the partridges, then pour this mixture into the casserole and bring to a boil.

Arrange the partridges in the center of a serving dish. Surround with the onions and the sauce.

HARE TERRINE

Pastel de liebre   Serves 6–8

Most cultures have versions of preserved game specialties. Although these dishes often involve time-consuming, intricate preparation, they can seem rather primitive and are certainly not for the fainthearted, as the concentration of strong flavors packs quite a punch. Served straight from the mold with thick hunks of coarse bread, this terrine is quite unforgettable.

1 hare (2 lb/1 kg), boned and soaked in water
  overnight to get rid of the strong taste

8 oz (250 g) cured ham, with fat

8 oz (250 g) pork, ground (minced)

8 oz (250 g) beef, ground (minced)

¼ cup (2 fl oz/60 ml) sherry

¼ cup (2 fl oz/60 ml) Cognac

salt

freshly ground pepper

1 truffle (canned), sliced

1 teaspoon finely chopped thyme

butter, for greasing the pan

15–20 bay leaves

Preheat the oven to 400°F (200°C/Gas 6).

Rinse and drain the hare, then grind.

Put all the meats in a large bowl. Add the sherry and Cognac and season with salt and pepper. Add the truffle and the liquid from the can, then sprinkle with the thyme and mix thoroughly.

Grease a deep rectangular pan with butter and fill with the meat mixture. Press down slightly and cover the surface with bay leaves. Cover with aluminum foil with a hole in the center. Bake in a bain-marie in the oven for 45–60 minutes.

Pierce with a thick needle to check if the terrine is cooked — there should be no red juice on it. Remove from the oven and turn out of the tin. Put a heavy board on the top and leave for 24 hours in the refrigerator. Bring to room temperature before serving.

Hare terrine

Marinated partridge (left); marinated rabbit (right)

Plate with hare, pottery from Manises (second half fifteenth century)

MARINATED PARTRIDGE

Perdices escabechadas   Serves 4

The common partridge has been a popular dish since the sixteenth century, although it was known in Spain for many centuries before then. It inhabits the vineyards, cereal fields and hillsides along the shores of the Mediterranean. The quality of the meat depends on age (young birds are best), climate and what the partridges have been fed on. The most important factor, however, is to know how to counteract the negative qualities in the cooking process. There are countless recipes for partridge in both Arab and European cuisine. This version of marinated partridge is very typically Spanish and keeps well for a long time. The cooking technique and ingredients show its medieval origins, as it includes no foods from the New World.

4 partridges (each 8 oz/250 g)
¾ cup (6½ fl oz/200 ml) olive oil
4 small onions (13 oz/410 g), finely chopped
4 cloves garlic, peeled
4 medium-size carrots, scraped and sliced
2 bay leaves
¼ cup (2 fl oz/60 ml) white wine vinegar
¾ cup (6½ fl oz/200 ml) dry white wine
4 black peppercorns
3 sprigs thyme
salt

Clean and singe the birds to ensure that no feathers remain; then rinse and dry them.

Heat the oil in a skillet (frying pan) and sauté the partridges over medium heat, turning to cook evenly. Transfer to a heatproof casserole.

Gently fry the onion, garlic and carrots with the bay leaves in the same oil.

Pour this mixture over the partridges, then add the vinegar, wine, peppercorns and thyme. Add water to cover, then add a little salt, cover and cook over low heat until very tender (1–1½ hours).

Before serving, cut the birds in half and arrange on a platter. Strain the sauce and pour over the top. This dish can be eaten hot or cold.

MARINATED RABBIT

Conejo en escabeche   Serves 4–6

The common rabbit is very abundant in the hills and woods of the Iberian peninsula. It has been used in home cooking in many different forms since ancient times and features in all the historical culinary documents. The medieval tradition of *escabeche* — a means of preserving food in oil, wine and vinegar with spices — is an ideal way of preparing rabbit and provides a handy addition to the larder. This recipe is eaten at room temperature and is a popular choice for outdoor meals.

> Roast the rabbits; cut them along the joints and take in a skillet [frying pan] two parts of vinegar, if it were weak vinegar, and one of water; and if it were strong, equal parts; and put salt to it until it has taste; add the salt in parts, not all at once, or it may become too salty; add oil which is sweet, whatever quantity you think fit, because some like a little, and some a lot; and boil it all without the rabbits; and put it all afterward together in a pot; and let it go cold; and put to it ginger, and cloves, and saffron; and this marinade will last a great many days.
>
> Ruperto de Nola, *Libro de Guisados*, 1520

4 lb (2 kg) rabbit
salt
¾ cup (6½ fl oz/200 ml) olive oil
1 head (bulb) garlic
2 bay leaves
1 tablespoon finely chopped parsley
1 tablespoon black peppercorns
4 cloves
4 slices orange
4 slices lemon
¾ cup (6½ fl oz/200 ml) dry red wine
2¼ cups (16 fl oz/500 ml) water
1 pinch saffron strands

Chop up the rabbit, add a little salt and sauté in the oil.

Transfer to a casserole together with the cooking oil and add the rest of the ingredients. Cover and cook slowly for approximately 1½ hours, or until the meat is tender.

Cool and allow to stand for 48 hours in the refrigerator. Bring to room temperature before eating.

Still-life, Luis Meléndez (1716–80); ART MUSEUM OF CATALONIA, BARCELONA   These melons have been prepared for hanging up through the winter months. Properly stored, Elche

SAUCES, PRESERVES AND MARINADES

melons managed to retain their freshness and juiciness because of their thick skins.

T 1174

SAUCES, PRESERVES AND MARINADES

Sauces feature in Spanish cuisine more often as a product of the cooking process, integrated in a dish, than as a separate element served in a sauce boat. All the same, as in all countries steeped in history, Spain has produced the occasional sauce that has attained international renown.

Garum provides an early example of a sauce being exported, which occurred during the Roman occupation: the Romans imported *garum* from Iberia in small glass flasks as if it were perfume from Paris. This sauce, which the Romans used in the most capricious ways, was the result of a complex fermentation process carried out in the fisheries of southern Spain from the most ignoble leftovers of the catch.

Garum is, sadly, no longer made, but anyone interested in a similar kind of recipe can try the sauce made from anchovies in brine that is typical of La Escala in the province of Gerona, which has a very intense, tart flavor.

During the middle ages there was a great number of acid sauces. Arnaldo de Vilanova, in his book *Regimen Sanitatis* (1480), describes the traditional summer sauces based on fresh vineshoots, lemon and lime juice, tart pomegranate, sugar, rosewater and vinegar. In winter these vinaigrettes were, however, prepared with wine, weak vinegar, meat-juice and a profusion of spices and aromatic herbs such as mustard, garlic, sage, parsley, thyme, mint, fennel, ginger, cinnamon, fragrant cloves and pepper.

Present-day Spanish vinaigrettes are characterized by the widespread use of onion and the colorful touch provided by red or green bell peppers (capsicums). It was the appearance of New World foods, such as these, that changed the character of medieval flavors. *All-i-oli* sauce is common in Spain, as in other Mediterranean countries, and is made by pounding garlic with oil in a mortar.

Spain has a long-standing disagreement with France on the subject of the origins of mayonnaise. The Spanish insist it was invented in Mahón, on the island of Menorca, as a result of British influence. Whatever the origins of mayonnaise, it is certainly a most surprising sauce — how can raw egg mixed with oil and vinegar or lemon turn into something so different from its basic ingredients? With its fresh, appetizing taste and creamy texture, it makes even the driest fish irresistible and turns a simple

Oranges and goldfinch, (1862) A. Mensaque; MUSEO ROMANTICO, MADRID
This painting suggests something of the poetry and romance associated with the orange groves of the south. The heavy-scented blossoms fill the evening air in spring. In the heat of summer there is the tangy fruit to quench one's thirst and the goldfinch's bright song echoing through the groves.

Still-life (1879), José Pinazo;
FINE ARTS MUSEUM, VALENCIA
The influence of Moorish potters on
Spanish pottery and ceramics has been
deep and enduring. Such classic
earthenware pots and vases all owe
their form to Moorish design.

mixture of vegetables into a sumptuous feast. Some people claim to be capable of dipping a loaf of long Spanish bread into mayonnaise and eating the lot. With mayonnaise as a base, the addition of mustard, pickles, tomato or orange juice, or brandy can create a variety of other sauces.

Romesco is a sauce whose antecedents can be found among the elaborate sauces mentioned in the medieval Catalan recipe book *Libre de Sent Sovi* (1324), and is still made by Catalans today. It is another example of a sauce made with oily ingredients, crushed with garlic and fried bread. In this case the distinctive character of *romesco* is created by the inclusion of hot *romesco* peppers, with almonds and tomatoes.

Another hot sauce, *mojo picón* (mojo dressing), is typical of the Canary Islands and is sharp, spicy and aromatic.

Salsa española (Spanish sauce) is used very widely in Spanish cooking and can be used to brighten up virtually any dish, whether meat-based or not. This sauce is made from toasted onion and carrot, thickened with flour and flavored with white wine, and tomato can also be added. Potatoes are transformed into a dish on their own by the addition of this sauce.

PRESERVES AND MARINADES
With the dry climate and, throughout history, the poverty in Spain, people have had to use all possible means of preserving foods. Fortunately, there has never been a

shortage of the essential preserving ingredients: salt, vinegar and oil.

The warm coasts of the Levante region and the south are highly suitable for saltworks. Trading with the north of Europe began long ago and one result of that trade was that the Spanish provided the Norwegians with salt in exchange for cod. The rich sources of oily fish caught by the Spanish were put to good use by taking advantage of salting and other preservation processes. Some very interesting recipes in Spanish cooking are based on these preservation processes, such as savory pies and other dishes that make use of the very tasty anchovy.

Thanks to a plentiful supply of wine and, consequently, vinegar, Spanish vegetables can be pickled. There is a wide range of pickled vegetables, many of which are used for *tapas* and appetizers. Eggplants (aubergines) from Almagro are perhaps the most surprising example of this sort of snack, because of their size.

The asparagus seller and the soldier,
Lorenzo Tiepolo (1696–1770);
COLLECTION OF THE DUCHESS OF SAINT MAURO

Vinegar is also used to make certain household recipes last for several days. This method, known as cooking in *escabeche*, works best with oily fish and some kinds of small game. As a method of preserving, it is very similar to Arab and medieval practices and has been used consistently since those times. In 1611, for example, Francisco Martínez Montiño, in his *Arte de Cocina, Pastelería Vizochería y Conservería*, mentioned two very up-to-date recipes for *escabeche de atún* (marinated tuna) and *escabeche de besugo* (marinated bream).

Escabeches are very popular in Spain and also very highly esteemed. If, before, their popularity was due to the economic good sense of preserving foods, now they are made for their own sake. They are even regarded as somewhat inconvenient by some people, whose appetites are greater than their patience, as they cannot wait the few hours required for an *escabeche* to take on its full flavor. On an upward scale, the range of foods cooked in *escabeche* goes from the simple *boquerón* (fresh anchovy) to the luxurious partridge. All involve previous preparation: generally, frying and stewing, then cooking and marinating in a broth (stock), usually with the inclusion of green (spring) onions, carrots, garlic and other vegetables, and suitable seasonings such as black pepper and bay leaves — together with just the right amount of Spanish vinegar, one of the most powerful and aromatic in the world.

Oil is another preservative for foods, which is used as a protection against oxidation caused by contact with air. It is a simple method, but requires ideal conditions of both temperature and storage. The same foods that are preserved in *escabeche* can be preserved in oil, which tempers tart flavors. Oil is also used for prolonging the natural preservation capacities of cheeses and sausages.

Other methods of preserving are taken care of by the sun, the cold climate of the *mesetas* (the high central plateaux) and the smoke from hearths.

The Spanish food-preserving industry has attained much prestige for its treatment of fish and vegetables. The canning industry, particularly, has developed apace and its high-quality results are being increasingly combined with fresh ingredients in a variety of dishes. Foods mass produced using all these preservation methods now form an important part of the cuisine, to the extent that some people prefer them to the original, fresh ingredients. This is why canned bonito is used in *empanada* savory pies and fillings in preference to fresh fish. Equally, top-quality asparagus is served in restaurants and hotels with no secrets as to its canned origin and the same goes for canned red bell peppers (capsicums), which are ideal for stuffing.

SALMORRETA SAUCE

Salsa salmorreta   Serves 4

Salmorreta is prepared in Valencia and Alicante to accompany fish broiled (grilled) and *arroz a banda* and is often served together with *all-i-oli*. The secret of this sauce is that the tomato is cooked beforehand and acquires a delicious smoky flavor, which creates very interesting results when mixed with the raw ingredients. The spicy flavor can be varied according to individual taste.

1 medium-size ripe tomato (4 oz/125 g)
1 piece chili pepper
1 tablespoon finely chopped parsley
3 cloves garlic, peeled and finely chopped
1 small onion (3½ oz/100 g), peeled and
   chopped

Limes, oranges, azaroles and watermelon, Luis Meléndez (1716–80); PRADO MUSEUM, MADRID
Bitter oranges came to Spain with the Moors and today are exported in large quantities to Britain for making marmalade. The famous sweet Valencian orange was a later introduction from China.

⅓ cup (3 fl oz/90 ml) olive oil
1 tablespoon white wine vinegar
freshly ground pepper
salt

Broil (grill) or bake the tomato. Peel and remove the seeds.

Crush the chili pepper with the parsley and garlic in a mortar, followed by the onion and finally the tomato or, alternatively, use a blender.

Drizzle in the oil drop by drop, stirring constantly. Add the vinegar and a little pepper. Add the salt last. If the sauce is too thick, dilute with fish broth.

Salmorreta sauce (left); egg, oil and garlic sauce (right)

EGG, OIL AND GARLIC SAUCE

All-i-oli con huevo   Serves 4–6

The two basic ingredients of this dressing — garlic and olive oil — represent the quintessence of traditional Mediterranean cuisine. Both are mentioned as flavorings, balsams and symbols of culture in classical literature. *All-i-oli* is the most popular sauce in Mediterranean cuisine and is used as a contrasting feature in a great many dishes. Successful results require a steady action with the pestle to blend the dressing smoothly in the mortar. It is a suitable accompaniment to salads, potatoes, rice dishes, fish and meat.

2 or 3 cloves garlic, peeled

1 egg yolk, at room temperature

1 cup (8 fl oz/250 ml) olive oil, at room temperature

salt

lemon juice

Crush the garlic in a mortar until creamy. Add the egg yolk and mix in with the pestle or, alternatively, use a blender. Trickle in the oil very slowly, stirring all the time in the same direction with the pestle to mix thoroughly.

Add a little salt and a dash of lemon juice if desired. The *all-i-oli* should be very thick.

SPICY MOJO DRESSING

Mojo picón   Serves 4

Just go up to the counter in any bar in the Canary Islands and there will soon be a little dish of spicy *mojo* served with "wrinkly potatoes" in front of you, just to get you in the swing of things. ("Wrinkly potatoes" are small unpeeled potatoes boiled in highly salted water. This method makes them wrinkly and salty on the outside but soft and sweet inside.)

The main ingredient of this sauce is hot chili pepper, which was brought to the Canaries from Latin America. Spicy *mojo* goes very well with potatoes but can also be eaten with meat, fish or salads.

1 head (bulb) garlic
1 tablespoon cumin
1 bay leaf
3 cayenne peppers
1 cup (8 fl oz/250 ml) olive oil
salt
white wine vinegar

Peel the garlic and crush in a mortar (or blender) with the cumin, bay leaf and peppers.

Drizzle in the oil drop by drop, then add a little salt and finally a dash of vinegar.

If you want to thicken the dressing a little, mash some stale bread and add it to the mixture.

ROMESCO SAUCE

Salsa romesco   Serves 4

When Angel Muro tasted this dish in 1892, he said of it: "It is a dish unique and exclusive to Tarragona, with a Roman flavor and a Cyclopean texture which could revive the dead." In his book, *El Practicon*, published in 1894, he states: "I would go as far as to bet a couple of pesetas that the Celts used to eat *romesco* in Tarragona, and that the recipe, which is indisputably of Phoenician origin, came from them."

What Angel Muro says is not true, because the ingredients came from America after 1492, but his comments extol the deep-rooted tradition and heritage of the dish.

2 dried peppers (Capsicum annuum), seeded
⅓ cup (3 fl oz/90 ml) olive oil
1 small piece chili pepper
8 cloves garlic, peeled
1 small slice bread (½ oz/15 g)
1 tablespoon finely chopped parsley
12 almonds, toasted
12 hazelnuts, toasted

1 medium-size ripe tomato (4 oz/125 g),
  baked or broiled (grilled)
2 tablespoons white wine vinegar
salt

Soak the dried peppers for 30 minutes.

Heat 2 tablespoons (1 fl oz/30 ml) of oil in a skillet (frying pan) and fry the dried peppers and chili pepper, taking care not to let them burn. Remove and set aside. Fry 4 cloves of garlic and the slice of bread in the same oil. Remove and set aside.

Crush the remaining 4 cloves of garlic in a mortar (not wooden), followed by the fried garlic, then the dried peppers and chili pepper, then the parsley, almonds and hazelnuts and finally the bread. Alternatively, you can use a blender.

Peel the cooked tomato, remove the seeds and chop finely, then mix with the other ingredients. Add the vinegar and oil drop by drop, stirring to blend thoroughly. Add a little salt. If the sauce is too thick, add more oil and stir. Check the seasoning and add more salt or vinegar if necessary.

VINAIGRETTE DRESSING

Salsa vinagreta   Serves 4

In hot weather, *vinagretas* and finely chopped ingredients are a colorful feature of Spanish tables. These are not actually dressings as such, because the seasonings are added directly to the foods and may include all sorts of fresh, flavorsome and natural ingredients: onions, herbs, capers, cucumbers, olives, tomatoes and other salad vegetables, together with virgin olive oil and vinegar. *Vinagretas* are used to season meat and fish, as well as boiled potatoes.

⅓ cup (3 fl oz/90 ml) olive oil
2 tablespoons (1 fl oz/30 ml) white wine
  vinegar
salt
freshly ground pepper
1 tablespoon finely chopped parsley
1 teaspoon finely chopped tarragon
1 small onion (3½ oz/100 g), finely chopped
1 hardcooked (hardboiled) egg, finely
  chopped

Blend the oil with the vinegar, salt and a little pepper. Add the parsley, tarragon, onion and hardcooked egg. Mix thoroughly and serve to accompany asparagus, other vegetables or fish.

Spicy mojo dressing (top); romesco sauce (bottom left); vinaigrette dressing (bottom right)

Mosaic floor, Manises (eighteenth century); NATIONAL CERAMICS MUSEUM, VALENCIA
For such eighteenth-century meals, rather than cooking everything in a sauce or serving food already garnished with the sauce, many sauces were separately prepared. Once the main dish had been served, the sauce was added to it at the table.

SPANISH TOMATO SAUCE

Salsa de tomates a la española   Serves 4–6

The use of tomatoes in the Indian and Creole cuisines of Mexico was documented by early travelers to the New World. In the course of the sixteenth and seventeenth centuries, tomatoes developed from being purely a botanical curiosity to a basic food. In *Lo Scalco alla Moderna* (1692), Antonio Latini gave a recipe for tomato sauce *alla espagnuola* which included spicy peppers — a clear indication of its origins. By 1747, when Juan de la Mata published *Arte de Repostería*, the umbilical cord had been cut and the sauce was presented as genuinely Spanish. Since then it has become a part of a great many dishes, both as a basic component and an accompanying sauce.

> After baking three or four Tomatoes, and removing their skin, chop them on a table as finely as possible, then put them in the sauce boat and add a little Parsley, Onion and Garlic, also chopped very finely, with a little Salt, Pepper, Oil and Vinegar; when everything is well mixed together, it may be served.
>
> Juan de la Mata, *Arte de Repostería*, 1747

⅓ cup (3 fl oz/90 ml) olive oil

1 medium-size onion, finely chopped

2 lb (1 kg) very ripe tomatoes, peeled, seeded and chopped

2 teaspoons sugar

salt

Heat the oil in a large skillet (frying pan) and sauté the onion for 5 minutes without letting it brown. Add the tomato and fry over low heat for 20–30 minutes, adding the sugar and salt at the end of the cooking time.

Put through a food mill to blend, and serve in a sauce boat.

MAYONNAISE SAUCE

Salsa mahonesa   Serves 4

Josep Plá, a leading twentieth-century Catalan writer, graphically compared *mahonesa* with *all-i-oli*: "*All-i-oli* is to *mahonesa* what a lion is to a pet cat." You are never afraid of a pet cat, and it always enjoys a caress. *Salsa mahonesa* can be used to "caress" any kind of dish.

1 egg yolk, at room temperature
1 cup (8 fl oz/250 ml) olive oil, at room temperature
salt
1 teaspoon lemon juice

Put the egg yolk in a marble or china (not wooden) mortar and stir with the pestle or, alternatively, use a blender.

Add the oil drop by drop, stirring steadily in one direction with the pestle, to blend smoothly.

When it thickens, add a little salt and the lemon juice. The mayonnaise should be thick.

Spanish tomato sauce (left); mayonnaise sauce (right)

211

Boy with a basket of fish, Joaquín Sorolla (1863–1923);
PRIVATE COLLECTION

BONITO PRESERVE

Bonito en aceite   2 lb (1 kg)

In ancient Iberia there were some very important fishing centers; there the fish was preserved in salt and sent off to the capital, where it was in great demand. Especially famous were the preserves made in Sexi, Abrera and Gades. A condiment was made, called *garo* by the Greeks and *garum* by the Romans. This preserve maintains this tradition by using olive oil, which blends very well with the flavor of the bonito.

1 fresh bonito tuna
salt
olive oil

Cut the bonito into thick slices, add salt and leave overnight.

The next day, boil the bonito until the flesh is tender and the bone comes away.

Allow to cool. Remove the skin and bones and transfer to sterilized jars. Add oil very gradually for the fish to soak up as much as possible. Keep adding oil until the bonito is covered.

Seal the jars, then simmer, covered with water, in a bain-marie for 3 hours. If using a pressure cooker, boil for 1½ hours.

OLIVE OIL WITH FIVE FLAVORS

Aceite a los cinco aromas   Makes 4 cups (1 qt/1 l)

Virgin olive oil is an extraordinary vehicle for absorbing and preserving the aromatic flavors that are added to it.

It is known as the "golden seasoner" because of its color, value and usefulness. I suggest you set up in your kitchen your own *olioteca*: little bottles of oil containing the widest possible range of aromatic herbs — which are rich in essential oils — to provide a variety of flavors for your dishes, evoking thousands of sensorial Mediterranean pleasures.

3 sprigs rosemary
3 sprigs thyme
3 sprigs oregano
3 sprigs mint
3 sprigs fresh basil
1 tablespoon kosher (medium coarse) salt
4 cups (1 qt/1 l) virgin olive oil

Wipe the herbs with paper towels — do not wash.

Crush them slightly in a mortar, then transfer to a wide-mouthed sterilized jar, sprinkling with salt as you go. Continue until the jar is three-quarters full.

Add the oil — it should be about 1 in (2–3 cm) deep — then seal the jar.

Leave in a sunny place for 3 weeks.

Filter through a fine sieve and pour into a clean bottle with a herb sprig or two inside.

GOAT'S CHEESE IN OLIVE OIL

Queso de cabra en aceite   2 lb (1 kg)

Shepherds have traditionally made delicious mild and cured cheeses from goat's milk. The wild herbs which the animals feed on as they ramble over the mountainside during the seasonal migrations give the cheese a slightly spicy flavor, which is accentuated by the olive oil, also seasoned with herbs. The oil keeps these small cheeses fresh and can afterward be filtered and used as a dressing or eaten with bread.

8 small goat's cheeses, with a diameter of
*   about 2 in (5 cm)*
4 sprigs thyme
4 sprigs rosemary
1 tablespoon fennel seeds
1 tablespoon black peppercorns
2 cups (16 fl oz/500 ml) olive oil

Put the goat's cheeses in a sterilized, sealable glass jar with the herbs and peppercorns in between. Add enough oil to cover completely. Seal and leave for 1 month before eating.

The oil can be used afterward to dress salads.

Bonito preserve (left); olive oil with five flavors (center); goat's cheese in olive oil (right)

Pickled olives

PICKLED OLIVES

Conserva de aceitunas Makes 2 lb (1 kg)

Methods of preserving olives are often closely linked to local traditions. Each region, village and even each family is proud of its own particular procedure, although they are perhaps unaware that these customs are a legacy from the oldest inhabitants of the Mediterranean region. This recipe reflects an Arab influence, with its use of cumin and orange rind, as well as the purely Mediterranean elements.

2 lb (1 kg) green olives
¼ cup (2½ oz/75 g) salt
2¾ cups (22 fl oz/600 ml) water
½ cup (4 fl oz/125 ml) white wine vinegar
3 tablespoons oregano
½ orange
3 sprigs thyme

1 bay leaf
1 teaspoon cumin
3 stalks fennel

Hit each olive, without breaking the pit, with a wooden pestle or a smooth stone. Put the olives in a vat with enough water to cover. Leave for 24 hours, then change the water. Repeat this process over 6–8 days, then drain.

Make a brine with the water and salt. Add the drained olives, vinegar, herbs and the remaining ingredients.

Marinate the olives in this mixture for 8 days. Once split, the olives (and the brine) should not be touched by either hand or metal utensils.

After 8 days the olives are ready to eat. Remove them from the marinade with a wooden spoon.

2 lb (1 kg) ripe apricots
1 cup (8 fl oz/250 ml) water
3 cups (1½ lb/750 g) sugar
½ vanilla pod, split lengthwise

Wash the fruits and cut in half, removing the pits.

Make a syrup by slowly dissolving the sugar in the water over low heat. Add the vanilla and cook for 2 minutes. Add the fruits and cook over low heat for 45 minutes, stirring frequently.

Transfer to sterilized jars and seal immediately.

The orange-seller at the Albanico Fountain, (detail)
José del Castillo (1737–93); MUNICIPAL MUSEUM, MADRID
The typical patter of a nineteenth-century Madrid orange-seller was: "Good day, my young masters. Murcian oranges, as you see; the genuine dragon's blood. Water sweet and cold."

APRICOT JAM WITH VANILLA

Confitura de albaricoques   Makes 3 lb (1.5 kg)
a la vainilla

The development of techniques for preserving food came about because of the widely differing climatic conditions throughout the year in Spain. Fruit preserves used as pie fillings are very common, particularly for special and symbolic occasions when the kind of fruit required is out of season. Apricots formed part of what the Spanish Jews called "Haman pouches," which were little triangular turnovers used as gifts on Purim. In *Arte de Reposteria* (1747), Juan de la Mata extols the virtues of apricots and suggests various ways of preparing and preserving them.

Nobody is unaware of the shape, size and color of Apricots: it is one of the least respected Fruits; but in the use of preserves, both liquid and dry, it rightly occupies one of the highest places. They are excellent for garnishing and decorating a dessert, with their colorful variety, particularly those which come in bunches.

The early apricots, which last from June until the end of July, have white flesh; but not because of this are they better than the yellow ones, which do not come until the middle of this latter month. Make them into compotes, and like this they are at their best. The fire and Sugar lend them a gentle fragrance, which is not there when they are uncooked.

Juan de la Mata, *Arte de Reposteria*, 1747

Apricot jam with vanilla

215

Marinated pork (left); pickled red bell peppers (right)

MARINATED PORK

Carne de cerdo en adobo   Serves 4

There are many different ways of preserving pork loin, and it is very handy to have some in the larder ready to pop on the broiler (grill) for quick and tasty sandwiches. It is a common *tapa* served on bread in bars, called *montaditos de lomo*.

2 lb (1 kg) pork loin, ribs or flank
4 cloves garlic, peeled
1 orange
1 lemon
1 heaped tablespoon paprika
1 teaspoon black peppercorns
1 teaspoon cinnamon
½ teaspoon cloves
12 cups (3 qt/3 l) water
⅓ cup (3 fl oz/90 ml) white wine vinegar
1 tablespoon oregano
3 tablespoons salt
olive oil

Cut the pork into 1¼ in (3 cm) slices.

Crush the garlic in a mortar.

Wash and dry the orange and lemon. Squeeze them, then chop up the peel.

In a large bowl, mix the spices with the water, vinegar, garlic, oregano and the peel and juice from the orange and lemon.

Add the pork — it should be covered by the marinade — and put in the refrigerator for 6 days.

After this time, fry the meat in plenty of oil. Transfer to a sterilized, glazed earthenware pot or jar and pour in the cooking oil.

If preferred, the meat can be stored in jars. Fill the jars with the pork and oil, then seal and simmer, covered with water, in a bain-marie for 2 hours.

PICKLED RED BELL PEPPERS

Conserva de   Makes 2 cups (16 oz/500 g)
pimientos

There are at least two reasons why making pickled red bell peppers is an essential chore — albeit an enjoyable one. First, in the summertime there is an abundant supply of exuberant bell peppers (capsicums), which are sun-dried on a massive scale. The other reason is that bell peppers are such an important

A Catalan woman (nineteenth century), from the Collection of Spanish National Costumes; NATIONAL LIBRARY, MADRID
In *La Ben Plantada* (1912) Eugenio d'Ors, writer and leading Catalanist, portrayed the main character with qualities held to be typically Catalan — as a tall, upright woman, poor but pious, industrious and down-to-earth. She was supposedly modeled on a Catalan woman from a small fishing village famed for her cooking prowess and such sayings as: "to make a good *dento a la marinesca* it takes three different people — a madman, a miser and a prodigal. The madman must tend the fire, the miser add the water and the prodigal add the oil."

element in Spanish cooking that it would be impossible to do without them throughout the winter. Used as both an ingredient and a condiment, bell peppers came originally from the New World.

2 lb (1 kg) red bell peppers (capsicums),
   without blemishes or bruises
1 teaspoon salt
1 tablespoon lemon juice

Rinse the bell peppers under the tap. Bake in a 400°F (200°C/Gas 6) oven, turning every 15–20 minutes.

Place in a deep container and cover with a lid or aluminum foil. Allow to cool a little.

Peel, remove the stalk and seeds and set aside the liquid yielded. Strain this juice and add the salt and lemon juice.

Put the peppers in sterilized jars, pressing down lightly, with 2 tablespoons of the liquid.

Cover and sterilize in a pressure cooker at 240°F (115°C) for 35 minutes.

Allow to cool, then store in a dry, cool, dark place.

Still-life, E. Lucas (1817–70); PRADO MUSEUM, MADRID There is a Valencian saying that says there are three uses for the watermelon: eating, drinking and washing one's face.

DESSERTS AND DRINKS

Sweet dishes do exist in Spain but more as vestiges of history than anything else since Spaniards no longer seem to be so fond of sweet meats. In other European countries, sweet foods occupy an important position in the diet, as a fundamental part of English teas and Central European meals. In Spain, however, the traditional man considers this kind of food to be a feminine weakness, while for women it is a disaster for the waistline. Maybe the explanation for all this is that in Spain bread really provides all carbohydrate requirements.

There is, therefore, no important collection of recipes for desserts, although there is a wealth of regional sweet dishes. Sometimes these recipes are named after appropriate patron saints. Others are named after the most characteristic ingredient, such as *roscos de vino*, made with wine; *anisados*, with aniseed; *encocadas*, with coconut; *almendrados*, with almonds; and *mantecados*, with butter. Others get their names from their texture — such as *sequillos*, with their implication of dryness — or method of preparation, as with *sobaos* (from kneading) and *buñuelos de viento* (from frying); *rosquillas tontas* are quite dry, while *rosquillas listas* have a syrupy fondant coating.

One of the classic treatises dealing with sweet dishes is *Los Quatro Libros del Arte de Confitería* (1592) by Miguel de Baeza, a confectioner in the city of Toledo, who discusses sugar in all its forms, varieties and ways of preparation. Another was the eighteenth-century *Arte de Repostería* by Juan de la Mata, which contains all kinds of ways to make sweets, dry and in liquid, sponges, *turrón* nougats, creams, and all kinds of frozen drinks. Other culinary *rosolis* writers detail a passionate array of sweet preparations, the majority of which are made to this day in convents, at home and in the traditional cake shops. This is particularly true of the smaller varieties — for example, marzipans, *turrón* nougats, cookies and candies — that feature in an almost identical form in the still-life paintings of centuries ago and in the window displays of present-day cake shops.

One way of classifying Spanish sweet recipes is by the main ingredient used in making them. Accordingly, first place would be taken by flour-based recipes. There is a wonderful variety of flour-based cookies and buns. Flour yields surprising results according to whether it is mixed with oil or lard, egg yolks or whites, a dash of aniseed, the liqueur *aguardiente* or nuts. Then, all these variations can be baked in a wide range of shapes: half-moons, stars, circles, ovals and even animals.

Boys eating fruit, Bartolomé Murillo (1617–82); PINAKOTHEK, MUNICH
Murillo effectively created the genre of using vagrant and beggar children as subjects for painting.

Still-life, Luis Meléndez (1716–80);
PRADO MUSEUM, MADRID
These fruits and nuts are associated predominantly with the northern Spanish provinces. Asturian apples and Basque pears were especially prized. Hazelnuts, probably introduced by the Greeks, were grown extensively near Tarragona and used for *turrón*, but in Basque areas they were made into a soup. Chestnut forests were a feature of Galicia and the highly nutritious fruit was a traditional staple of peasant diet there.

Recipes based on milk and other dairy products are traditionally more associated with the north of Spain, because that was where milk was more readily available. *Sobaos* from the Pas valley in Santander are a type of sponge cake made neither with the traditional oil nor with the popular pork lard but, surprisingly, with butter.

Milk from the north is used to make the delicate *cuajada* (curds), which is a result of the first and most elemental curdling process that milk undergoes, and has a gelatinous texture with no trace of acidity.

The regions with plentiful supplies of milk put it to good use and make *arroz con leche* (rice pudding). *Leche frita*, thick custard cut into squares and then fried, is another of the few typically Spanish desserts. It can be described as a thick, sweet *béchamel* that is then coated with egg and fried.

Many traditional Spanish sweet dishes are based on eggs, which were always widely available. Such dishes, therefore, are not restricted to regional boundaries: the sweet known as *yema* (candied egg-yolk), for instance, is to be found in every village in Spain. The most commercialized and best-known are *yemas de Santa Teresa, la flor de Castilla* (candied egg-yolks of St Teresa, the flower of Castile). These are made with egg yolks, coagulated to varying degrees of consistency, in syrup and covered by a layer of sugar, which may either be in grains or fondant. *Yemas*, thus, can have a characteristic smoothness or a varying granular texture — and it is hard to believe how extremely noticeable the difference between them is.

Huevo hilado (candied egg-thread) is also made with sugared egg yolk in the form of many extremely thin sweet threads. Despite being a very old recipe, you might think it had been conceived for the more recent international cuisine of banquets and conferences. Its attractive appearance and delicious flavor make it an ideal accompaniment for all kinds of cold meats.

Fruit in Spain is excellent and plentiful; it also occupies an important position in confectionery, as can be seen in a great many of the old still-lifes in Spanish art. In these paintings, sweets made from quince appear in beautiful boxes of very fine wood. Candied fruit that maintains its original shape is one of the most attractive elements in these paintings. It looks like normal fresh fruit, but is frozen by sugar.

One can, however, only hazard a guess at the contents of the *arropes* (fruit drinks) in the pitchers in the background of these paintings. These are maybe the sweetest of all sweet recipes, and for this reason nowadays are not to many people's taste. *Arrope* is made by mixing all kinds of fruit together with honeys and juices, and boiling the mixture; then, as if this were not enough, sugar is added until the desired syrupy consistency is attained. It sometimes even starts to ferment, which lends a very characteristic flavor.

The abundant supply of nuts in Spain, together with Arab influence, have led to the invention of *turrón*, a high-quality almond nougat. It is very good for exporting and is typical Christmas fare. It is widely manufactured in Spain, and much of what is made is sold in Latin America.

The Arabs introduced the most characteristic methods of making sweet things, one of which is frying. Many of the flour-based sweets are fried and sweetened with syrups and honey in typical Arab style.

Wedding at Cana, Bartolomé Murillo (1617–82); BARBER INSTITUTE OF FINE ARTS, BIRMINGHAM UNIVERSITY, UK
In this depiction of Christ's turning the water into wine, it is not just the food that reminds us, instead, of Murillo's seventeenth-century Seville. The ceramic jars are actually examples of Seville craftsmanship and the beautifully enameled vase (on the left) is of a type still found in Seville churches. The tablecloth beneath, embroidered with Chinese pheasants, together with the oriental clothing worn by some guests, recalls the presence of oriental goods in the marketplace of Seville. Perhaps even the water itself came from a source in the nearby Sierra, and it became the finest Andalusian wine.

223

There is also a long tradition of confectionery making by the nuns, and many convents have their own specialties. They use marzipan to recreate mystic symbols such as the sacrificial lamb, the entrails of which are made out of the most exquisite candied fruits. Even today there are many convents, some of them founded as long ago as the twelfth and thirteenth centuries, that continue to make their confectionery just as they have always done. Thus, in these convents the long and extremely valuable traditions of confectionery making have been maintained continuously from the middle ages.

Spain has two interesting soft drinks: *granizado de limón* (iced lemon crush), a logical consequence of the plentiful supplies of lemons, and *horchata* (orgeat or tiger-nut milk). The taste of *horchata* may seem rather strange at first, and is definitely something that has to be acquired, but most people are soon hooked. It is a white, milky liquid with a marbly, grayish tinge and a starchy, earthy taste. The basic ingredient comes from a very strange tuber, similar to a small potato, less than half an inch (1 cm) in diameter, called the *chufa (Cyperus esculentus)*, which is cultivated only in one area of Valencia. *Horchata* is like a milk that has been drawn from the earth, and it has been used to feed a great many Spanish children. Nowadays, it is the most popular refreshment in summer, but sometimes is adulterated with other ingredients, ruining the flavor.

Café, Maestro Palmero (born 1901);
MUSEO PALMERO, BARCELONA
This café has a slightly Bohemian air — just the place to go, late, after the show. For this couple the night is probably just beginning; and what better start than with this apricot dessert accompanied by champagne.

Tilework (nineteenth century);
DECORATIVE ARTS MUSEUM, MADRID
It was important to take great care with preparation of desserts so that the meal should conclude happily. As an early nineteenth-century writer put it: "When the time comes to serve the dessert, it will be close at hand. These agreeable objects, after having diverted the eye, will thus crown the pleasure of the senses."

ICE CREAMS

To fully appreciate the pleasure of eating ice cream, we have to think back to what life was like before the invention of artificial ice. Nowadays there are refrigerators to produce ice, but before that it came only from the sky in the form of snow. This had to be collected and stored or, later, mined, all of which involved extremely hard labor just to provide a minute supply.

The geography of the Granada area is perfect for this industry, and the Arabs made the most of its advantages. It is not so far to travel from the highest peaks of the peninsula, the Sierra Nevada, right down to sea level; snow from the highest mountains could, therefore, be brought down with relative ease to the lowest areas of the province.

Madrid, the capital of the kingdom, also has the good fortune to be close to a mountain range. The first large storage pit would be dug out right in the middle of the snow field and throughout the winter the collectors deposited snow in the pit. It was compounded until its own weight turned it to ice and was then cut into blocks for transportation. On reaching the markets, the ice was stored again in shady pits provided in the city. Straw and cork were used to insulate the ice blocks.

The ice was mostly used for chilling drinks. Ice holders for bottles, called *enfri-adores*, are featured in the still-lifes by the eighteenth-century painter Meléndez. These are small cork cylinders with a lid and a central opening for the neck of the bottle; the ice was kept in the hollow inside.

In the seventeenth century, Doctor Matías de Porres gave an account of how the custom of using snow was fast taking hold in Spain. The expansion of the industry provided enough ice to supply all levels of society. As Matías de Porres said, "Everyone drinks with snow." Legend attributes the death of Prince Don Carlos at El Escorial Palace to poisoning, but the official version was always that he died of an excess of cold drinks. Even now, to back up this story, two snow pits are maintained, one

Still-life (detail), Juan van der Hamen y León (1596–1631);
ROYAL ACADEMY OF SAN FERNANDO, MADRID

for collecting snow on the highest mountain, and another for storage alongside the Friars' Garden at El Escorial.

The origin of ice cream in Spain can be traced back to when the *Alojeros*, who were drink manufacturers, obtained official permission to dispense "snow water," which was actually water chilled with snow, during the warm times of the year. The water was soon replaced by lemonade, sour cherry or cinnamon water and iced milk. These drinks were sometimes frozen to soft ice, which was the immediate antecedent of ice cream, and were called *garapiña*. With time, a distinction was made between sorbets without milk and ice cream with milk, which was made in different flavors and called *mantecado*.

Like the inhabitants of all Mediterranean countries, Spanish people are very fond of ice cream, which must have been the most sybaritic experience one could have had in a dry, hot country before the advent of refrigeration. Until very recently, the Levante region had a wonderful local ice-cream-making tradition, which operated with total disregard for modern industrial processes.

CHOCOLATE

The Spaniards discovered Aztec chocolate and brought it to Spain in 1520, subsequently introducing it to Europe. But they were not capable of developing its possibilities to the heights later achieved by the confectionery industry elsewhere in Europe. The Spaniards added sugar to the cocoa tablets, which was an important contribution, and later cinnamon and vanilla. The cocoa tablet was conceived not to be used raw, but for the sole purpose of being heated with water, resulting in thick, liquid hot chocolate. Archeological museums have examples of the *molinillo* — a kind of wooden whisk with an artichoke-shaped end-piece and diamond-shaped spikes — which was used by the Mexicans to help dissolve the chocolate and create froth just before serving. The more modern version sometimes also had a couple of loose rings to increase the effect.

Hot chocolate gradually changed in character as it became more widespread throughout Europe. Spain zealously guarded the secret of chocolate production as long as it could and maintained a monopoly on the supply of cocoa, which came from its American colonies. But, gradually, chocolate spread and was certainly known in Paris by the end of the seventeenth century, where a small volume was published in 1687 describing the "proper" use of tea, coffee and chocolate. The French replaced the water with milk. They also gave greater importance to the froth and added butter and cream, thus topping it with whiteness and creating a surprising cold touch that hid the dark soul underneath.

Over the years, *chocolate a la española* (Spanish chocolate) has caused a great deal of confusion. This Spanish version is the thickest hot chocolate possible. Aficionados check it is just right by tilting the cup for a few seconds to ensure that the contents are too thick to spill. Another test used to be the dipping of a particular kind of sponge cake, called *bizcocho de soletilla*, into the middle of the chocolate. The longer the cake remained upright, the better the chocolate. The Spaniards enjoyed this form of hot chocolate for centuries, and in Spanish literature it was always vaunted as a temptation to clergymen.

The generally excessive consumption of chocolate in all social circles caused a great deal of controversy. Various books canvassed opinions on the virtues and vices generated by chocolate. Antonio Colmenero de Ledesma was a Seville doctor who in 1631 published *Curioso Tratado de la Naturaleza y Calidad del Chocolate* (*Curious Treatise on the Nature and Quality of Chocolate*). Another book, by the Peruvian Antonio de León Pinelo, appeared in 1636, called *Questión Moral de si el Chocolate Quebranta el Ayuno Eclesiástico* (*Moral Question of Whether Chocolate Breaks the Ecclesiastical Fast*).

But chocolate has undergone something of a decline: consumption levels are not as excessive as they used to be. This has been brought about by a reduction in price due to more widespread and increased production, together with a progressive improvement in the means of transportation. Until this occurred, chocolate had been an expensive product, an item of value to be mentioned in people's wills. It was drunk from a special cup, called a *jícara*, which was very small and enabled the thick liquid to be consumed with no danger to health. The mistake was to try to drink the same chocolate in large tea cups, just because it had become much cheaper.

Hearing, or the allegory of autumn,
Miguel March (1638–70);
FINE ARTS MUSEUM, VALENCIA
Autumn symbolizes both maturity and decay. Like these fruits, the last of summer's fullness, everything has reached its peak and will begin to fade, just as the sounds of this boy's pipe fade on the oncoming winds of winter.

A serving of chocolate, Luis Meléndez (1716–80); PRADO MUSEUM, MADRID

The French could do this, with their much lighter mixture. But for the Spaniards, national pride made it difficult to maintain this new custom in the middle of the War of Independence, when they were resisting French armies. So the Spaniards therefore stubbornly went on insisting that "chocolate should be thick and everything else clear."

LIQUEURS

There is no doubt that liqueurs were one of the many products that alchemists obtained in their vain search for the philosopher's stone. The Arabs were expert distillers and were the first to make use of this process. The most specific date is provided by the mystic, saint and traveler Ramón Lull, who called alcohol the "fifth essence" when he obtained it for the first time towards the end of the thirteenth century.

Once the Spanish had managed to dissolve sugar in alcohol, by means of syrup, they obtained a drink they called *agua divina* (holy water) because of the extraordinary medicinal properties attributed to it. From then on, everything was very straightforward: the burning, sweet drink needed only the addition of the most appropriate juice or essence to turn it into some kind of liqueur.

Developments in the *aguardiente* (a spirituous liquor, usually made from grape) industry have historically occurred in the wine-producing areas. Galicia, which produces low-alcohol wines, has traditionally used its stills to distill *orujo*, a kind of clear brandy.

The most famous European liqueurs are made with herbs typical of alpine regions: Benedictine, Chartreuse and Grand Marnier are well known. For its part, Spain has only very small areas of alpine land in the Pyrenees, but has developed a range of aniseed-based, white liqueurs with various alcohol and sugar contents. *Orujo* and *cazalla* are extremely dry, with a barely discernible flavor. Owing to traditional bans on the private distillation of alcohol, these white liqueurs are sweetened and flavored by other manufacturers. The most popular is the dry *pacharán*, which is traditionally made with aniseed and sloes to produce a cheerful red color and a fresh flavor. There is a range of dry anisettes, with greater emphasis on the spicy flavor of the aniseed. The sweeter anisettes have a lower alcohol content.

The torrid heat of the summer led to the invention of a mixed drink, based on water and anisette and sweetened to taste, with a lovely iridescent white color. This drink, called *palomita* (little dove), became most popular in Madrid, coinciding with the summer festivals for the Virgin de la Paloma. The way of drinking it, sweetened with a kind of sugar that looks like pumice stone, gave its name to a *zarzuela* (musical comedy), *Agua, Azucarillos y Aguardiente* (*Water, Lemon Candy and Liqueur*).

The nuns and monks in convents and monasteries began creating their own liqueurs, and even though these brews did not usually achieve any great renown, people visiting them at least recognized the spirit of the order. Some people even experiment with their own potions at home, and even if the results are not that successful, at least it gives ordinary people a chance to dabble in alchemy.

During the sixteenth and seventeenth centuries, there were two drinks that were much in demand: *hipocras*, made from mature wine fortified with cinnamon, cloves, amber and sugar; and *carraspada*, made from watered-down wine, boiled honey and spices. *Carraspada* was considered to be medicinal, hence its widespread acceptance.

At the court, however, the most popular of all drinks was *aloja*. This refreshing drink was perhaps a legacy from the Arabs, who may in turn have derived it from hydromel. Hydromel was a drink based on water and honey, popular in ancient times. *Aloja*, similarly, consisted of a mixture of water with honey, flavored with spices such as cinnamon, ginger, pepper and nutmeg. It was drunk at the royal palace, by the aristocracy, and by ordinary people, too. The towns were full of establishments called *alojerías*, where it was sold in varying degrees of quality, but always cold. When it was chilled with snow and ice, it was called *aloja de nieve*.

Although it may seem overly simple, one of the perennially favorite drinks of the Spaniards has been clear water from the fountain, nice and cold. There have always been street sellers hawking their refreshing wares through the towns: frozen water, fresh as snow! Such scenes always drew the attention of people traveling around the peninsula, and in the nineteenth century the French writer Théophile Gautier was one who was moved to comment on this aspect of Spanish life, in his book *Journey through Spain*.

The chocolate-drinking (detail), tile from the Marquis of Castellvell's house in Alella, Barcelona (1710);
CERAMICS MUSEUM, BARCELONA
By the eighteenth century chocolate-drinking virtually attained the status of a cult, complete with the trappings of ceremonious ostentation, at least among the fashionably well-off. Some of this flavor comes through in this vignette of bewigged gentlemen, on bended knee, proffering their ladies cups of the precious beverage.

Santiago almond cake

SANTIAGO ALMOND CAKE

Tarta de Santiago   Serves 4–6

Although the period of Arab rule in Spain had little effect on Galicia, the region boasts numerous sweet dishes of Mediterranean and eastern origin, such as this almond and egg-yolk cake often decorated with the cross of Saint James, the symbol of the pilgrimage to Santiago de Compostela.

4 eggs
3½ oz (100 g) butter, at room temperature
¾ cup (6 oz/185 g) sugar
¾ cup (3 oz/90 g) all-purpose (plain) flour
1 tablespoon baking soda (bicarbonate of soda)

¾ cup (6 fl oz/185 ml) water
2 cups (10 oz/315 g) raw almonds, ground
zest (rind) of 1 lemon
confectioners' (icing) sugar for decorating

Preheat the oven to 325°F (170°C/Gas 3).

Beat the eggs with the butter and sugar. Beat in the flour and baking soda, gradually adding the water. Add the ground almonds and lemon zest.

Grease a 9 in (25 cm) round cake pan and pour in the mixture.

Bake for 30–35 minutes. Prick with a long needle to check whether it is cooked. If it comes out clean, the cake is ready.

Remove from the oven, allow to cool, then turn out of the pan.

Draw a cross or other design on a piece of cardboard and cut it out. Place on the cake, then sprinkle all over the top with confectioners' sugar. Lift off the cardboard carefully, taking care not to spoil the edges of the design.

ANISEED COOKIES

Tortas de anís   Makes 8 small cookies

Andalusia has been described as a vast sweet olive grove, exuding the aromas of cinnamon, syrup, aniseed, sesame, sugar and toasted almonds. Every village has its own sweet recipes. Everybody loves *tortas de anís*, which are made by the most highly regarded confectioners and are characterized by sulfurized paper wrappers. Although the commercially produced ones are delicious, these cookies are very quick and easy to make at home.

¼ cup (2 fl oz/60 ml) olive oil
¼ cup (2 fl oz/60 ml) beer
1 tablespoon dry anisette liqueur (similar to grappa)
1 teaspoon salt
1 cup (4 oz/125 g) all-purpose (plain) flour

6 tablespoons sesame seeds
6 tablespoons aniseeds
⅔ cup (5 oz/155 g) sugar

Preheat the oven to 400°F (200°C/Gas 6).

Put the oil, beer, anisette and salt in a large bowl. Add the flour gradually. Mix to a dough with your hands.

Knead the dough roughly on a work surface, then divide into 8 pieces.

Flour the work surface and roll out the pieces, starting in the center and working outward, to form very thin rounds.

Sprinkle on the sesame seeds, aniseeds and sugar.

Roll again to stick the seeds firmly into the dough, then trim the edges and transfer to a baking sheet.

Bake for 8 minutes, watching in case they burn.

When the cookies are almost ready, put them under the broiler (grill) for 2 minutes to caramelize the sugar.

Remove from the baking sheet immediately.

Aniseed cookies

231

NUNS' SIGHS

Suspiros de monja   Makes 24

This is a good example of how the nuns in convents devised imaginative recipes for delicious cakes which were traditionally given to donors to thank them for their generosity.

6½ oz (200 g) lard
2 cups (13 oz/410 g) sugar
zest (rind) of 1 lemon
2¼ cups (18 fl oz/500 ml) water
8 cups (2 lb/1 kg) all-purpose (plain) flour

5 eggs, beaten
olive oil, for deep-frying
confectioners' (icing) sugar, for dusting

Heat the lard, sugar, lemon zest and water. Cook over low heat, adding the flour gradually and stirring constantly. Cook the mixture until it comes away easily from the bottom of the pan.

Stir the eggs into the mixture.

Roll out on a flat surface and cut into squares. Fry in plenty of hot oil in several batches. Drain on paper towels and sprinkle with the confectioners' sugar.

Nuns' sighs (left); syrup-coated buns (right)

The Plandiura family, Ricardo Canals (1876–1931); ART GALLERY, BARCELONA
Salvador Dali recalls that, at the age of 7, he used to visit a neighboring family, where "every day at about six, around a monumental table in a drawing room a group of fascinating creatures would sit and take *maté*" (South American herbal tea). "I would in turn sip the tepid liquid, which to me was sweeter than honey."

SYRUP-COATED BUNS

Almojábanas   Makes 16

*A*lmojábanas are of Arab origin, and variations of the original recipe are still made in different regions of Spain. They are mentioned in *Libro de Guisados* (1520) by Rupert de Nola, who calls them *taronges de Xàtiva*. The buns were originally cheese-based, but the recipe has changed over the centuries.

1⅔ cups (13 fl oz/410 ml) water
¾ cup (6½ fl oz/200 ml) olive oil
2 tablespoons sugar
4 cups (1 lb/500 g) all-purpose (plain) flour
6 eggs

Syrup:
2¾ cups (22 fl oz/600 ml) water
2½ cups (1 lb/500 g) sugar
zest (rind) of 1 lemon

Preheat the oven to 300°F (150°C/Gas 2).
    Heat the water with the oil and sugar. When it comes to a boil, remove from the heat and add the flour all at once.

    Stir well with a wooden spoon to avoid lumps and put back on very low heat, stirring constantly, until the mixture comes away from the sides. Remove from the heat, allow to cool a little, then add the eggs 1 at a time. Wait for each egg to be completely absorbed before adding the next. The dough should be thick but not hard.

    Grease a baking sheet with oil. Use 2 spoons to transfer blobs of the dough. Grease your finger and make a hole in the center of each one.

    Bake for 20–25 minutes until golden.

    Meanwhile, make the syrup by heating the water and dissolving the sugar. When it boils, add the lemon zest and cook for 5 minutes.

    When the buns have cooled, dip into the hot syrup and arrange on a platter. Serve cold.

ORANGE GATEAU

Tarta de naranja   Serves 6

This is a specialty of Valencia, a homage to the exuberance of the *huerta*, where the orange groves provide a series of sensuous delights throughout the year: bright green leaves, intoxicating orange blossoms — very popular for bridal bouquets — and the bittersweet fruit which is used in a wide variety of cakes and pastries.

Cake mixture:

3½ oz (100 g) butter
2 cups (8 oz/250 g) all-purpose (plain) flour
2 egg yolks
¼ cup (2 oz/60 g) sugar
1 pinch salt

Filling:

juice of 3 oranges
⅞ cup (6½ oz/200 g) sugar
2 oz (60 g) butter, melted
5 eggs, beaten

Decoration:

1 orange
¼ cup (2 oz/60 g) sugar
1 cup (8 fl oz/250 ml) water

Syrup:

2 teaspoons orange juice
2 teaspoons water
¼ cup (2 oz/60 g) sugar

Valencian procession, Joaquín Sorolla (1863–1923);
SPANISH SOCIETY, NEW YORK
The painting depicts a religious Valencian procession, possibly for corpus Christie.

Orange gateau

Preheat the oven to 350°F (180°C/Gas 4).

Make the cake mixture by cutting the butter into small pieces and mixing with the flour. Add the egg yolks, sugar and salt. Mix thoroughly to form a light, moldable mixture.

Grease a 10–12 in (25–30 cm) pan with a removable base with butter, then line it with the mixture.

For the filling, mix the orange juice with the sugar, melted butter and beaten eggs. Heat in a bain-marie to thicken, stirring continuously with a wooden spoon, then pour into the cake pan.

Bake for 20 minutes. Remove and allow to cool.

For the decoration, wash the orange and cut into thin slices without peeling. Cook in a saucepan with the water and sugar until soft but not disintegrating. Remove and drain.

Make the syrup by heating the orange juice, water and sugar together for 5 minutes.

Arrange the orange slices on the cake and pour the syrup over the top.

Almond cake

ALMOND CAKE

Tortada de almendra   Serves 8–10

The utmost care goes into preparing this pie from Alicante, which really is a work of art. The ground almonds are usually untoasted and unpeeled, lending a certain primitive touch to this highly refined recipe. The pie is usually decorated with meringue, which is often colored pink.

12 eggs, separated
1¾ cups (12 oz/375 g) sugar
2¼ cups (12 oz/375 g) ground almonds
zest (rind) of 1 lemon
½ cup (2 oz/60 g) all-purpose (plain) flour
ground cinnamon
confectioners' (icing) sugar

Syrup (optional):
¾ cup (6½ fl oz/200 ml) water
½ cup (3½ oz/100 g) sugar

Preheat the oven to 250°F (130°C/Gas ½).

Beat the eggwhites until very stiff, gradually adding the sugar. Stir in the yolks, then gradually add the ground almonds, lemon zest and flour. Mix thoroughly.

Line a 15 in (37 cm) round mold with baking parchment (paper) and fill with the mixture. Bake for approximately 1 hour.

Prick with a thick needle to check that it is cooked; the needle should come out clean when it is done.

Remove from the oven and leave to cool. Turn out of the mold and sprinkle with ground cinnamon and confectioners' sugar.

If you prefer, make a light syrup by heating the water with the sugar for 5 minutes, until the sugar has dissolved. Allow to cool. Carefully prick the surface of the pie and sprinkle with the cold syrup.

235

DIAMOND MERINGUE CAKE

Punta de diamante   Serves 6–8

This sumptuous dessert is typically eaten at Easter in the Valencia region. The meringue topping is shaped to resemble a diamond. The filling is traditionally obtained from the cucurbit plant (squash or calabash), the flesh of which is split into fine strands, called "angel hair" in Spanish.

Sponge:

4 eggs, separated
½ cup (3½ oz/100 g) sugar
1 cup (4 oz/125 g) all-purpose (plain) flour
1 teaspoon baking soda (bicarbonate of soda)
butter, for greasing

Custard filling:

8 egg yolks
1¼ cups (8 oz/250 g) sugar

Meringue:

8 eggwhites
1¼ cups (8 oz/250 g) sugar

Filling:

1½ cups (12 oz/375 g) candied squash or
  canned candied yams (sweet potatoes)

Preheat the oven to 400°F (200°C/Gas 6).

To prepare the sponge, beat the eggwhites very briskly, gradually adding the sugar.

Mix the flour with the baking soda and sift. Blend gradually with the eggwhites.

Beat the yolks a little and add to the mixture.

Grease a round 12 in (30 cm) cake pan with butter and fill with the sponge mixture.

Bake for 10 minutes, then allow to cool and turn out of the pan.

To prepare the custard filling, heat the 8 egg yolks with the sugar over very low heat, whisking vigorously to thicken.

Remove from the heat.

To make the meringue, beat the eggwhites until very stiff, gradually adding the sugar. The meringue must be very smooth.

Place the sponge in an ovenproof dish and spread with the candied squash, followed by the custard. Top with the meringue and form into a point with flat sides to resemble a diamond. Sprinkle lightly with sugar and bake for a few minutes until golden.

Allow to cool before serving.

Still-life, Luis Meléndez (1716–80); PRADO MUSEUM, MADRID

COCONUT PUFFS

Pastelitos de coco   Serves 4–6

The coconut palm grows in abundance on the coasts of the warm regions of Asia, Africa and America. According to José de Acosta in *Historia Natural de Las Indias*, it existed in Puerto Rico in the sixteenth century. Hernández, his contemporary, called it by the non-native name used by the Mexicans, *coyolli*, and Oviedo also included it in his descriptions. We do not know how these little golden mouthfuls first came to be introduced into Spanish cuisine, but they are still very popular. It is often the first sweet recipe children learn to make and they love the intense aroma which emanates from the oven as the puffs are baking. On the beaches of the south in summer, salesmen walk along shouting the local name for them, "*Sultanas, sultanas!*"

3 small eggs, beaten
1¼ cups (8 oz/250 g) sugar
2⅔ cups (8 oz/250 g) shredded (desiccated)
  coconut
oil, for greasing

Preheat the oven to 300°F (150°C/Gas 2).

Mix the beaten eggs with the sugar and coconut.

Grease a baking sheet with oil and spoon on blobs of the mixture.

Bake for 20 minutes until golden.

Diamond meringue cake (left); coconut puffs (right)

FRIED ANISEED PASTRIES

Pestiños   Makes about 50 small pastı

These fried pastries are extremely popular. Sometimes flavored with aniseed, sometimes with sweet wine or cinnamon, they are always bathed in a honey syrup. Each region has its own particular version, but all use a very fine dough which is rolled up and folded before frying. The pastries are eaten with hot chocolate for breakfast or afternoon tea and are also made in larger quantities for family celebrations.

zest (rind) of 1 lemon
⅓ cup (3 fl oz/90 ml) mild-flavored olive oil
2 tablespoons (½ oz/15 g) aniseeds
⅓ cup (3 fl oz/90 ml) dry white wine
2½ cups (10 oz/315 g) all-purpose (plain) flour
olive oil, for deep-frying
1 cup (8 oz/250 g) runny honey
confectioners' (icing) sugar

Heat the oil with the lemon zest. Remove from the heat and take out the zest, then add the aniseeds and allow to cool.

When the oil is cold, pour it into a bowl and add the wine and flour. Blend well to form a smooth dough, then turn out onto a floured surface. Allow to rest for 30 minutes.

Roll the dough out thinly. Cut into 4 × 2½ in (10 × 6 cm) rectangles. Roll up, starting from one of the corners, to form wide, flat cylinders.

Dip your fingers in cold water and press down the edges to seal, so that the pastries will keep their shape when fried.

Fry a few at a time in plenty of hot oil. Drain well and allow to cool.

Heat the honey with a little water, bringing to a boil very slowly. Pour over the aniseed pastries. Drain on a rack, sprinkle with confectioners' sugar and serve.

ALMOND BRITTLE

Turrón de guirlache   Makes 24

Turrón is made from almonds and honey and is clearly of Jewish and Arab origin. It is sometimes flavored with aniseed, especially in Aragón. A dispute has been going on between Catalonia and Alicante for hundreds of years over who actually invented it, on the basis of documents and events dated between the fourteenth and sixteenth centuries. *Turrón* is the Christmas candy *par excellence* and is sent all over the world

at this time of year to ease the homesickness of all those Spaniards unable to spend the holiday with their families.

2½ cups (1 lb/500 g) sugar
a few drops lemon juice
3 cups (1 lb/500 g) raw almonds, peeled
2 tablespoons sweet almond oil

Heat the sugar in a (preferably) copper pan or any heavy pan with a few drops of lemon juice. Stir gently with a spatula so it will dissolve thoroughly and not stick to the sides of the pan.

When it has completely dissolved, add the almonds and stir until golden. Grease a marble slab with the sweet almond oil, then pour on the contents of the pan. Grease a rolling pin with almond oil and roll out to a thickness of ½ in (1.5 cm).

Before it cools completely, cut into 1¼ × 4 in (3 × 10 cm) strips.

Fried aniseed pastries (top); almond brittle (left); peaches with meringue topping (right)

PEACHES WITH MERINGUE TOPPING

Melocotónes con merengue   Serves 4

Peaches are one of the fruits which herald the arrival of summer and reflect the plenty and warmth of the season. The best peaches in Spain are grown in Aragón. The rich taste is perfectly complemented in this dish by the airy touch of the meringue, contrasted in turn with the dates, which are reminiscent of sultrier climes.

2¼ cups (18 fl oz/500 ml) water

¼ cup (4 oz/125 g) sugar

4 large peaches, peeled and halved with the pits removed

1 tablespoon (½ oz/15 g) butter

3½ oz (100 g) dates, finely chopped

Meringue:

2 eggwhites

1 pinch salt

¾ cup (4 oz/125 g) confectioners' (icing) sugar

Preheat the oven to 400°F (200°C/Gas 6).

Heat the water in a large saucepan. Dissolve the sugar. Bring to a boil and cook for 2 minutes.

Poach the peaches in this syrup for 10 minutes, turning them over and coating with the syrup occasionally.

Soften the butter and mix with the dates.

Drain the peaches, transfer to a baking dish and fill the centers with the date mixture.

For the meringue, beat the eggwhites with a pinch of salt until stiff. Gradually add the confectioners' sugar to form meringue. Spoon the mixture onto the peaches, making decorative peaks.

Bake for 10 minutes until golden.

A large dresser (1961), Antonio Lopez; PRIVATE COLLECTION

CREAMY RICE PUDDING

Crema de arroz   Serves 4–6

In *Libro de Guisados* (1520), the writer Ruperto de Nola says, "Of all the foods there are in the world, the main ones and the best are these three: turkey sauce, *mirrauste* [a sauce made of milk, almonds, breadcrumbs, sugar and cinnamon] and blancmange, which should each receive a royal crown, because generally they are the cream of all the others and especially of the common sauces." One of his versions of this dish is called "blancmange for invalids who cannot eat anything." It is a very old recipe, featured in all European medieval and Renaissance recipe books. Given the Arab origins of rice and sugar, and the plentiful supply of almonds in Spain, it would not be surprising to find that the recipe originally came from Spain as researchers on Medieval Catalan and Arab cookbooks have claimed.

1½ cups (8 oz/250 g) almonds, peeled
4 cups (1 qt/1 l) water
7½ teaspoons (¾ oz/20 g) cornstarch (cornflour)
1¼ cups (6½ oz/200 g) rice flour
zest (rind) of 1 lemon
1 stick cinnamon
2 cups (13 oz/410 g) sugar
1 pinch salt

Wash the almonds, then purée them in a blender with the water. Press through a piece of cheesecloth or other fine cloth and squeeze thoroughly to obtain the almond milk.

Dissolve the cornstarch and rice flour with half the almond milk. Heat the rest of the almond milk with the lemon zest, cinnamon, sugar and salt. Add the dissolved cornstarch and rice flour and stir continuously with a wooden spoon until smooth.

Pour into individual glass molds and serve well chilled.

CATALAN CUSTARD

Crema catalana   Serves 4–6

This is a delicious, traditional dessert with a very smooth texture, providing a sharp contrast with the caramelized sugar which decorates the surface. The custard is even nicer if made with free-range eggs and dairy milk.

½ cup (2 oz/60 g) cornstarch (cornflour)
4 cups (1 qt/1 l) milk
1 stick cinnamon
zest (rind) of ½ lemon (yellow part only)
6 egg yolks
1¼ cups (10 oz/315 g) sugar

Dissolve the cornstarch in 1 cup (8 fl oz/250 ml) of the milk.

Heat the rest of the milk in a deep pan with the cinnamon and lemon zest. Bring to a boil.

Meanwhile, blend the egg yolks with 1 cup (8 oz/250 g) of the sugar.

Strain the boiled milk through a fine sieve, then pour over the egg mixture. Add the dissolved cornstarch, mix well and heat again gently, stirring constantly in one direction. Do not allow to boil as the mixture might separate.

When it thickens, remove from the heat and strain again through a fine sieve. Transfer to a serving dish or individual bowls. When the mixture has cooled completely, heat a salamander (or metal spatula) over a naked flame or hot griddle until red hot. Sprinkle the remaining sugar over the custard and quickly caramelize with the salamander before the sugar is absorbed, to form a thin, firm caramel layer.

Creamy rice pudding (top); Catalan custard (bottom)

The lemon, Juan Gris (1887–1927); PRIVATE COLLECTION, MADRID
The lemon itself is a classical Spanish theme in art and, in placing the glass at its side, perhaps Gris was remembering the sharp, refreshing taste of *granizado de limón*.

RICH EGG CRÈME CARAMEL

Tocino de cielo   Serves 6–8

Sweet dishes based on egg yolks and sugar — sometimes in the form of a syrup — are of Arab origin. *Tocino de cielo* originated from the sherry-making cellars of Jerez, where beaten eggwhites were used to clarify the wines. The leftover yolks were usually offered to the nuns at the convents and were used to make a great variety of delicacies.

> To make a plate of beaten eggs, make a syrup from a pound of sugar, and beat twenty and four egg yolks, and put the sugar where it will cook very quick; then add all the eggs together in the syrup, in such a way that the syrup comes up above all the eggs, and thus make the ball of beaten eggs; and if you like, serve them in the pot, or put them on a plate with some pancakes, or some slices of bread, or otherwise in bowls, and decorate with some preserves.
>
> Francisco Martínez Montiño, *Arte de Cocina, Pastelería, Vizcochería y Conservería*, 1611

2 cups (16 oz/500 g) sugar
1⅔ cups (13 fl oz/410 ml) water
12 egg yolks
1 egg

Preheat the oven to 300°F (150°C/Gas 2).

Dissolve 1¾ cups (14 oz/440 g) of the sugar slowly in the water over low heat. When a syrup has formed, cook for a further 10 minutes, then leave to cool.

Put the rest of the sugar in a 10 in (25 cm) shallow, round metal mold and heat until it caramelizes.

Beat the egg yolks with the whole egg, then strain through a fine sieve into the cold syrup. Pour this mixture into the mold, cover with aluminum foil and bake in a bain-marie in the oven for approximately 30 minutes.

Prick with a thick needle to check that it is cooked. The needle should come out clean.

Allow to cool. Turn the caramel out of the mold and serve.

ROYAL CAKE

Torta real Serves 6–8

The effects of Moorish influences on Spanish cuisine are reflected by the widespread use of almonds, eggs and cinnamon in recipes which are traditionally prepared for local festivals and religious celebrations. This is perhaps due to the fact that nuns in cloistered orders have always used old recipes in their cooking. The nuns offered these elaborate cakes and candies to almsgivers to show their gratitude to the people who made their frugal existence possible. Travelers in Andalusia will still find these cakes at certain convents.

12 eggs, beaten
2½ cups (1 lb/500 g) sugar
9 cups (2 lb/1 kg) ground almonds
zest (rind) of 1 lemon
confectioners' (icing) sugar and ground cinnamon, for dusting

Preheat the oven to 300°F (150°C/Gas 2).

Mix the beaten eggs with the sugar, then gradually add the ground almonds, followed by the lemon zest.

Line a 15 in (37 cm) round mold with brown paper. Grease with a little oil, then pour in the egg mixture.

Bake for 45 minutes. Remove from the oven and allow to cool. Turn out of the mold and sprinkle with confectioners' sugar and cinnamon to serve.

Rich egg crème caramel (left); royal cake (right)

Chocolate-drinking (detail), tile from the Marquis of Castellvell's house in Alella, Barcelona (1710); CERAMICS MUSEUM, BARCELONA
Entitled "Banquet of the high bourgeoisie," this is a section of the tilework on the subject of chocolate-drinking. It further emphasizes the class rituals and images of wealth that surrounded chocolate at this time. This was especially so in Barcelona, fast becoming the great center for chocolate production in Spain. After the opening of the first chocolate mill there in 1654, consumption rapidly increased during the following century. In one 40-year period the number of chocolate-makers increased sixfold and, this was the type of lifestyle they aspired to, made rich by the demand for their products.

ICED COFFEE CRUSH

Granizado de café   Serves 4–6

Granizado de café was all the rage back in the thirties. At the counters of cafés and casinos, at the tables in parks, alongside the bandstands, drinking a *granizado* was regarded as a risqué sign of modernity. It can be mixed with lemon crush and is then called *mazagran*.

3⅓ cups (27 fl oz/750 ml) strong coffee, made by brewing 8 cups (2 qt/2 l) water with 8 oz (250 g) ground coffee (half light, half dark roast), hot
1½ cups (10 oz/315 g) sugar
1 small piece lemon zest (rind) (optional)

Dissolve the sugar in the coffee. Add a little lemon zest if desired, then cover and allow to cool.

When it has cooled completely, remove the lemon zest and transfer to an ice-cream maker to turn into crushed ice. Alternatively, put in the freezer and stir frequently with a fork when it starts to freeze (although the texture will not be the same). Repeat this operation 4 or 5 times.

Spoon into chilled glasses just before serving.

CREAMY CINNAMON ICE CREAM

Mantecado   Serves 4–6

Of all the milk-based ice creams, *mantecado* is the true classic, the oldest and the best-loved in Spain. It combines very well with other flavors, such as strawberry or chocolate. When a scoop of *mantecado* is served in a glass with *granizado de café* (iced coffee crush), it is called a *blanco y negro* ("white and black"). It is very popular in sidewalk cafés throughout Spain.

4 cups (1 qt/1 l) milk
1 small piece lemon zest (rind)
1 small cinnamon stick
6 egg yolks
1½ cups (10 oz/315 g) sugar

Heat half the milk in a pan with the lemon zest and cinnamon. Remove from the heat.

Beat the yolks with the other half of the milk and mix in the sugar. Add to the pan and heat again until the milk thickens, but do not allow to boil. Stir continuously with a wooden spoon.

Remove the lemon zest and cinnamon stick.

Allow to cool, then chill in the freezer until smooth and creamy.

Iced coffee crush (left); creamy cinnamon ice cream (right)

ICED LEMON CRUSH

Granizado de limón   Serves 4–6

In the sixteenth century it was customary to use snow to chill fruit drinks, wine and water. On the tables of the well-to-do, digestive sorbets and ice creams were served halfway through the meal to cleanse the palate between the various spicy dishes. In the course of the seventeenth and eighteenth centuries, the fashion for cold drinks snowballed. In *Don Quixote*, Cervantes relates how things could not be all that bad in a peasant's house, because "his wife, while making her way through a pound of wine, had an overflowing jug of delicate snow drinks at her side, as well as perfumes, flowers, song and music."

Many documents of the time mention the convenience of cold drinks and give detailed descriptions of suitable containers for this practice.

> To make twelve glasses of lemonade you need a large lemon and a pound of sugar. You make it in the following way: peel the lemon as if it were an apple; when it is peeled, cut it up and put it in the mortar. Pound it well and when it is almost ready, add sugar and finish mashing it. Take a bottle which will hold the twelve glasses of water, and mix what is in the mortar with the water, for it to take on the lemon taste. Strain it twice.
>
> Bring it out in the afternoon, after a good lunch, particularly in midsummer, as it refreshes the body.
>
> Fray Sever de Olot, *Libro de Arte de Cocina*, 1787

zest (rind) and juice of 3 lemons
4 cups (1 qt/1 l) water
⅞ cup (6½ oz/200 g) sugar

Iced lemon crush

Creamy ice milk

Heat the lemon zest in ¾ cup (6½ fl oz/200 ml) of water for 5 minutes.

Strain, then add the rest of the water, lemon juice and sugar.

Transfer to an ice-cream maker to turn into crushed ice. Alternatively, chill in the freezer (although the texture will not be the same). Stir frequently with a fork to prevent it from setting hard.

CREAMY ICE MILK

Leche merengada   Serves 4–6

The practice of making iced drinks began in the seventeenth century, when snow was used to chill liquids in containers known as *garrafas* or *garapiñeras*, the precursors of modern freezers. Tradesmen prepared different iced combinations, using milk, lemons, sour cherries, cinnamon or chocolate. Although it is virtually an ice cream, *leche merengada* is nowadays not served as a dessert after meals but as a refreshing drink in open air cafés.

4 cups (1 qt/1 ¹) milk
1½ cups (10 oz/315 g) sugar
1 piece lemon zest (rind)
2 eggwhites
ground cinnamon

Heat the milk with the sugar and lemon zest, stirring frequently to dissolve the sugar and prevent sticking. Boil for 2 minutes, then take off the heat and allow to cool.

When it has cooled completely, strain through a fine sieve and chill in the freezer until it starts to set.

Beat the eggwhites until stiff, then blend into the mixture.

Chill again. It should be creamy and slightly crystallized.

Sprinkle with cinnamon and serve.

Tiger nut orgeat

TIGER NUT ORGEAT

Horchata de chufas   Serves 4–6

At the end of spring the people of Valencia and Alicante travel the length and breadth of the country to sell their local production of *horchata de chufas, granizado de limón* and iced barley water. The famous *horchaterías*, where this drink is made and sold, are transformed into shops selling fig bread with almonds, mats, pottery and blinds at the end of the season.

Horchata can also be made from almonds or rice. Sometimes, as an extra-nourishing treat for the children, it is made of all three ingredients — tiger nuts, almonds and rice — mixed with sugar and flavored with lemon. It is very tasty indeed and is a great pick-me-up, served either crushed or as a very cold, smooth liquid, and is often accompanied by a sweet bun called a *fartón*. It can be drunk at any time of day or night in hot weather, either outdoors at a sidewalk café or in the cool, shady *horchaterías*.

8 oz (250 g) tiger nuts (or almonds)

4 cups (1 qt/1 l) water

1¼ cups (8 oz/250 g) sugar for making crushed ice (use only ⅔ cup/5 oz/155 g if making liquid orgeat)

lemon zest (rind) and whole cinnamon stick (optional)

Wash the tiger nuts and discard any blemished ones. Soak in water for 12 hours. Rinse twice and pick over them again.

Grind in the blender with 1⅔ cups (13 fl oz/410 ml) of water. Let stand for 2 hours.

Strain through a cloth filter in small amounts, gradually adding the remaining water. Add the sugar and stir to dissolve, then, if desired, add a little lemon zest (rind) and cinnamon.

Turn into crushed ice using an ice cream maker or serve very cold.

248

SPANISH THICK HOT CHOCOLATE

Chocolate a la española   Serves 4

Hot chocolate — a traditional drink of the Aztecs and other Mexican peoples — first came to Spain by means of religious orders at the beginning of the Conquest. It has been arousing passionate emotions since the seventeenth century. Many writers have extolled its virtues, such as Dr Cárdenas, who wrote from Mexico in 1606: "What a benefit chocolate is, whether or not it is a healthy drink." A surgeon, Ledesma, published *Tratado de la naturaleza y calidad del chocolate* in Spain in 1631, giving healthy and explanatory prescriptions.

Hot chocolate came to be sold on street stalls and in shops and candy stores, and was very popular with women who claimed it had aphrodisiacal and energy-giving properties. In fact, it aroused as much controversy as its contemporary, tobacco. It became established as a nutritious drink and was also used as an ingredient in cakes throughout European salons. It was originally highly seasoned with all sorts of strong spices, but this version was soon modified to achieve a milder flavor. Nowadays it is served almost nostalgically at breakfasts and afternoon teas on special occasions. *Chocolate a la española* is thick and traditionally drunk from cups called *jicaras* or from the traditional shape called *mancerina*.

10–12 oz (315–375 g) semisweet chocolate, grated
2¼ cups (18 fl oz/500 ml) water
1 teaspoon cornstarch (cornflour), dissolved in a little cold water

Heat the grated chocolate with the water in a saucepan. Stir to mix thoroughly. When it comes to a boil, add the dissolved cornstarch. Bring back to a boil 3 times, whisking vigorously and removing from the heat each time it starts to bubble to prevent the mixture from boiling over.

Ladle into cups from a suitable height to make it nice and frothy.

Spanish thick hot chocolate

AROMATIC HERB LIQUEUR

Licor de hierbas   Makes 4 cups (1 qt/1 l)
aromaticas

The Arab secret of distilling wine was taken up by the Spanish humanists Arnaldo de Vilanova and Ramón Lull. They worked to improve the technique and finally managed to make the long-anticipated *aqua vitae*, which was so strong that people called it *aqua ardens*. Being from the Mediterranean, both men valued the extraordinary concentration of essential oils contained in the aromatic plants which grew locally on the dry land. They decided to add these herbs to their *aguardiente* both to disguise its awful taste and to take advantage of their medicinal value. As well as a curative balsam, it became a refined drink. It is still very popular and highly esteemed and is often made at home for family consumption.

3 sprigs thyme
3 sprigs rosemary
3 sprigs savory
1 sprig lemon verbena
6 sage leaves
6 mint leaves
2¼ cups (18 fl oz/600 ml) dry anisette liquer
2¼ cups (18 fl oz/600 ml) sweet anisette liqueur
peel of ½ orange, washed, dried and cut into strips

Put the herbs, without washing them, in a dry sterilized jar. Add the 2 kinds of anisette and the orange peel. Seal and macerate for 2 months in a cool, dark place.

Filter through a cloth sieve, then pour into a bottle with a couple of sprigs of herbs inside and put the top on.

ROSE PETAL LIQUEUR

Licor de petalos   Makes 3⅓ cups (27 fl oz/750 ml)
de rosas

The most noteworthy Arab alchemists, including the philosophers Avicenna (eleventh century) and Averroës (twelfth century), used to distill wine to obtain alcohol. Their writings mention the distillation of rose water, spikenard and many perfumes.

In Valencia roses are one of the basic pleasures of everyday life, decorating gardens, parks and balconies. During local festivals millions of rose petals float through the air, a symbol of gay abandon and good cheer. Rose petals are therefore the obvious choice as the essential ingredient in one of the favorite local drinks and are also used in cakemaking.

Still-life with fruit, Juan de Espinosa (early seventeenth century); PRADO MUSEUM, MADRID
Grapes hanging like this recall the method used to create one of the most exquisite grape-products — *lagrimas*. This is a wine from Malaga made out of the "tears" (*lagrimas*), or moisture that naturally drips from bunches of ripe grapes suspended to dry in the sun.

8 oz (250 g) insecticide-free fragrant red rose petals (about 24 roses)
2½ cups (13 oz/410 g) confectioners' (icing) sugar with 6 drops vanilla extract (essence) added
1 cup (8 fl oz/250 ml) water
24 insecticide-free rose-scented geranium leaves
1 teaspoon cilantro (coriander) seeds
2¼ cups (18 fl oz/600 ml) orujo (similar to marc or grappa)

Trim the roses around the calyx, removing the white part of the petals.

Make a syrup by dissolving the sugar in the water over low heat for 5 minutes. Add the rose and geranium petals and the cilantro seeds. Cook over low heat for another 5 minutes, then remove from the heat, cover and leave to cool.

Pour into a sterilized jar, add the *orujo* and stir. Seal and store in a cool, dark place for 1 month.

After this time the liqueur is ready to be filtered and bottled.

Aromatic herb liqueur (left); rose petal liqueur (right)

BIBLIOGRAPHY

Alonso, J. C. *La cocina de Sevilla en su salsa (The Cuisine of Seville "in its Element")* Seville: Algaida, 1988

Andrews, C. *Cocina Catalana (Catalan Cuisine)* Barcelona: Martinez Roca, 1989

Aragonés Subero, A. *Castronomía de Guadalajara (Gastronomy of Guadalajara)* Guadalajara: Marqués de Santillana Cultural Institution, 1973

Bolens, L. *La cuisine andalouse: un art de vivre XI–XIII ème siècle (Andalusian Cuisine: A Way of Living, 11th–13th Century)* Paris: Albin Michel, 1990

Capel, J. C. *Comer en Andalucía (Eating in Andalusia)* Madrid: Penthalon, 1981

Capel, J. C. *Pícaros, ollas, inquisidores y monjes (Scoundrels, Stewpots, Inquisitors and Monks)* Barcelona: Argos Vergara, 1985

Carbajo, M. J. & García, G-Ochoa, L. *Los dulces de las monjas de Castilla y León (The Confectionery of the Nuns of Castile and Leon)* Toledo: Castille and León Regional Council, 1988

Castroviejo, J. M. & Cunqueiro, A. *Viajes por los montes y chimeneas de Galicia (Journeys through the Mountains and Chimneys of Galicia)* Madrid: Espasa Calpe, 1962

Culinary Talks at the Menéndez y Pelayo International University 1981–82, Barcelona: Tusquets, 1982

Crosby, A. W. *The Columbian Exchange* Westport: Greenword Press, 1972

Cunqueiro, A. *A cociña galega (Galician Cuisine)* Vigo: Galaxia, 1973

Davidson, A. *Mediterranean Seafood* London: Allen Lane, 1981

Defourneaux, M. *La vida cotidiana en la España del Siglo de Oro (Everyday Life in the Spain of the Golden Age)* Barcelona: Argos Vergara, 198

Diaz Párraga, M. A. *Comer en Murcia (Eating in Murcia)* Madrid: Penthalon, 1982

Domingo, E. *Comer en mi Castilla (Eating in My Castille)* Madrid: Penthalon, 1980

Domingo, X. *La mesa del Buscón (The Swindler's Table)* Barcelona: Tusquets, 1981

Domingo, X. *De la olla al mole (From "olla" to "mole")* Madrid: ICI, 1984

Elexpuru, I. & Serrano, M. *Al Andalus — Magia y seducción culinarias (Al Andalus — Culinary Magic and Seduction)* Madrid: Al Fadila, 1991

Entrambasaguas de, J. *Gastronomia Madrileña (Gastronomy of Madrid)* Madrid: Institute of Madrid Studies, 1971

Espinet, M. *El espacio culinario (The Culinary Space)* Barcelona: Tusquets, 1984

Esteban, J. *Breviario del Cocido (Breviary of "Cocido" Stews)* Madrid: Mondadori, 1988

Fábrega, J. *La cuina Gironina (The Cuisine of Gerona)* Barcelona: Grafitti y Laia, 1985

Ferrand, M. *Gastronomía Sevillana (Gastronomy of Seville)* Seville: Caja de Ahorros, 1985

Fernandez Duro, C. *La cocina del Quijote (The Cuisine of Quijote)* Madrid: José Esteban, 1983

Ford, R. *Comidas y vinos de España (Foods and Wines of Spain)* Madrid: Almarabu and José Esteban, 1985

Gallego-Morell, A. *De la cocina andaluza (About Andalusian Cooking)* Granada: Don Quijote, 1985

García Gómez, E. *Foco de antigua luz sobre la Alhambra (Spotlight from the past Over the Alhambra)* Madrid: Egyptian Institute for Islamic Studies, 1988

García Martín, P. *La mesta (The "Mesta")* Madrid: Historia 16, 1990

G. Seijo-Alonso, F. *Gastronomía de la Provincia de Alicante (Gastronomy of the Alicante Province)* Alicante: Seijo, 1977

G. Seijo-Alonso, F. *La cocina valenciana (Valencian Cooking)* Alicante: Seijo, 1981

Lasierra Rigal, J. V. *La cocina aragonesa (The Cuisine of Aragon)* Zaragoza: Librería General, 1979

Luján, N. *La vida cotidiana en el Siglo de Oro Español (Everyday Life in the Spanish Golden Age)* Barcelona: Planeta, 1988

Llanodosa i Giró, J. *La cocina medieval (Medieval Cooking)* Barcelona: Laia, 1984

Mapelli, E. *Málaga a mesa y mantel (Malaga with a Table and Cloth)* Malaga: Mapelli, 1983

Mapelli, E. *Escritos malagueños (Malaga Writings)* Malaga: Mapelli, 1986

March, L. *El libro de la paella y los arroces (The Book of Paella and Rice Dishes)* Madrid: Alianza, 1985

March, L. *Hecho en casa: conservas, mermeladas y licores (Homemade: Preserves, Jams and Liqueurs)* Madrid: Alianza, 1986

March, L. *La cocina mediterránea (Mediterranean Cooking)* Madrid: Alianza, 1988

March, L. & Rios, A. *El libro del aceite y la aceituna (The Book of Olive Oil and Olives)* Madrid: Alianza, 1989

Martínez Llopis, M. & Irizar, L. *Las cocina de España (The Cuisines of Spain)* Madrid: Alianza, 1990

Martínez Llopis, M. & Ortega, S. *La cocina típica de Madrid (The Typical Cooking of Madrid)* Madrid: Alianza, 1987

Martínez Llopis, M. *Historia de la gastronomía española (History of Spanish Gastronomy)* Madrid: Editora Nacional, 1981

Martínez Llopis, M. *Guisos de la Abuela — 81 (Grandmother's Cooking — 81)* Madrid: Grupo Gasterea, 1981

Millo, L. *La taula i la cuina (The Table and the Kitchen)* Valencia: Diputacio Provincial, 1984

Molí, D. *A la recerca d'una cuina garrotxina (In Search of a Garrotxan Cuisine)* Olot: Aubert Impressor, 1982

Muro, A. *El practicón (The Expert)* Barcelona: Tusquets, 1982

Pérez, D. *Post-Thebussem Guía del buen comer español (Post-Thebussem, Guide to Good Spanish Eating)* Madrid: Velázquez, 1977

Revel, J. F. *Un festín de palabras (A Feast of Words)* Barcelona: Tusquets, 1980

Simon Palmer, C. *Bibliografía de la gastronomía española (Bibliography of Spanish Gastronomy)* Madrid: Velázquez, 1977

Soler, M. C. *Banquetes de amor y muerte (Banquets of Love and Death)* Barcelona: Tusquets, 1981

Tannahil, R. *Food in History* New York: Stain and Day, 1973

Thebussem, Dr *La mesa moderna (The Modern Table)* Barcelona: Laia, 1986

INDEX

Page numbers in italics indicate photographs

ACKNOWLEDGMENTS

FOOD PHOTOGRAPHY

Food Stylists:

Isabel D'Olaberriague: pp. 43, 52, 167, 188, 193, 195, 231.

Carmen Lasquetti: pp. 56 (top), 64, 128, 131, 136, 141, 152, 155, 157, 161, 162, 165, 180, 190, 191, 194, 196, 241.

Lourdes March: pp. 29, 30, 31, 32, 38–39, 42, 55, 57, 61, 79, 81, 113, 114, 126, 127, 132, 153, 166, 184, 192, 197, 198, 213, 215 (bottom), 216, 245, 247, 248, 249, 251.

Alicia Rios: pp. 29, 30, 32, 35, 36, 38–39, 41, 42, 53, 55, 59, 60, 63, 76, 77, 80, 81, 83, 85, 98–99, 101, 102 (top and bottom), 105, 106–107, 108, 111, 113, 114, 116–117, 132, 133, 135, 138, 139, 142–143, 153, 158 (top and bottom), 159, 163, 169, 181, 183, 184, 187, 189, 192, 197, 198, 206–207, 209, 211, 213, 214, 215 (bottom), 216, 230, 232, 234 (bottom), 235, 237, 238–239, 243, 245, 246, 247, 248, 249, 251.

All food photography by Alejandro Pradera.

Weldon Russell would like to thank the following people and restaurants for their help in food preparation: Juan Diego Bolufer, Panaderia y Pasteleria Bolufer, Benissa, Alicante; Josefa Fullana, Restaurante "Casa Cati", Xaló, Alicante; Julia Garcia de Paredes; Luis Irizar, Restaurante Irizar Jatetxea, Madrid; Ximo Ivars, Restaurante Canto', Benissa, Alicante; Lourdes March; Maria Del Pilar Bertomeu, Pasteleria Francis, Xaló, Alicante; Restaurante "Casa Baydal", Calpe, Alicante; Restaurante "Carmen de San Miguel", Alhambra, Granada; Restaurante "La Fonda Real", Madrid; Alicia Rios; Luis Sendra, Denia, Restaurante Sendra, Alicante; Vicente Soriano, Restaurante "Venta La Chata", Calpe, Alicante.

HISTORICAL PICTURES

Weldon Russell would like to thank the following photographic libraries, photographers and institutions for supplying pictures for reproduction:

Alvaro Garcia Pelayo: pp. title page, 17, 27, 56, 62, 65, 71, 74, 88, 103, 106, 112, 115, 123, 130, 137, 143, 146, 154, 168, 179, 210, 215, 225, 226.

Archivo gráfico AISA: pp. back cover, endpapers, 4–5, 12, 15, 19, 20, 22–23, 26, 33, 37, 44–45, 46, 50, 58, 66–67, 68, 72, 73, 86–87, 90 (top and bottom), 92, 96 (bottom), 99, 104, 110, 122, 125, 140, 148, 149, 150, 156, 170–71, 174, 178, 182, 185, 199, 200–201, 204, 212, 217, 220, 229, 233, 244.

Archivo gráfico Oronoz: pp. 18, 28, 34, 48, 49 (top and bottom), 51, 75, 78, 95, 97, 118–119, 120, 124, 144–145, 151, 160, 172, 175, 202, 205, 223, 227, 234 (top), 240, 242, 250.

Dagli Orti: pp. front cover, 24.

Fine Arts Museum, Bilbao: p. 224.

La Casa de Valencia, Madrid: p. 100.

Mapfre Vida Cultural Foundation, Mapfre: p. 38.

National Library, Madrid: 10, 176.

Prado Museum, Madrid: pp. opposite title page, 6, 8–9, 13, 14, 16, 40, 70, 84, 91, 94, 96 (top), 164, 177, 186, 206, 218–19, 222, 228, 236.

Copyright information: Salvador Dali © Demart Pro. Arte—1922; Antonio Lopez © Visual; Joan Miró © ADAGP; Pablo Picasso © DACS; Pérez Villalta © Visual.

OVEN TEMPERATURE CONVERSIONS

° Celsius	° Fahrenheit	Gas Mark
110°C	225°F	¼
130	250	½
140	275	1
150	300	2
170	325	3
180	350	4
190	375	5
200	400	6
220	425	7
230	450	8
240	475	9